ENTREPRENEUR MAGAZINE
Guide to Raising Money

The *Entrepreneur* Magazine Small Business Series

Published:

Bringing a Product to Market
Guide to Integrated Marketing
Human Resources for Small Businesses
Making Money with Your Personal Computer
Small Business Legal Guide
Starting a Home-Based Business
Starting an Import/Export Business
Successful Advertising for Small Businesses
The Entrepreneur Magazine Small Business Advisor
The Entrepreneur Magazine Small Business Answer Book
Guide to Professional Services
Guide to Raising Money
Organizing and Promoting Seminars
Encyclopedia of Entrepreneurs

ENTREPRENEUR MAGAZINE
Guide to Raising Money

Entrepreneur Media, Inc.

John Wiley & Sons, Inc.

New York • Chichester • Weinheim • Brisbane • Singapore • Toronto

This text is printed on acid-free paper.

Copyright © 1998 by Entrepreneur Media, Inc.
Published by John Wiley & Sons, Inc.

Library of Congress Cataloging-in-Publication Data:

Entrepreneur magazine : guide to raising money / by Entrepreneur
   Media, Inc. (The Entrepreneur magazine small business series)
         p.   cm.
   Includes bibliographical references and index.
   ISBN 0-471-17995-7 (alk. paper)
   1. Venture capital.   2. Small business—United States—Finance.
   I. Entrepreneur Media, Inc.   II. Entrepreneur (Santa Monica, Calif.)
   HG4751.E58   1998
   658.15'224—dc21   97-30941

Printed in the United States of America

10   9   8   7   6   5   4   3   2   1

CONTENTS

Chapter 1 • Introduction   1

    Phases of Business Development / 4
    Sources of Financing / 5

Chapter 2 • Business Plan   7

    The Business Plan / 8
    Business Plan Structure / 16
    Financial Components / 39

Chapter 3 • Start-Up Financing   49

    Evaluating Your Financial Situation / 50
    Start-Up Financing Starts with You / 53

Chapter 4 • SBA Loans   78

    Types of SBA Loans / 78
    Specialized Programs / 84
    Types of Lenders / 89
    Loan Restrictions / 90
    SBA Loan Structure / 92
    Collateral / 103

Chapter 5 • Bootstrap Financing   107

    Trade Credit / 108
    Factoring / 110
    Customers / 110
    Real Estate / 111
    Equipment Suppliers / 112
    Leasing / 112
    Managing Cash Flow / 114

Chapter 6 • Credit   117

    Trade Credit: Tips and Traps / 118
    Establishing Credit / 123

Collections / 124
The Collection Process / 128

Chapter 7 • Expansion Financing   **137**
When Do You Need Expansion Capital? / 137
Expansion Capital / 148
Sources of Expansion Capital / 149
Venture Capital / 156

Chapter 8 • Public Offerings   **166**
Advantages and Disadvantages of Taking Your
    Company Public / 166
Preparing a Public Offering / 169
The Process of Going Public / 170
Operating as a Public Company / 173
Additional Methods of Going Public / 173

Chapter 9 • Internet Financing   **175**
History of the Internet / 175
The Net Hits the Big Time / 176
Electronic Financial Services / 177

Appendix A   Sample Business Plan—Backbay
**   Brewing Company**   **179**

Appendix B   Business Resources   **209**

Appendix C   Small Business Resources   **219**

Appendix D   Government Listings   **229**

Appendix E   Business Banks   **241**

Glossary   **262**

Notes   **267**

Index   **269**

1

INTRODUCTION

You have this great idea for a start-up business or to expand your current operations that will enable you to hit the jackpot. You have the technology, you have people willing to pursue this adventure with you, but how do you get the capital? Most entrepreneurs start by charging everything to their personal credit cards; then they borrow money from family and friends; they may even try a traditional approach and secure a bank loan. Soon they realize that this is not enough and that there must be a better way to finance their business. That's when they go after information.

Information is power. Success in business depends on what you know and how well you can apply the information you have. No one can tell you the best way to apply the information you have; in fact, your ability to do so in the way that is right for you is what makes your business distinctive from your competitors'. What we can do, though, is offer you a wealth of information to broaden your understanding of financial matters. That is what the *Entrepreneur Magazine's Guide to Raising Money* intends to do.

Raising money requires discipline and a thorough knowledge of the rules of the game. You probably already know the first rule, the "Golden Rule": He or she who has the "gold" makes the rules. The second rule is that new money only funds new or expanding opportunities; it does not solve old problems. With these ideas in mind, you are ready to start digging into this book. First, here are some thoughts on resources and on the best approach to raising money efficiently and effectively.

As you may imagine, there is a lot of help online. America Online's Microsoft Small Business Center has topics such as Finance, Starting a Business, and Women in Business that are full of magazine stories, videotape transcripts, and organizational literature. Under Finance, for instance, you can find "Alternative Ways to Find Capital," defining techniques like factoring and bartering. You can then browse the bulletin boards. In one such bulletin board (titled Partnerships), you'll find a lot of business opportunities; on another (the Venture Capitalist), you can get help in searching for investors; and, finally, you may go to the Small Business Administration (SBA) bulletin board where you can find detailed, easy-to-read materials explaining essentials such as how to write a business plan. Your curiosity dictates the amount of information you can get from the Internet.

If you are considered part of a specific target group, such as women or ethnic categories, there are now several publications geared to your business. Some examples of these publications are *Klein's Handbook on Building a Profitable Business* (see the chapter on " Special Groups") and Gustav Berle's book, *Retiring to Your Own Business: How You Can Launch a Satisfying, Productive, and Prosperous Second Career.* There are also publications on foreign sources of financing that reflect the increasing globalization of the economy. All these sources agree on one thing: Entrepreneurs need to start their search for financing with a close examination of themselves and their companies or proposed businesses. Translated to the individual level, this means you need to develop a business plan and evaluate your request for financing from the point of view of the potential funding source. A time line may help you in the process of getting the funding you need.

The Four-Month Project Time Line	Days
Preparation of a Business Plan	30–45
Preparation of a Private Placement Memorandum	15–30
Attracting Potential Investors	30
Due Diligence, Final Negotiations, Closing	30

For entrepreneurs, the old adage rings true: "It takes money to make money." Or, as Shakespeare put it, "Nothing comes of nothing." If you're just starting out, you need money; if you're already in business, you need a way to operate, grow, and develop. From marketing new products to meeting payroll, nothing happens without sufficient capital to drive it. Innovation, hard work, and the willingness to take chances are traits at the heart of every entrepreneur, but you risk forfeiting all of that when you don't have a solid base of capital upon which to stand.

Veteran financial planners are the first to admit that raising money is a complicated and often frustrating process. Some entrepreneurs spend years trying to secure funds for a start-up or growth effort, courting both public and private interests in their search for the best way to fuel their business dreams, often to no avail. Why? There are hundreds of possible explanations. In many cases, though, it is because entrepreneurs don't know how to present themselves and their business to interested investors or lenders. They have promising ideas and a wealth of business experience, but no practical means of implementing those ideas because they lack the necessary financial resources, or the resources necessary to secure financing. In other words, they don't know how to raise money, which is precisely the reason Entrepreneur Magazine has produced this book.

The choice seems simple enough at first: Use your own money or someone else's. Entrepreneurs with a shortage of the former don't have a choice: They must find financing. Their first order of business, then, is to locate a source; and each possible source or combination of sources has its own set of advantages and drawbacks. Finding an investor willing to provide you with all the capital you need, for instance, enables you to avoid self-financing your business and cut short your search for investors; but you may wind up being asked to give up more control of your company than you originally intended. You narrow the selection by carefully assessing the value or proposed value of your business, the amount of capital you require, and the repayment terms of money borrowed or rate of return expected by the investor.

From your collection of prospective sources, you decide on the exact source or sources to target. It could be a single investor, a friend or relative, the Small Business Administration, a securities firm, or any number of other possibilities. You may have a single financier or an assortment of loans, partners, and investors. But note, while it may seem like you are the one making choices about the money's origin, the amount of money, the borrowing terms and the likelihood of receiving funds, it is the financing source that chooses you. It represents the supply; you represent the demand. One side cannot exist without the other, but nowhere does it say yours is the business that deserves the money outright. The supply side has to loan money, but it does it on its terms. Your goal is to differentiate your business from other capital-hungry enterprises. Unfortunately, it is a talent that many entrepreneurs have yet to develop.

Early in the process, you need to set a limit on the cost you are willing to incur in the course of raising money. To do this, you have to know what to expect. Investors identify two critical pieces of information before they make a commitment: the risk involved and the rate of return. This applies to all individuals and organizations who loan money (providers of grant money and similar awards do not expect monetary compensation). When venture capitalists invest their money in businesses they believe are poised for rapid growth and high profit, they expect a high rate of return to reward their acceptance of the risk. Likewise, lenders will charge higher rates of interest on their loans if a borrower has a shaky credit history and only a small down payment. Risk-averse investors make safer investments and earn correspondingly modest returns. If you are willing to take risks for the sake of big profits and exceptionally fast growth, venture capitalists may be the answer—but their money will cost you. In the end, some things may never be worth sacrificing, such as ownership of your business. Stipulating certain boundaries enables you to avoid costs you are unwilling to incur.

PHASES OF BUSINESS DEVELOPMENT

This book is not devoted to a single event in the life of a business. Instead, it is designed to be a companion for entrepreneurs in search of financing through all phases of the business growth cycle. There are at least 11 distinct stages of business development that require an inflow of resources:[1]

1. *Seed.* Developing the idea, market research, and study of concept feasibility.
2. *Research and development.* Development of a new technology or product.
3. *Start-up.* Planning and preparation for a new business.
4. *First stage.* Initial expansion and development of an existing, profitable business.
5. *Second stage.* Second significant funding effort.
6. *Recapitalization.* Refinancing or consolidating debt.
7. *Mezzanine (expansion).* Third significant funding.
8. *Acquisition.* The purchase of another company or facility.
9. *Bridge.* Financing between stages of significant funding.
10. *Leveraged buyout.* Using the assets of the acquired company to fund acquisition by another business interest.
11. *Management buyout.* A business is purchased by its management.

A business requires a different mixture of resources as it evolves from one growth stage into the next, and every business has distinct resource requirements distinguishing it from other businesses. Manufacturing operations, for instance, require a lot of start-up money up front, whereas the bulk of the cash that goes to high-tech businesses is in the form of seed money. Service businesses may have a desperate need for financing at the Mezzanine level. Some entrepreneurs never reach the later stages of development, and are content with that. Your particular business and the direction you want to take it are additional factors determining the amount of financing.

SOURCES OF FINANCING

The subjects covered in this book create a broad list of possible capital sources available to entrepreneurs who either own or are planning to own a business. Whether starting up a new enterprise (phases 1, 2, and 3), looking for money to fund ongoing operations (phases 4, 5, and 6), or planning for further development and expansion (phases 7 through 11), they have a wealth of options at their disposal, including:

- *Personal savings.* This includes 401(k) savings, pension plans, unused vacation pay, or severance.
- *Family and/or friends.*
- *Corporate partners.*
- *Joint ventures.*
- *Bank loans.*
- *Nonbank lending.*
- *Government sources.*
- *Private placements.*
- *Customers.* When customers pay cash, you have no accounts receivable and, therefore, can place orders in advance and secure long-term contracts.
- *Vendors.* They offer installment terms or delayed payments, as well as support services such as consulting and marketing.
- *Leasing.* This allows you to update equipment more often.
- *Venture capital.* This includes money from sources such as venture capital funds, equity investors (business "angels"), institutional investors, buyout specialists, investment bankers, and other entrepreneurs.

institutional investors, buyout specialists, investment bankers, and other entrepreneurs.

- *Financiers.*
- *Reverse merger.*
- *Initial Public Offering (IPO).*

Regardless of the source you pursue, you're going to need a formal business plan that declares the courses of action you will take. You have to be persistent and adhere to your business plan relentlessly until you meet your goals—or the business proves unfeasible. If your product or service has merit, chances are you will find someone willing to finance you.

2

THE BUSINESS PLAN

Would you get on an airplane if you did not know where it was going to land? If you were taking a long trip and wanted to cover several cities and states, planned to see the main attractions and stay in fine hotels, what would be the first thing you would do? You would go to the bank, pick up a lot of cash, hop in your car, and take off, right? Wrong. You would make advance reservations, stay in hotels of your choice, map out where you wanted to go, and so on. If you didn't do this before going, you'd find that you didn't bring enough money to cover expenses, because you didn't know how much gasoline or hotels would cost. When you arrived at the hotel, you might find that it was booked; no reservation, no room.

This sort of thing isn't the result of bad luck. It's the result of poor planning. You may get tired of hearing about the necessity for planning when starting a business, but we can't stress the importance of a sound business plan enough. In short, it is essential if you are serious about having any chance for success in your business venture. And the sad truth is, most people plan trips and vacations more carefully than they plan their business ventures. It doesn't occur to them that a business plan can help—tremendously.

All entrepreneurs, regardless of the business they run or plan to start, stand to benefit from using business plans. An AT&T Small Business Study reports that fewer than 42 percent of businesses with less than $20 million in sales during 1992 use formal business plans to guide their daily operations. Among businesses with sales of less than $500,000, which make up 68 percent of the total, only one-third have carried out even the most basic planning efforts. Those who do, however, are likely to be rewarded: More than half (59 percent) of the small businesses that exhibited growth over the past two years said they used formal business plans.

Very few owners, principals, or executives in charge of small businesses identify long-term planning as one of the strengths they bring to their company. Only 6 percent of these individuals say long-term planning is a strength, despite the fact that a finished business plan has long been regarded by business professionals as a very powerful management tool. It is the chief instrument for communicating ideas to others—businesspeople, bankers, and partners—and is the basis for your loan proposal.

The majority of entrepreneurs prepare a business plan only when raising capital becomes an issue, and their intent or sole purpose is to raise financing. Preparing a business plan is time-consuming and can cost money. Many entrepreneurs assert that their plan is in their head. "Prior proper planning prevents poor performance" has been quoted for years, yet this admonition is rarely followed. For example, Steve Jobs and Steve Wozniak created Apple Computers without a formal business plan. Can you imagine the difficulty in projecting a market that did not yet exist?

THE BUSINESS PLAN

Without a formal business plan to follow, your chances of building an effective, efficient, profitable business are dramatically reduced. And just as important as the plan itself is its preparation. Far too many individuals who prepare plans concentrate on form and neglect the content. The result is often a business plan that looks good but doesn't tell the prospective audience anything.

There is no question that form is an important factor when writing effective business plans, but just as important, if not more so, is content—the information that is conveyed through the plan. The goal of this book is to provide you with not only the correct form of a business plan, but also to guide you through the methods of researching and producing the proper information required to add substance to the plan. Generally, most business plans will require information on several topics that will affect the marketing and support of the product. Those topics are usually:

- Industry.
- Competition.
- Customer.
- Company.
- Technology.

Whether your goal is to prepare a business start-up, reorganize your business and give it new direction, or expand your existing venture, a business plan is vital. This is a difficult concept for many entrepreneurs who are more comfortable with the tangible outcome than the many benefits generated by the process itself: crystallizing one's thoughts, identifying one's options, and selecting strategic choices to optimize the business.

The Business Plan for a New Start-Up

When developing a business plan for a new start-up, offering a new product that would require revising an existing business plan, or developing a marketing plan, it is important to keep in mind that the business will concentrate its efforts on marketing a product of some sort. In the traditional sense, product has always referred to something tangible, and many books on business plans have dealt exclusively with this concept; but with the emergence of the service sector, the term product has taken on a different meaning. Today there are two types of products:

1. *Hard product.* Refers to product in the traditional sense, meaning a manufactured item or good that is physically tangible, such as an item of clothing or a book.
2. *Service product.* Refers to an intangible product, where the business is performing a service for a client, such as washing and polishing a car or landscaping a yard.

Goods versus Services

When it comes to the production of the business plan, in many instances, there is little difference between hard and service products. In those areas where there are differences, they are sometimes drastic, and you need to be aware of them.

Goods

Tangible.
Inventoriable.
Deferred consumption.
Often perishable.
Consistent goods.

Services

Intangible.
Noninventoriable.
Simultaneous production and consumption.
Consumer-oriented.
Inconsistent service.

The following sections will take you through the intricacies of developing a business plan, explain its value and use, and point out those areas where hard product plans differ from those of a service-oriented business.

Why You Need a Plan

The process of creating a business plan forces you to take a realistic, more or less detached look at your business in its entirety, which may be difficult for most entrepreneurs cuddling their newborn. Why is it so important to see your venture in full view? Most people who have business ideas deal with them in a scattered manner. Putting a business plan together by writing down specifics provides you with the opportunity to evaluate your business as a whole so that you can proceed to implement it. The process involves putting your thoughts on paper in a structured, cohesive document, from which others can critique your direction and specific approaches.

A finished business plan becomes a management tool that will help you manage your business and work toward its success. The final, completed plan is the chief instrument for communicating your ideas to others—businesspeople, bankers, partners, key employees, and relevant others. If you seek financing for your business, the plan will become the basis for your loan proposal.

In the preopening period of a business, the business plan becomes incredibly useful. It helps you gather and analyze information that you can apply to the overall concept. Essentially, it becomes the animating force behind a concept that puts some life into it. All of us at some time have had great ideas that we believe would have made us a million dollars. But if we were so smart, how come we're not rich? The answer is simple: We didn't do anything beyond generating an idea. To be successful in business, you have to take the next step: putting the idea into action.

The business plan allows you to take nebulous thoughts and put them in concrete form. It is the difference between those who merely have an idea and those who make money on one. To repeat: The importance of planning cannot be overemphasized. It is the key to unlocking the door to success. Unfortunately, once you open that door, there are approximately a thousand more doors with all kinds of variables, problems, and situations. And the only way you can effectively handle those variables in a business venture is to have a logical, well-organized business plan. By taking an objective look at your business, you can identify areas of strength and weakness. You can pinpoint your needs and other details you might normally overlook just by "thinking about" your idea. A business plan will also give you enough information to help you spot problems before they arise. Planning will help you determine how you can best achieve your business goals.

A business plan does several things for you:

- Helps you identify your objectives.
- Helps you develop strategies to meet those objectives.
- Helps you earmark problems and suggests ways to solve them.
- Helps you avoid problems altogether.
- Helps create a structure for your business by defining activities and responsibilities.
- Helps you obtain the necessary financing to start your business.

For a plan to be effective, it is imperative that *you* do as much of the work, as much of the research, and as much of the investigation of your business as possible. In short, *you* must do the planning. A commonly asked question is, "Can I hire somebody to do this for me?" Sure you can. There are companies that will organize and write a business plan for you. They will charge you several hundred dollars for their services, and you will receive a very professional and polished plan—one that will become a very valuable tool. But in our opinion, a business plan becomes even more valuable when you devote the time to organize and write it. It helps you to better understand just what you and your business are capable of doing, and it will make you a better manager when your business is up and running.

Just as you cannot expect the vision of your business to come to life without your active involvement, neither can you expect a business plan to do everything for you without controlling its creation. When you thoroughly research and pull your business plan together, you derive an enormous amount of financial and operational information about your business, information that promotes business knowledge and confidence. Confidence, in turn, promotes enthusiasm and makes you the best salesperson for your business. The bottom line is that if you're going to use your business plan for the purpose of raising money, you will have to be able to sell your idea, your plan, and your business. If you don't know everything about your program—all the ins and outs, ups and downs, pros and cons—you're not going to be the best salesperson for it. This doesn't mean you must be a super-salesperson to go into business; it does mean that the owner of any business must be able to talk about the benefits and risks in an intelligent and straightforward manner—and anyone can achieve this level of knowledge.

You must take plenty of time to put your plan together correctly. Some people take two weeks, others four months. If you're working full-time right now, you'll find it's almost impossible to put together a plan quickly. It takes time and effort if you're serious about your business. Throughout the course of your business career, you can always hire somebody to perform certain tasks. But you can't hire anyone to do your thinking; no one can read your mind. You are the one with the vision; and even if you hire a writer to organize that vision into a business package with an acceptable form, you're the person who must decide what you want to do with your business. If you're not yet in business, a good business plan will give you important information. First of all, a well-organized plan will tell you whether your idea makes sense. Why is this seemingly obvious fact important? Frequently, when an entrepreneur presents an idea to individuals or organizations with a view toward obtaining financing, one of the potential investors asks, "Why don't you give me a business plan on it?" When the entrepreneur starts working on the plan, he or she may find one factor has been left out that can materially affect the chief variable of any business: the net profit. Accordingly, a business plan can tell the entrepreneur whether there is enough net profit in a business to make it an enterprise worth his or her time or investment.

A business plan forces you to analyze your market from your point of view as business operator and from your potential customer's point of view. You must determine the potential demand for the product or service you plan to offer. Additionally, you must evaluate your ability to provide a product or service. Therefore, the second thing a business plan will tell you is whether your idea has a chance in the marketplace.

Third, when you prepare a business plan, you're forced to see both the pitfalls and potential in your idea. Simply put, this means a plan will tell you whether you're kidding yourself. The fourth thing a business plan will tell you is whether you're capable—physically, mentally, and emotionally—of taking on the chore of setting up, running, and operating a small business over the long term.

Clearly, a good business plan will save you time and money. Whether you're in business for yourself or for somebody else, you will soon realize that time and money are the keys in any enterprise.

What Will Happen without a Plan

As much as we would like to say that you stand a very good chance of developing a successful business without a business plan, the odds are stacked against you. Starting a business is a risky venture, and when you're not prepared, it becomes even more so.

Much has been written about business failures. Every year, thousands of businesses of every size and variety fail. Although business failures know no size boundaries, the majority are classified as small businesses. According to data from the Administrative Office of the U.S. Courts, more than 98 percent of businesses that have filed for bankruptcy since 1980 have been small. Most small-business surveys show that the primary reasons for business failure lie in the following areas:

1. Inefficient control over costs and quality of product.
2. Stock control failures.
3. Underpricing of goods sold.
4. Poor customer relations.
5. Failure to promote and maintain a favorable public image.
6. Poor relations with suppliers.
7. Inability of management to reach decisions and act on them.
8. Failure to keep pace with the management system.
9. Illness of key personnel.
10. Reluctance to seek professional assistance.
11. Failure to minimize taxation through tax planning.
12. Inadequate insurance.
13. Loss of impetus in sales.
14. Poor personnel relations.

15. Loss of key personnel.
16. Lack of staff training.
17. Lack of knowledge of merchandise.
18. Inability to cope adequately with competition.
19. Competition disregarded due to complacency.
20. Failure to anticipate market trends.
21. Loose control of liquid assets.
22. Insufficient working capital or incorrect gearing of capital borrowings.
23. Growth without adequate capitalization.
24. Poor budgeting.
25. Ignoring data on the business's financial position.
26. Inadequate financial records.
27. Extending too much credit.
28. Poor credit control.
29. Overborrowing or using too much credit.
30. Poor control over receivables.
31. Loss of control through creditors' demands.

Most business experts cite the top two reasons for small-business failures to be either incompetent management or lack of adequate financial working capital.[1]

The last quarter of the twentieth century has witnessed the parallel phenomena of more new businesses being started and failing each year. This suggests that while business owners display a good deal of confidence and enthusiasm in opening their businesses, they also experience a high mortality rate. A careful examination of the preceding list reveals that a lack of planning is the principal or underlying cause of business difficulty: Inefficient control . . . , Failure to promote and maintain . . . , Failure to keep pace . . . , Inability to cope . . . and so on, including money-related causes for failure, are indicators of poor planning. Other things being equal, planning can make the difference between success and failure in business.

A business plan can help protect you from going into a venture that is doomed to failure from the start. Think about it: Would you prefer to know earlier or later? Sometimes, visioning your plan and preparing your plan may not be a prudent course of action, because the feedback you receive is from one primary source: yourself. As such, the necessary different perspectives may engender arranging assistance when preparing the plan—recruiting an independent professional to prepare the plan. This may prove to be the wisest investment you have ever made.

Many people fail in business because they don't prepare a substantive business plan. Had they prepared one, perhaps they would have found that there was not enough profit potential, that the market wasn't right for their business, or that they were missing one of the key success factors to achieve their goals. They would have been able to determine in advance whether going into the business they chose in the way they anticipated was a good course of action.

Not only can a business plan assist you when your business is marginal, but it can also address the critical constraints for expansion. It can help you avoid the high price of failure and the high cost of breaking even. And make no mistake, breaking even has plenty of cost attached to it. Suppose someone makes $20,000 a year. If he or she starts a business and grosses only $20,000 a year, why (except for emotional reasons, which may be significant) should he or she endure the heartache, headache, pain, and frustration involved in running a business, just to be his or her own boss? Nontraditional motives aside, it's far cheaper not to begin an ill-fated business than to learn by experience what business planning could have revealed at the outset.

The Business Plan as a Management Tool

Many people intend to use their business plan to obtain money. A business plan will provide information needed by others who evaluate your venture, and a comprehensive plan can become a financing proposal that will meet the requirements of most lenders.

As mentioned earlier, there are many types of lenders or investors. Private funds, friends and family, Small Business Investment Companies (SBICs), single investors, private placements, public offerings, credit cards, banks, commercial finance companies, venture capitalists, and government agencies are the most obvious sources.

Keep in mind, however, that you will get money from such sources only by making them confident that your business is going to be secure and profitable over the next several years. Lenders have not been thinking about your business as long as you have. They have not been digging out facts on it for several months. They are seeing it on paper for the first time. Therefore, you must present something to them that clearly, succinctly, and reasonably assures them that you're going to make money—and, equally important, that they are not going to lose any. Whichever kind of lender you finally find, you're going to have to present a cogent business plan.

BUSINESS PLAN STRUCTURE

A strong business plan holds few surprises for its audience. It conforms to generally accepted guidelines of form and content. Each section should denote specific elements that will clarify your business goals. Your plan should address all the relevant questions that will be asked by individuals such as investors who review it. If your business plan is not structured to provide the appropriate information in a concise and logical progression, then your chances of answering the key questions concerning development and operations will decrease.

There are seven major components that generally make up a business plan. They are:

1. Executive summary and key success factors.
2. Business description.
3. Market strategies.
4. Industry and competitive analysis.
5. Design and development plans.
6. Operations, management and personnel plans.
7. Financial projections.

An optional component is a section for SBA materials, which should be incorporated only if the purpose of developing your business plan is to obtain SBA financing. The documents required by the SBA may also be useful to you in setting up your business.

Title Page and Table of Contents

While the business plan can be divided into the seven components just listed, there are three elements that don't fall within these broad classifications but are, nevertheless, critical to the plan's success. These elements include the *cover, title page,* and *table of contents.*

First, the business plan should have a cover, which is not to say you must have your work bound in leather; all that is required is a neat cover of adequate size to hold your material. Buy a blue, black, or brown binder at a stationery store. A lender is more likely to think well of you if your presentation is conservative than if you spend money on unnecessary ornamentation. Subtle factors like this reflect your business judgment. In some respects, the way a person reads your business plan will affect his or her judgment of your management ability.

Also include a title page to precede your business plan. On this page, put the name of the business, the name(s) of the principals, as well as the business address and phone number. If you have a professional, businesslike logo, use it to dress up your title page. On some plans, the first page includes the name of the packager or person who assisted the business owner in preparing the plan. We believe this is a mistake. A business plan should be represented as a personal document by only the principals. There is a place in the plan where you can acknowledge professional assistance, but the business and the plan itself should be presented as yours.

You also must have a table of contents following the *executive summary* or *statement of purpose* (discussed in the next section). Although the table of contents is included toward the beginning of the book, you will naturally prepare this last. When you or others look over your plan, you and they should be able to quickly find certain information, financial data, market information, and the like.

The Business Definition

The first component of the business plan should describe the nature of the business through several elements that include the *executive summary* or *statement of purpose* and the *business description*. These two elements serve to define the business, the type of product it will offer, and its role within the context of the overall industry.

Executive Summary and Key Success Factors

Within the overall outline of the business plan, the executive summary will follow the title page. The summary should tell the reader what *you* want and answer for him or her what's called WIIFM, or "what's in it for me." This is very important. Too often, what the business owner desires is buried on page 8. Be sure to clearly state what you are asking for in the summary. Keep the statement short and businesslike, generally no more than half a page, although it may be longer, depending on how complicated the use of funds may be. In total, the summary of a business plan, like the summary of a loan application, is generally no more than one to three pages. Within that space, you'll need to provide a synopsis of the entire business plan. The key elements to include are:

1. *Business concept.* Describes the business, its product, and the market it will serve. Points out exactly what will be sold, to whom, and why the business will hold a competitive advantage.
2. *Financial projections.* Highlights the important financial points of the business, including sales, profits, cash flows, and return on investment.

3. *Financial requirements.* Clearly states the capital needed to start the business and to expand it. Details how the capital will be used, and the equity, if any, that will be provided for funding. If the loan for initial capital will be based on security instead of equity within the company, specify the source of collateral.

4. *Current business position.* Furnishes relevant information about the business, its legal form of operation, when it was formed, the principal owners, and key personnel.

5. *Major achievements.* Details any developments within the company that are essential to its success. Major achievements include items like patents, prototypes, location of a facility, crucial contracts that need to be in place for product development, or results from any test marketing that has been conducted.

When writing your executive summary, don't waste words. If the executive summary is eight pages, nobody is going to read it because it will be very clear that the business, no matter what its merits, won't be a good investment because the principals are indecisive and don't really know what they want. Make it easy for the reader to realize, at first glance, both your needs and capabilities.

The Business Description

The business description usually begins with a short description of the industry. When describing the industry, discuss the present outlook as well as future possibilities. You should also provide information on all the various markets within the industry, including any new products or developments that will benefit or adversely affect your business. Base all of your observations on reliable data and be sure to footnote sources of information as appropriate. This is important if you're seeking funding because the investor will want to know just how dependable your information is. Investors won't risk money on assumptions or conjecture.

When describing your business, the first thing to concentrate on is its structure, by which we mean the type of operation (i.e., wholesale, retail, food service, manufacturing, or service-oriented). State this immediately in the description, along with whether the business is new or already established.

In addition to structure, legal form should be reiterated again. Detail whether the business is a sole proprietorship, partnership, or corporation, who the principals are and what they will bring to the business. Also mention whom you will sell to, how the product will be distributed, and the business support systems. Support may come in the form of advertising, promotions, or customer service.

Once you've described the business, define the products or services you intend to market. The product description statement should be complete enough that the reader can ascertain a clear idea of your intentions. This might mean a discussion on the application and the end uses. You may want to emphasize any unique features or variations from similar concepts found in the industry. The investor will be looking for any proprietary information that will set your concept apart from the crowd. Most investors call this the USP, or unique selling proposition. Almost every business has one. It can be a patented product or a trade secret like Kentucky Fried Chicken's recipe. Note, however, that this element has come into question of late since it is becoming increasingly difficult to have a unique feature.

As we may be in an era of commoditization, determine early whether your basis for competing is (a) low cost, (b) differentiation in some manner, or (c) focus on a particular market niche that you can serve better than anyone else. Be specific in identifying how you will give your business a competitive edge. For example, your business will be better because you will supply a full line of products while Competitor A does not have a full line, making your differentiation one-stop shopping. Or perhaps you are going to provide service after the sale, and Competitor B doesn't support anything he or she sells. Or your merchandise will be of higher quality. You'll give a money-back guarantee. You'll provide parts and labor for up to 90 days after the sale. Or since Competitor C has the reputation for selling the best french fries in town, you're going to sell the best Thousand Island dressing.

Next you must be a classic capitalist and ask yourself, "How can I turn a buck? And why do I think I can make a profit this way?" Answer these questions for yourself, and then convey those answers to others in the business concept section. You don't have to write 25 pages on why your business will be profitable. Just explain the factors you think will make it successful: For instance, it's a well-organized business; it will have state-of-the-art equipment; its location is exceptional; the market is ready for it; it's a dynamite product at a fair price.

If you're using your business plan as a document for financing purposes, explain why the added equity or debt money is going to make your business more profitable. Show how you will expand your business or be able to create something by using that money. State how the money will help your business.

Next, show why your business is going to be profitable. A potential lender is going to want to know how successful you're going to be in this particular business. Factors that support your claims for success can be broad-brushed here because they will be detailed later. Give the reader an idea of the experience of the other key people in the business. They will want to know which suppliers or experts you've spoken to about your business and their response to your idea. They may even ask you to clarify your choice of location or reasons for selling this particular product.

The business description can be a few paragraphs in length to a few pages depending on the complexity of your plan. If your plan is not too complicated, keep your business description short, describing the industry in one paragraph, the product in another, and the business and its success factors in three or four paragraphs to conclude the statement. A lengthy business description is called for in some cases, but it is our opinion that a short statement conveys the required information in a much more effective manner. It doesn't require holding the reader's attention for an extended period of time, and this is important since there will be other plans that the investor is expected to read as well. If the business description is long and drawn out, you may lose the reader's attention—and possibly any chance of receiving the necessary funding for the project.

Market Strategies

Market strategies are formulated as the result of a meticulous market analysis, and a market analysis forces you, the entrepreneur, to become familiar with all aspects of the market so the target customer can be defined and the business can be positioned in order to garner its share of sales. A market analysis also enables you to establish pricing, distribution, and promotional strategies that will enable the business to become profitable within a competitive environment. In addition, it provides an indication of the growth potential within the industry, and this will allow you to develop your own estimates for the future of your business. Begin your market analysis first by defining your target customer, the resultant market in terms of size, structure, growth prospects, trends, and sales potential.

The total aggregate sales of your competitors will provide you with a fairly accurate estimate of the *total potential market.* For instance, within the beer brewing industry, the total market potential would be the total sales of malt beverages in the United States, which is $35 billion. (For a sample plan of a microbrewery, see Appendix A.)

Once the size of the market has been determined, the next step is to define the specific consumer target market. Defining the target market narrows the total market, forcing you to concentrate on segmentation factors that will determine the total addressable market—the total number of users within the sphere of the business's influence. The segmentation factors can be any or all of the following: geographic (where they live); demographic (who they are—age, sex, income); psychographic (why they buy—lifestyle factors); and synchographic (when they buy). For instance, if the distribution of your product is confined to a specific geographic area, then you would want to further define the target market to reflect the number of users or sales of that product within that geographic segment.

Once the target market has been detailed, it must be further defined to determine the total feasible market. This can be done in several ways, but most professional planners will delineate the feasible market by concentrating on product segmentation factors that may produce gaps within the market. In essence, this is a reachable market segment for you. In the case of the microbrewery that plans to brew a premium lager beer, for example, the total feasible market could be defined by determining how many drinkers of premium pilsner beers there are in the target market.

It is important to understand that the total feasible market is the portion of the market that can be captured provided every condition within the environment is perfect and there is very little competition. In most industries, this is simply not the case. There are other factors that will affect the *share* of the feasible market a business can reasonably capture. These factors are usually tied to the structure of the industry, the impact of competition, strategies for market penetration and continued growth, and the amount of capital the business is willing to spend in order to increase its market share.

Arriving at a projection of the *market share* for a business plan is a very subjective estimate. It is based not only on an analysis of the market, but also on highly targeted and competitive distribution, pricing, and promotional strategies. For instance, even though there may be a sizable number of premium pilsner drinkers to form the total feasible market, you need to be able to reach them through your distribution at a price point that is competitive, and then you have to let them know your product is available and where they can buy it. How effectively you can achieve your distribution, pricing, and promotional goals is the extent to which you will be able to garner market share.

In your business plan, you must be able to estimate market share for the time period the plan will cover. In order to project market share over the time frame of the business plan, you will need to consider two factors:

1. Industry growth, which will increase the total number of users or number of uses of the product. This is determined by growth models. Most projections utilize a minimum of two growth models by defining different industry sales scenarios. The industry sales scenarios should be based on leading indicators of industry sales, most likely industry sales, industry segment sales, demographic data, and historical precedence.

2. Conversion of users from the total feasible market (see Figure 2–1). This is based on a sales cycle similar to a product life cycle with five distinct stages: early pioneer users, early users, early majority users, late majority users, and late users. Using conversion rates, market growth will continue to increase your market share during the period from early pioneers to early majority users, level off through late majority users, and decline with late users.

Defining the market is but one step in your analysis. With the information you gain through market research, you need to develop strategies that will allow you to fulfill your objectives. When discussing market strategy, it is inevitable that positioning will be brought up. Positioning a product in the market is essential because it forms part of its identity in the eyes of the purchaser. A business positioning strategy is affected by a number of variables that are closely tied to the motivations and requirements of customers within the target market, as well as to the actions of primary competitors.

Figure 2–1   Revenue Model for Backbay Brewing Company

Revenue Summary	1995	1996	1997
Product One—Six-Packs			
No. of customers	13,778	14,742	16,510
Units/Customer	24	24	24
Total units	330,672	353,808	396,240
New customers	13,778	964	1,768
Price/Unit	$ 3.85	$ 3.85	$ 3.85
Revenue	$1,273,087	$1,362,161	$1,525,524
Product Two—22-oz. Bottles			
No. of customers	11,273	12,062	13,508
Units/Customer	48	48	48
Total units	541,104	578,976	648,384
New customers	11,273	789	1,446
Price/Unit	$ 1.20	$ 1.20	$ 1.20
Revenue	$ 649,325	$ 694,771	$ 778,061
Product Three—15-Gallon Kegs			
No. of customers	172	178	199
Units/Customer	12	12	12
Total units	2,064	2,136	2,388
New customers	172	6	21
Price/Unit	$ 105	$ 105	$ 105
Revenue	$ 216,720	$ 224,280	$ 250,740
Total Revenue	$2,139,132	$2,281,212	$2,554,325

The strategy used to position a product is usually a result of an analysis of your customers and competition. Before a product can be positioned, you need to answer several strategic questions:

1. How are your competitors positioning themselves?
2. What specific customer benefits does your product have that your competitors' don't?
3. What customer needs or wants does your product fulfill?
4. Is there anything unique about the place of origin of the product?

Once you've answered these strategic questions based on your market research, you can begin to develop your positioning strategy and illustrate that in your business plan. A positioning statement for a business plan doesn't have to be long or elaborate. It should point out exactly how you want your product perceived by both customers and the competition. For example, Ford's statement is "Quality Is Job One."

How you price your product is also important because it will have a direct effect on the marketing and financial success of your business. Though pricing strategy and computations can be complex, the basic rules of pricing are straightforward:

1. All prices must cover costs.
2. The best and most effective way of lowering your sales prices is to lower costs.
3. Your prices must reflect the dynamics of cost, demand, changes in the market, and response to your competition.
4. Prices must be established to assure sales. Do not price against a competitive operation alone; rather, price to sell.
5. Product utility, longevity, maintenance, and end use must be judged continually; target prices must be adjusted accordingly.
6. Prices must be set to preserve order in the marketplace.

There are many methods of establishing prices available. These are:

- *Cost-plus pricing.* Used mainly by manufacturers, cost-plus pricing assures that all costs, both fixed and variable, are covered and that the desired profit percentage is attained.
- *Demand pricing.* Used by companies that sell their product through a variety of sources at differing prices based on demand.

- *Competitive pricing.* Used by companies that are entering a market where there is already an established price and where it is difficult to differentiate one product from another.
- *Markup pricing.* Used mainly by retailers, markup pricing is calculated by adding your desired profit to the cost of the product.

Distribution includes the entire process of moving the product from the factory to the end user. The type of distribution network you choose will depend upon the industry and the size of the market. A good way to help make your decision is to analyze your competitors to determine the channels they are using, then choose to use the same type of channel or an alternative that may provide you with a strategic advantage.

Some of the more common distribution channels are:

- *Direct sales.* The most effective distribution channel given the parameters of the basic model is to sell directly to the end user.
- *OEM (Original Equipment Manufacturer) sales.* When your product is sold to the OEM, it is incorporated into their finished product and distributed to the end user.
- *Manufacturer representatives.* One of the best ways to distribute a product, manufacturer reps (as they are known), are salespeople who operate out of agencies that handle an assortment of complementary products and divide their selling time between them.
- *Wholesaler distributors.* Using this channel, a manufacturer sells to a wholesaler, who in turn sells it to a retailer or other agent for further distribution through the channel until it reaches the end user.
- *Brokers.* Third-party distributors who often buy directly from the distributor or wholesaler and sell to retailers or end users.
- *Retail distributors.* Distributing a product through this channel is important if the end user of your product is the general consuming public.
- *Direct mail.* Selling to the end user through a direct mail campaign.

As mentioned, the distribution strategy you choose for your product will be based on several factors that include the channels being used by your competition, your pricing strategy, and your internal resources.

After a distribution strategy is formed, a promotion plan must also be developed. The promotion strategy, in its most basic form, is the controlled distribution of communication designed to sell your product or service. In order to accomplish this, the promotion strategy encompasses every marketing tool utilized in the communication effort:

- *Advertising.* Includes the advertising budget, creative message(s), and at least the first quarter's media schedule.
- *Packaging.* Provides a description of the packaging strategy. If available, mock-ups of any labels, trade, or service marks should be included.
- *Public relations.* Gives a complete account of the publicity strategy, including a list of media that will be approached as well as a schedule of planned events.
- *Sales promotions.* Establishes the strategies used to support the sales message. This includes a description of collateral marketing material as well as a schedule of planned promotional activities such as special sales, couponing, contests, and premium awards.
- *Personal sales.* Outlines the sales strategy, including pricing procedures, returns and adjustment rules, sales presentation methods, lead generation, customer service policies, salesperson compensation, and salesperson market responsibilities.

Once the market has been researched and analyzed, conclusions need to be drawn that will supply a quantitative outlook concerning the potential of the business. The first financial projection within the business plan must be formed utilizing the information drawn from defining the market; positioning the product; and pricing, distribution, and promotional strategies. The sales or revenue model (as depicted in Figure 2–1) charts the potential for the product, as well as the business, over a set period of time. Most business plans will project revenue for up to three years, although five-year projections are becoming increasingly popular among lenders.

When developing the revenue model for the business plan, the equation used to project sales is fairly simple. It consists of the total number of customers and the average revenue of each customer. In the equation, T = total number of people, A = average revenue per customer, and S = sales projection. The equation for projection sales is:

$$T \div A = S$$

Using this equation, the annual sales for each year projected within the business plan can be determined. Of course, there are other factors that you need to evaluate from the revenue model. Since the revenue model is a table illustrating the source for all income, every segment of the targeted market that is treated differently must be accounted for. In order to determine any differences, the various strategies utilized in order to sell the product have to be considered. As we've already mentioned, those strategies include distribution, pricing, and promotion.

Competitive Analysis

The competitive analysis is a statement of the business strategy and how it relates to the competition. The purpose of the competitive analysis is to determine the strengths and weaknesses of the competitors within your market, strategies that will provide you with a distinct advantage, barriers that can be raised in order to prevent competition from entering your market, and any weaknesses that can be exploited within the product development cycle.

The first step in a competitive analysis is to identify the current and potential competition. There are essentially two ways you can identify competitors. The first is to look at the market from the customer's viewpoint and group all your competitors by the degree to which they contend for the buyer's dollar. The second method is to group competitors according to their various competitive strategies so that you understand what motivates them.

Once you have grouped your competitors, you can start to analyze their strategies and identify areas where they are most vulnerable. This can be done through an examination of your competitors' weaknesses and strengths, which are usually based on the presence and absence of key assets and skills needed to be competitive in the market.

To determine just what constitutes a key asset or skill within an industry, David A. Aaker in *Developing Business Strategies*[2] suggests concentrating your efforts in four areas:

1. Reasons behind successful, as well as unsuccessful, firms.
2. Prime customer motivators.
3. Major component costs.
4. Industry mobility barriers.

According to theory, the performance of a business within a market is directly related to the possession of key assets and skills. Therefore, an analysis of strong performers should reveal the causes behind their successful track record. This analysis, in conjunction with an examination of unsuccessful companies and the reasons behind their failure, should provide a good idea of the key assets and skills that are needed to be successful within a given industry and market segment.

For instance, in the personal computer operating system software market, Microsoft reigns supreme with DOS, Windows, and Windows97. It has been able to establish dominance in this industry because of superior marketing and research as well as strategic partnerships with a majority of the hardware vendors that produce personal computers. This has enabled DOS and Windows to become the operating environments, maybe not of choice, but of necessity for the majority of personal computers on the market.

Microsoft's primary competitors, Apple and IBM, both have competing operating systems with a great deal of marketing to promote them. However, both suffer from weaknesses that Microsoft has been able to exploit. Apple's operating system for its Macintosh line of computers, while superior in many ways to DOS, Windows, and Windows97, is limited to the Macintosh personal computers. Therefore, it doesn't run many of the popular business applications that are readily available to users of DOS, Windows, and Windows97. To an extent, IBM's OS/2 operating system suffers from the same problem. While it will run on all of the personal computers that DOS, Windows, and Windows97 can run on, and even handle Windows applications, the number of programs produced for OS/2 in its native environment is very small. This is the type of detailed analysis you need to make when evaluating an industry.

Through your competitor analysis, you will also have to create a marketing strategy that will generate a unique asset or skill that will provide you with a distinct and enduring competitive advantage. Since competitive advantages are derived from key assets and skills, you should sit down and put together a competitive strength grid. This is a scale that lists all your major competitors or strategic groups based upon their applicable assets and skills, and indicates where your business fits on this scale.

To lay out a competitive strength grid, list all the key assets and skills down the left margin of a piece of paper. Along the top, insert two column headers: Weakness and Strength. In each asset or skill category, place all the competitors that have weaknesses in that particular category under the weakness column, and all those that have strengths in that specific category in the strength column. After you've finished, you'll be able to determine just where you stand in relation to the other firms competing in your industry.

Once you've established the key assets and skills necessary to be successful in the business you are researching and have defined your distinct competitive advantage, you need to communicate the results in a strategic form that will attract market share as well as defend it. Competitive strategies usually fall into five areas:

- Product.
- Distribution.
- Pricing.
- Promotion.
- Advertising.

Many of the factors leading to the formation of a strategy should already have been highlighted in previous sections, specifically in marketing strategies. Strategies primarily revolve around establishing the point of entry in the product life cycle and defining an endurable competitive advantage. As we've already discussed, this involves defining the elements that will set your product or service apart from your competitors or strategic groups. You need to clearly establish this competitive advantage so the reader understands not only how you will accomplish your goals, but why your strategy will work.

Design and Development Plans

The purpose of the design and development plan section is to provide investors with a description of the product's design; chart its development within the context of production, marketing, and the business itself; and create a development budget that will enable the business to reach its goals. There are generally three areas you will cover in developing the plan section:

1. Product development.
2. Market development.
3. Organizational development.

Each of these elements needs to be examined from the funding of the plan to the point where the business begins to experience a continuous income. Although these elements will differ in nature concerning their content, each will be based on structure and goals.

The first step in the development process is to set goals for the overall development plan. From your analysis of the market and competition, most of the product, market, and organizational development goals will be readily apparent. Each goal you define should have certain characteristics within it. Your goals should be:

- *Quantifiable,* in order to set up time lines.
- *Directed,* so they relate to the success of the business.
- *Consequential,* so they have impact upon the company.
- *Feasible,* so that they aren't beyond the bounds of actual completion.

Goals for product development should center around the technical as well as the marketing aspects of the product so that there is a focused outline from which the development team can work. For example, a goal for product development of a microbrewed beer might be "Produce recipe for premium lager beer" or "Create packaging for premium lager beer." In terms of market development, a goal might be, "Develop collateral marketing material." Organizational goals would center around the acquisition of expertise in order to attain your product and market development goals. This expertise usually needs to be present in areas of key assets that provide a competitive advantage. Without the necessary expertise, the chances of bringing a product successfully to market diminishes.

With your goals set and expertise in place, a set of procedural tasks or work assignments should be delineated for each area of the development plan. Procedures have to be determined for product development, market development, and organization development. If the list of procedures is short enough, product and organization can be combined. Procedures should include how resources will be allocated, who will be in charge of accomplishing each goal, and how everything will interact. For example, to produce a recipe for a premium lager beer, you would need to do the following:

1. Gather ingredients.
2. Determine optimum malting process.
3. Gauge mashing temperature.
4. Boil wort and evaluate which hops provide the best flavor.
5. Determine yeast amounts and fermentation period.
6. Determine aging period.
7. Carbonate the beer.
8. Decide whether to pasteurize the beer.

Although the development of procedures provides a list of work assignments that need to be accomplished, one thing it doesn't provide are the stages of development that coordinate the work assignments within the overall development plan. To do this, you first need to amend the work assignments created in the procedures section so that

Figure 2–2   Development Expenses

Item	Budgeted Amount
Materials	$ 129,000
Direct labor	21,840
Overhead	376,790
G&A	14,560
Equipment	485,000
Miscellaneous	2,000
Total	$1,029,190

all the individual work elements (a detailed breakdown of the work assignments—basically, who, what, when) are accounted for in the development plan. The next stage involves setting deliverable dates for components as well as the finished product for testing purposes. Terence P. McCarty's book *Business Plans That Win Venture Capital*[3] identifies three steps that must be taken before the product is ready for final delivery:

1. *Preliminary product review.* All the product's features and specifications are checked.
2. *Critical product review.* All the key elements of the product are checked and gauged against the development schedule to make sure everything is going according to plan.
3. *Final product review.* All elements of the product are checked against goals to assure the integrity of the prototype.

In discussing procedures, we mentioned scheduling, one of the most important elements in developing a plan. Scheduling should include all of the key work elements as well as the stages the product must pass through before customer delivery. The schedule should also be tied to *development expenses* (see Figure 2–2) so that expenditures can be tracked. But its main purpose is to establish time frames for completion of all work assignments and to juxtapose those within the stages through which the product must pass. When producing the schedule, provide a column for each procedural task name, duration of time, start and stop dates. If you want to provide a number system for each task, include a column in the schedule for the task number.

Scheduling leads to the development of a budget. When itemizing your development budget, you need to take into account not only all the expenses required to design the product, but also those to take it from prototype to production. Costs that should be included in the development budget are:

- *Material.* All raw materials used in the development of the product.
- *Direct labor.* All labor costs associated with the development of the product.
- *Overhead.* All overhead expenses required to operate the business during the development phase, such as taxes, rent, phone, utilities, office supplies, and others.
- *G&A costs.* The salaries of executive and administrative personnel, along with any other office support functions.
- *Marketing and sales.* The salaries of marketing personnel required to develop prepromotional materials and plan the marketing campaign that should begin prior to delivery of the product.
- *Professional services.* Those costs associated with consultation of outside experts such as accountants, lawyers, and business consultants.
- *Miscellaneous costs.* Costs related to product development.
- *Capital equipment.* To determine the capital requirements for the development budget, you first have to establish the type of equipment you will need; decide whether to acquire the equipment or use outside contractors; and, finally, if you decide to acquire the equipment, whether you will lease or purchase it.

As mentioned, the business has to have the proper expertise in key areas in order for it to succeed; however, not everyone will start a business with the requisite expertise in every key area. Therefore, the proper personnel should be recruited, integrated into the development process, and managed so that a team is formed, one that is focused on the achievement of the development goals.

Before you begin recruiting, you should determine the areas within the development process that will require additional personnel. This can be done by reviewing the goals of your development plan to establish key areas that need attention. After you have determined the positions that need to be filled, you should produce a *job description* and *job specification* for them.

Once you've hired the proper personnel, you need to integrate them into the development process by assigning tasks from the work assignments you've developed. Finally, each member needs to know his or her role within the company and how he or she interrelates with all others on the development team. In order to do this, you should draw up an organizational chart for your development team.

Finally, the risks involved in developing the product should be assessed and a plan designed to address each one. The risks during the development stage will usually center around technical development of the product, marketing, personnel requirements, or financial problems. By identifying and addressing each of the perceived risks during the development period, you not only quiet some of your major fears concerning the project, but those of investors as well.

Operations, Management, and Personnel

The operations and management plan is designed to describe just how the business functions on a continuing basis. The operations plan will highlight the logistics of the organization such as the various responsibilities of the management team, the tasks assigned to each division within the company, and capital and expense requirements related to the operations of the business. In fact, within the operations plan, you'll develop the next set of financial tables that will serve as the foundation for the Financial Components section. The financial tables to develop within the operations plan are:

- The operating expense table.
- The capital requirements table.
- The cost of goods table.

The factors that will affect these financial tables are directly attributable to the operations of the business. They should cover a time frame that corresponds to the overall projections that the scope of your plan will cover.

Two areas need to be accounted for when planning the operations of your business. The first is the organizational structure of the business, and the second is the expense and capital requirements associated with its operation.

Organizational structure is an essential element within a business plan because it provides a basis from which to project operating expenses. This is critical to the formation of financial statements that are heavily scrutinized by investors; therefore, the organizational structure has to be well defined and based within a realistic framework given the parameters of the business. Although every business will differ in its organizational structure, most can be divided into several broad areas:

- Marketing and sales (includes customer relations and service).
- Production (including quality assurance).
- Research and development.
- Administration.

These are very broad classifications and it is important to keep in mind that not every business can be divided in this manner. Every business is different, and each must be structured according to its own requirements and goals.

McCarty's *Business Plans That Win Venture Capital*[4] lists four stages for organizing a business:

1. Establish a list of the tasks using the broadest of classifications possible.
2. Organize these tasks into departments that produce an efficient line of communication between staff and management.
3. Determine the type of personnel required to perform each task.
4. Establish the function of each task and how it will relate to the generation of revenue.

Once you have structured your business, you next need to consider your overall goals and the personnel required to reach those goals. In order to determine the number of employees you'll need to meet the goals you've set for your business, apply the following equation to each department listed in your organizational structure:

$$C \div S = P$$

In this equation, C = the total number of customers, S = the total number of customers that can be served by each employee, and P = the personnel requirements. For instance, if the number of customers for first year's sales is projected at 10,110, and one sales employee is required for every 200 customers, you would need 51 employees within the sales department.

$$10{,}110 \div 200 = 51$$

Once you calculate the number of employees that you'll need for your organization, the next step is to determine the labor expense. The factors that need to be considered when calculating labor expense (LE) are the personnel requirements (P) for each department, multiplied by the employee salary level including benefits (SL). Therefore, the equation would be:

$$P \times SL = LE$$

Using the previous marketing example, the labor expense for that department would be:

$$51 \times \$40,000 = \$2,040,000$$

Once the organization's operations and labor expenses have been determined, the expenses associated with the operation of the business can be identified. These are usually referred to as *overhead expenses,* and include all nonlabor costs required to operate the business. Expenses can be divided into *fixed*—those expenses that must be paid, usually at the same rate, regardless of the volume of business—and *variable* (or semivariable)—those that change according to the amount of business. Some common overhead expenses are:

- Travel.
- Maintenance and repair.
- Equipment leases.
- Rent.
- Advertising and promotion.
- Supplies.
- Utilities.
- Packaging and shipping.
- Payroll taxes and benefits.
- Uncollectible receivables.
- Professional services.
- Insurance.
- Loan payments.
- Depreciation.

In order to develop the overhead expenses for the expense table used in this portion of the business plan (refer to Figure 2–3), multiply the number of employees by the expense of each employee. Therefore, if NE represents the number of employees and EE is the expense per employee, the following equation can be used to calculate the sum of each overhead (OH) expense:

$$OH = NE \times EE$$

Figure 2–3   Operating Expenses

	1995	1996	1997
Marketing expenses	$ 85,000	$ 90,950	$101,864
Sales expenses	80,000	85,600	95,872
Brewery operations expenses	70,000	74,900	83,888
Administrative expenses	35,000	37,450	41,944
Overhead	410,224	438,940	491,613
Total Expenses	$680,224	$727,840	$815,181

In addition to the expense table, you'll also need to develop a capital requirements table (see Figure 2–4) that depicts the amount of money necessary to purchase equipment that will establish and continue operations. It also illustrates the amount of depreciation your business will incur based on all equipment elements purchased with a lifetime beyond one year.

In order to generate the capital requirements table, you first have to establish the various elements within the business that will require capital investment. For service businesses, capital is usually tied to the various types of equipment used to serve customers. For instance, a janitorial service would need a vehicle, cleaning equipment, computer equipment, and cleaning supplies.

Capital for manufacturing companies, on the other hand, is based on the equipment required to produce the product. Manufacturing equipment usually falls into three categories:

1. Testing equipment.
2. Assembly equipment.
3. Packaging equipment.

With these capital elements in mind, you need to determine the number of units or customers, in terms of sales, that can be adequately handled by each equipment factor. This is important because capital requirements are a product of income, which is produced through unit sales. In order to meet the demand of sales, a business usually has to invest money so it can increase production or supply better service. In the business plan, capital requirements are tied to projected sales, discussed earlier in this chapter.

For instance, if the capital equipment required is capable of handling the needs of 10,000 customers at an average sale of $10 each, that would be $100,000 in sales, at which point additional capital will be required in order to purchase more equipment should the business grow. This leads to another factor within the capital requirements equation:

Figure 2–4   Capital Summary

	1995	1996	1997
Initial capital	$ 0	$ 0	$ 0
Net capital	0	370,476	358,395
Malting equipment			
No. barrels	10,000	10,700	11,984
ME/Barrel	3,500	3,500	3,500
ME capital	11,500	11,500	11,500
ME capital requirement	32,857	35,157	39,376
New ME capital	32,857	2,300	4,219
Mashing Brewing Equipment			
No. barrels	10,000	10,700	11,984
MBE/Barrel	1,700	1,700	1,700
MBE capital	15,500	15,500	15,500
MBE capital requirement	91,176	97,559	109,266
New MBE capital	91,176	6,383	11,707
Fermentation/Aging Equipment			
No. barrels	10,000	10,700	11,984
FAE/Barrel	840	840	840
FAE capital	10,500	10,500	10,500
FAE capital requirement	125,000	133,750	149,800
New FAE capital	125,000	8,750	16,050
Finishing Equipment			
No. barrels	10,000	10,700	11,984
FE/Barrel	3,500	3,500	3,500
FE capital	22,000	22,000	22,000
FE capital requirement	62,857	67,257	75,328
New FE capital	62,857	4,400	8,071
Packaging Equipment			
No. barrels	10,000	10,700	11,984
PE/Barrel	7,500	7,500	7,500
PE capital	75,000	75,000	75,000
PE capital requirement	99,750	107,000	119,840
New PE capital	99,750	7,250	12,840
Total new capital	411,640	29,083	52,887
Total capital	411,640	399,559	408,374
Depreciation	41,164	44,072	49,361

equipment cost. If you multiply the cost of equipment by the number of customers it can support in terms of sales, it would result in the capital requirements for that particular equipment element. Therefore, you can use an equation where capital requirements (CR) equals sales (S) divided by number of customers (NC) supported by each equipment element multiplied by average sale (AS), which is then multiplied by the capital cost (CC) of the equipment element. Given these parameters, your equation would look like the following:

$$CR = [(S \div NC) \, AS] \, CC$$

The capital requirements table is formed by adding all your equipment elements to generate the *total new capital* for that year. During the first year, total new capital is also the *total capital* required. For each successive year thereafter, the total capital (TC) required is the sum of total new capital (NC) plus total capital (PC) from the previous year, less depreciation (D), once again, from the previous year. Therefore, your equation to arrive at total capital for each year portrayed in the capital requirements model would be:

$$TC = NC + PC - D$$

Keep in mind that depreciation is an expense that shows the allocation of the cost of the equipment throughout its effective lifetime. For many businesses, depreciation is based upon schedules that are tied to the lifetime of the equipment. Be careful to choose the schedule that most appropriately fits your business. Depreciation may also serve as the basis for a tax deduction as well as the flow of money for new capital. You may need to consult an expert in this area.

The last table that has to be generated in the operations, management, and personnel section of your business plan is the cost of goods table (Figure 2–5). This table is used only for businesses in which the product is placed into inventory. For a retail or wholesale business, *cost of goods sold*, or *cost of sales*, refers to the purchase of products for resale—the inventory. The products sold are logged into cost of goods as an expense of the sale, while those that aren't sold remain in inventory.

For a manufacturing firm, *cost of goods* is the cost incurred by the business to manufacture its product. This usually consists of three elements:

1. Material.
2. Labor.
3. Overhead.

Figure 2–5   Cost of Goods—Barrels

	1995	1996	1997
Barrels sold	10,00	10,700	11,984
Begin FB	0	4,500	4,815
FB% Sales (Barrels)	45	45	45
End FB	4,500	4,815	5,393
Inventory/FB	4,500	315	578
Begin PB	0	3,500	3,745
PB% Sales (Barrels)	35	35	35
End PB	3,500	3,745	4,194
Inventory/PB	3,500	245	449
Begin I	0	2,000	2,140
1% Sales (Barrels)	20	20	20
End I	2,000	2,140	2,397
Inventory/I	2,000	140	257
Barrels sold	10,000	10,700	11,984
Barrels FBI	4,500	315	578
Barrels PBI	3,500	245	449
Barrels II	2,000	140	257
Total barrels inventory	20,000	11,400	13,268
Ingredients/Barrel ($)	32	32	32
Ingredient costs ($)	640,000	364,800	424,576
Barrels sold	10,000	10,700	11,984
Barrels FBI	4,500	315	578
Barrels PBI	3,500	245	449
Total L&OH barrels	18,000	11,260	13,011
Labor/PA % (Barrels)	50	50	50
Labor/Barrel ($)	39	39	39
OH/Barrel ($)	18	18	18
Labor costs ($)	633,750	434,363	498,674
OH Costs ($)	292,500	200,475	230,157
Total L&OH ($)	926,250	634,838	728,831
Inventory/I ($)	64,000	4,480	8,224
Production costs ($)	1,502,250	995,158	1,145,183
Inventory/PB ($)	211,750	14,823	27,165
COG Production ($)	1,290,500	980,334	1,118,018
Inventory/FB ($)	400,500	28,035	51,442
COG Sold ($)	890,000	952,299	1,066,576
COGS/Barrel ($)	89	89	89
Begin II ($)	0	64,000	68,480
Change II ($)	64,000	4,480	8,224
End II ($)	64,000	68,480	76,704
Begin PBI ($)	0	211,750	226,573
Change PBI ($)	211,750	14,823	27,165
End PBI ($)	211,750	226,573	253,738
Begin FBI ($)	0	400,500	428,535
Change FBI ($)	400,500	28,035	51,442
End FBI ($)	400,500	428,535	479,977
Begin inventory ($)	0	676,250	723,588
Change inventory ($)	676,250	47,338	86,831
End inventory ($)	676,250	723,588	810,419
Revenue/Barrel ($)	213.91	213.19	213.14
Revenue ($)	2,139,132	2,281,212	2,554,325
Inventory turn	3.16	3.15	3.15

Like retail, the merchandise that is sold is expensed as a cost of goods, while merchandise that isn't sold is placed in inventory. Cost of goods has to be accounted for in the operations of a business. It is an important yardstick for measuring a firm's profitability for the cash flow statement and income statement.

In the income statement, the last stage of the manufacturing process is the item expensed as cost of goods, but it is important to document the inventory that is still in various stages of the manufacturing process because it represents assets to the business. This is important not only from a cash flow point of view, but also when it comes to producing the balance sheet—which is what generating the cost of goods table helps to do. It is one of the most complicated tables you'll have to develop for your business plan, but it is an integral part of portraying the flow of inventory through your operations, the placement of assets within the company, and the rate at which your inventory turns.

In order to generate the cost of goods table, you need a little more information in addition to the cost of labor and material per unit. You also need to know the total number of units sold for the year, the percentage that will be fully assembled, the percentage that will be partially assembled, and the percentage that will be in unassembled inventory. Much of this information is dependent on the capacity of your equipment as well as the inventory control system you develop. Along with these factors, you also need to know at what stage the majority of labor is performed.

FINANCIAL COMPONENTS

Once the product, market, and operations have been defined, it is time to address the real backbone of the business plan: the financial statements. The set of financial statements that you'll need to develop include the *income statement*, the *cash flow statement*, and the *balance sheet*.

The Income Statement

The income statement (Figure 2–6) is a simple and straightforward report on the proposed business's cash-generating ability. It is akin to a video scorecard on the financial performance of your business that reflects when sales are made and when expenses are incurred for a period of time. It draws information from the various financial models developed earlier, such as revenue, expenses, capital allocation (in the form of depreciation), and cost of goods sold. By combining these elements, the income statement illustrates just how much your business

Figure 2-6 Income Statement

	Jan	Feb	Mar	Apr	May	Jun	Jul	Aug	Sep	Oct	Nov	Dec	1995	Qtr 1	Qtr 2	Qtr 3	Qtr 4	1996	1997
Income	42,783	64,174	85,565	128,348	149,739	171,131	181,826	203,218	213,913	246,000	310,174	342,261	2,139,132	410,618	501,867	638,739	729,988	2,281,212	2,554,325
Cost of goods	17,800	26,700	35,600	53,400	62,300	71,200	75,650	84,550	89,000	102,350	129,050	142,400	890,000	171,414	209,506	266,644	304,736	952,299	1,066,576
Gross profit	24,983	37,474	49,965	74,948	87,439	99,931	106,176	118,668	124,913	143,650	181,124	199,861	1,249,132	239,204	292,361	372,096	425,252	1,328,913	1,487,749
Margin %	58	58	58	58	58	58	58	58	58	58	58	58	58	58	58	58	58	58	58
Expenses	34,011	40,813	47,616	47,616	49,656	52,377	55,778	63,261	71,424	71,424	72,104	74,144	680,224	160,125	167,403	196,517	203,795	727,840	815,181
Net profit	-9,029	-3,339	2,350	27,332	37,783	47,563	50,398	55,407	53,490	72,227	109,020	125,717	568,908	79,080	124,958	175,579	221,457	601,073	672,568
Margin %	-21	-5	3	21	25	28	28	27	25	29	35	37	27	19	25	27	30	26	26
Depreciation	3,430	3,430	3,430	3,430	3,430	3,430	3,430	3,430	3,430	3,430	3,430	3,430	41,164	11,018	11,018	11,018	11,018	44,072	49,361
Net profit before interest	-12,459	-6,770	-1,081	23,902	34,353	44,123	46,968	51,976	50,059	68,796	105,590	122,286	527,744	68,062	113,940	164,561	210,439	567,001	623,207
Margin %	-29	-11	-1	19	23	26	26	26	23	28	34	36	25	17	23	26	29	24	24
Interest	13,350	13,200	13,050	12,900	12,750	12,600	12,450	12,300	12,150	12,000	11,850	11,400	150,000	36,135	34,903	33,671	32,166	136,875	127,716
Net profit before taxes	-25,809	-19,970	-14,131	11,002	21,603	31,523	34,518	39,676	37,909	56,796	93,740	110,886	377,744	31,927	79,037	130,890	178,273	420,126	495,491

makes or loses during the year by subtracting cost of goods sold and expenses from revenue to arrive at a net result—that is either a net profit or a net loss.

For a business plan, the income statement should be generated on a monthly basis during the first year, quarterly for the second, and annually for each year thereafter. It is formed by listing your financial projections in the following manner:

1. *Income.* All the revenues generated by the business and its sources.

2. *Cost of goods.* All the costs related to the sale of products in inventory.

3. *Gross profit margin.* The difference between revenue and cost of goods sold. Gross profit margin can be expressed in dollars, as a percentage, or both. As a percentage, the GP margin is always stated as a percentage of revenue.

4. *Operating expenses.* All overhead and labor expenses associated with the operations of the business.

5. *Total expenses.* The sum of all overhead and labor expenses required to operate the business.

6. *Net profit.* The difference between gross profit margin and total expenses, the net income depicts the business's debt and capital capabilities.

7. *Depreciation.* Reflects the allocation of costs of capital assets used to generate income. Also used as the basis for a tax deduction and as an indicator of the flow of money into new capital.

8. *Net profit before interest.* The difference between net profit and depreciation.

9. *Interest.* All interest derived from debts, both short-term and long-term. Interest is determined by the amount of investment within the business.

10. *Net profit before taxes.* The difference between net profit before interest and interest.

11. *Taxes.* All taxes on the business.

12. *Profit after taxes.* The difference between net profit before taxes and the taxes accrued. Profit after taxes is the bottom line for any business.

Accompanying the income statement should be a short note analyzing the results of the statement, emphasizing key points within the income statement.

Cash Flow Statement

The cash flow statement (Figure 2–7) is one of the most critical information tools for your business, showing how much cash will be needed to meet obligations, when the cash is going to be required, and from where it will come. It shows a schedule of the money coming into the business and expenses that need to be paid. The result is the profit or loss at the end of the month or year. In a cash flow statement, both profits and losses are carried over to the next column to show the cumulative amount. Keep in mind that if you run a loss on your cash flow statement, it is a strong indicator that you will need additional cash in order to meet expenses.

Like the income statement, the cash flow statement takes advantage of previous financial tables developed during the course of formulating the business plan. The cash flow statement begins with cash on hand and the revenue sources. It next lists expenses, including those accumulated during the manufacture of a product. The capital requirements are then logged as a negative after expenses. The cash flow statement ends with the net cash flow during a period of time.

The cash flow statement should be prepared on a monthly basis during the first year, and each year thereafter if considered prudent; or on a quarterly basis during the second year and on an annual basis thereafter. Items that you'll need to incorporate into the cash flow statement and the order in which they should appear are:

1. *Cash sales.* Income derived from sales paid for by cash.
2. *Receivables.* Income derived from the collection of receivables.
3. *Other income.* Income derived from investments, interest on loans that have been extended, and the liquidation of any assets.
4. *Total income.* The sum of total cash, cash sales, receivables and other income.
5. *Material/Merchandise.* The raw material used in the manufacture of a product (for manufacturing operations only), the cash outlay for merchandise inventory (for merchandisers such as wholesalers and retailers), or the supplies used in the performance of a service.
6. *Direct labor.* The labor required to manufacture a product (for manufacturing operations only) or perform a service.
7. *Overhead.* All fixed and variable expenses required for the production of the product and the operations of the business.
8. *Marketing/Sales.* All salaries, commissions, and other direct costs associated with the marketing and sales departments.

Figure 2-7 Cash Flow Statement

	Jan	Feb	Mar	Apr	May	Jun	Jul	Aug	Sep	Oct	Nov	Dec	1995	Qtr 1	Qtr 2	Qtr 3	Qtr 4	1996	1997
Cash sales	17,113	25,670	34,226	51,339	59,896	68,452	72,730	81,287	85,565	98,400	124,070	136,904	855,652	164,247	200,747	255,496	291,995	912,485	1,021,730
Receivables	0	0	25,670	38,504	51,339	77,009	89,844	102,678	109,096	121,931	128,348	147,600	892,019	458,720	261,317	323,540	398,190	1,441,767	1,552,160
Other income	0	0	0	0	0	0	0	0	0	0	0	0	0	0	0	0	0	0	0
Total income	17,113	25,670	59,896	89,843	111,235	145,461	162,574	183,965	194,661	220,331	252,418	284,504	1,747,671	622,967	462,064	579,036	690,185	2,354,252	2,573,890
Material	0	0	0	0	0	0	0	0	0	0	0	0	0	0	0	0	0	0	0
Direct labor	7,800	11,700	15,600	23,400	27,300	31,200	33,150	37,050	39,000	44,850	56,550	62,400	390,000	91,806	95,979	112,671	116,844	417,300	467,376
Overhead	0	0	0	0	0	0	0	0	0	0	0	0	0	0	0	0	0	0	0
Marketing/Sales	8,250	9,900	11,550	11,550	12,045	12,705	13,530	15,345	17,325	17,325	17,490	17,985	165,000	38,841	40,607	47,669	49,434	176,550	197,736
Operations/R&D	3,500	4,200	4,900	4,900	5,110	5,390	5,740	6,510	7,350	7,350	7,420	7,630	70,000	16,478	17,227	20,223	20,972	74,900	83,888
G&A	1,750	2,100	2,450	2,450	2,555	2,695	2,870	3,255	3,675	3,675	3,710	3,815	35,000	8,239	8,614	10,112	10,486	37,450	41,944
Taxes	0	0	40,528	0	0	40,528	0	0	40,528	0	0	40,528	162,113	41,538	41,538	41,538	41,538	166,150	186,451
Capital	3,430	3,430	3,430	3,430	3,430	3,430	3,430	3,430	3,430	3,430	3,430	3,430	41,164	11,018	11,018	11,018	11,018	44,072	49,361

9. *R&D.* All the labor expenses required to support the research and development operations of the business.

10. *G&A.* All the labor expenses required to support the administrative functions of the business.

11. *Taxes.* All taxes, except payroll, paid to the appropriate government institutions.

12. *Capital.* The capital requirements to obtain any equipment elements that are needed for the generation of income.

13. *Loan payment.* The total of all payments made to reduce any long-term debts.

14. *Total expenses.* The sum of material, direct labor, overhead expenses, marketing, sales, G&A, taxes, capital, and loan payments.

15. *Cash flow.* The difference between total income and total expenses. This amount is carried over to the next period as beginning cash.

16. *Cumulative cash flow.* The difference between current cash flow and cash flow from the previous period.

As with the income statement, analyze the cash flow statement to create a short summary in the business plan. Again, cover only the key points derived from the cash flow statement.

The Balance Sheet

The last financial statement you need to develop is the balance sheet (Figure 2–8). Like the income and cash flow statements, the balance sheet is akin to a snapshot at a point in time, and utilizes information from all of the financial models developed in earlier sections of the business plan; however, unlike the previous statements, the balance sheet is generated solely on an annual basis for the business plan and is, more or less, a summary of all the preceding financial information broken down into three areas:

1. Assets.
2. Liabilities.
3. Equity.

To obtain financing for a new business, you may need to provide a projection of the balance sheet over the period of time the business plan covers. More important, a *personal* financial statement or balance sheet

Figure 2–8 Balance Sheet

	1995	1996	1997
Assets			
Current assets			
Cash	$ 855,653	$ 912,485	$1,021,730
Accounts receivable	892,018	1,441,768	1,552,160
Inventory	676,250	723,588	810,419
Total Current Assets	$2,423,921	$3,077,841	$3,384,309
Fixed assets			
Capital/Plant	$ 370,476	$ 399,559	$ 408,374
Investment	41,164	44,072	49,361
Miscellaneous assets	0	0	0
Total Fixed Assets	$ 411,640	$ 443,631	$ 457,735
Total Assets	$2,835,561	$3,521,472	$3,842,044
Liabilities			
Current liabilities			
Accounts payable	$ 717,303	$1,034,785	$1,075,601
Accrued liabilities	660,000	706,200	790,944
Taxes	162,113	166,150	186,451
Total Current Liabilities	$1,539,416	$1,907,135	$2,052,996
Long-term liabilities			
Bond payable	$ 0	$ 0	$ 0
Notes payable	300,000	300,000	300,000
Total Long-Term Liabilities	$ 300,000	$ 300,000	$ 300,000
Total Liabilities	$1,839,416	$2,207,135	$2,352,996
Owner's Equity			
Owner's equity	$ 996,145	$1,314,337	$1,489,048
Total Liability/Equity	$2,835,561	$3,521,472	$3,842,044

will be required instead of one that encompasses the business. A personal balance sheet is generated in the same manner as one for a business. Refer to the balance sheet included in the sample business plan of this chapter as well as the personal balance sheet in Chapter 3, Start-Up Financing.

As mentioned, the balance sheet is divided into three sections. The top portion of the balance sheet lists your company's assets, which are classified as current assets and long-term or fixed assets. Current assets are those that will be converted to cash or will be used by the business in a year or less. Current assets are:

1. *Cash.* The cash on hand at the time books are closed at the end of the fiscal year. This refers to all cash in checking, savings, and short-term investment accounts.
2. *Accounts receivable.* The income derived from credit accounts. For the balance sheet, it is the total amount of income to be received that is logged into the books at the close of the fiscal year.
3. *Inventory.* This is derived from the cost of goods table. It is the inventory of material used to manufacture a product not yet sold.
4. *Total current assets.* The sum of cash, accounts receivable, inventory, and supplies.

Other assets that appear in the balance sheet are called long-term or fixed assets because they are durable and will last more than one year. Examples of this type of asset are:

1. *Capital and plant.* The book value (original cost or value) of all capital equipment and property (if you own the land and building), less cumulative depreciation.
2. *Investment.* All investments by the business that cannot be converted to cash in less than one year. For the most part, companies just starting out have not accumulated long-term investments.
3. *Miscellaneous assets.* All other long-term assets that are not capital and plant or investments.
4. *Total long-term assets.* The sum of capital and plant, investments, and miscellaneous assets.
5. *Total assets.* The sum of total current assets and total long-term assets.

After the assets are listed, you need to account for the liabilities of your business. Like assets, liabilities are classified as current or long-term. If the debts are due in one year or less, they are classified as current liabilities; if they are due in more than one year, they are long-term liabilities. Examples of current liabilities are as follows:

1. *Accounts payable.* All expenses incurred by the company that are purchased from regular creditors on an open account and are due and payable.
2. *Accrued liabilities.* All expenses incurred by the business that are required for operation but that have not yet been invoiced

and recorded as accounts payable at the time the books are closed. These expenses are usually the company's overhead and salaries.

3. *Taxes.* Taxes that are still due and payable at the time the books are closed.
4. *Total current liabilities.* The sum of accounts payable, accrued liabilities, and taxes.

Long-term liabilities include:

1. *Bonds payable.* The total of all bonds at the end of the year that are due and payable over a period exceeding one year.
2. *Mortgage payable.* Loans taken out for the purchase of real property that are repaid over a long-term period. The mortgage payable is that amount still due at the close of books for the year.
3. *Notes payable.* The amount still owed on any long-term debts that will not be repaid during the current fiscal year.
4. *Total long-term liabilities.* The sum of bonds payable, mortgage payable, and notes payable.
5. *Total liabilities.* The sum of total current and long-term liabilities.

Once the liabilities have been listed, the final portion of the balance sheet should be calculated. This portion is owner's equity. The amount attributed to owner's equity is the difference between total assets and total liabilities. The amount of equity the owner has in the business is an important yardstick used by investors when evaluating the business. Many times, it determines the amount of capital they feel they can safely invest in the business.

In the business plan, you'll need to create an analysis statement for the balance sheet just as you need to do for the income and cash flow statements. The analysis of the balance sheet should be kept short; it need cover only the most salient features of the business.

PROFESSIONALLY PREPARED BUSINESS PLANS

You can have your business plan professionally prepared: researched, written, printed—the works—but there are pros and cons to this practice. You can hire a business consultant who writes business plans for a living, and we believe that a knowledgeable consultant can be an extremely useful advisor to anyone contemplating opening a business. But if you plan to make a profit in your business, if you plan to control its operation, you must understand every word, every dollar amount and item entry, every penny, every paragraph of any plan you submit to a banker, a landlord, a lawyer, or a venture capitalist. Why? At some point, that consultant is going to move on. You have to stay with your business, on your own, and run it yourself. Or you will have to make a presentation to this or that loan officer by yourself, who are going to be taking a good look at you and asking you a lot of questions. If you have to look to your consultant to answer fundamental issues, neither you nor your business prospects are going to be viewed favorably.

In the planning phase of your business, therefore, we encourage you to do the work yourself. If you're not a writer, you must nevertheless be the principal supplier of data to the writer who puts your information into the business plan form. If you can explain the concept of your business to someone who needs to understand it in order to put your plan into final form, then chances are good you will be able to make lenders and others understand it as well.

In any case, remember that understanding comes from being involved with your business idea from the beginning. A business plan will do you no good if you don't use it. When you prepare your plan, do so with the idea of implementing it fairly quickly. Business plans are little time capsules, valid only for a certain period of time. If you devise your business plan today and don't use it until next year, much of the information in it may be outdated. You will have to revise it, restructure it, and go through the preparation process again.

3

START-UP FINANCING

One key resource to starting up a business is cash or financial capital. Raising money is one of the most basic of all business activities, yet is often underestimated by budding entrepreneurs in terms of planned effort. Because it can be a complex and frustrating process, many entrepreneurs quickly discover that raising money is not easy. In fact, it may become so time-consuming that they find little time to complete product or market development or recruit the right individuals or organizations to progress with their vision.

The amount of money it takes to transform an idea into a business hinges upon factors ranging from the nature of the product or service to the aptitude of the entrepreneur. Most manufacturing businesses cost considerably more to put into operation than most service-based businesses because of the sizable equipment purchases required. Retail and food service establishments by and large are also capital-intensive ventures. On the other hand, a manufacturing company run by an efficient manager who knows how to maximize the return on every dollar invested may spend less on start-up than the owner of a service business who doesn't know what a budget looks like. The point is, if you perform sufficient research and formulate a thorough business plan, you should gain a clear idea of the amount of money you need to begin your venture, as well as the best sources to approach for financing.

49

Traditionally, it has been hard for small, entrepreneurial ventures to obtain capital, especially in the start-up phase. This has been magnified by the increasing cost of money in the financial markets, which in turn has constricted the flow of money into the small business realm. Today, the importance of planning has never been more obvious. If you're well prepared when you seek start-up financing, or any kind of financing for that matter, you'll be a long way toward alleviating the doubts lenders exhibit when the owner of a small business comes knocking on their door.

There are two concerns of foremost interest in lenders' minds: (a) use of proceeds and (b) repayment of principal and payment of interest. Bankers, for instance, will not want to make a loan that puts them in the position of investing in your business. They want to stay liquid, which helps them minimize their risk. In essence, most bankers seek security to provide them with a second way out should the repayment of the loan not materialize. As an entrepreneur, you must always have a clear understanding of how much cash you need at any given time and how you propose to use it. By doing this, you can determine the best source for raising money to finance your business.

Many entrepreneurs start their business with little of their own cash and rely upon the doctrine of Other People's Money (OPM). The following examples illustrate it can be done—with perseverance.

Company	Start-Up Capital	1994 Revenues
Campus Concepts	$ 48	$ 2.5 Million
Combined Resource Technology	$14 Million	$ 2 Million
BOWA Builders	$5,000	$ 1.7 Million
Logo Athletic	$ 250	$230 Million
Buschman Corporation	$ 500	$ 2.7 Million
MC2 Microsystems	$ 200	$ 3.2 Million
Metro Services Group, Inc.	$ 900	$ 7.5 Million
Kitty Hawk Group, Inc.	$ 0	$108 Million
Value Added Distribution Inc.	$ 100	$ 11 Million
Tomkats	$2,000	$ 4.5 Million
Time Line Productions, Inc.	$2,500	$ 2 Million
Domino's Pizza	$4,500	$ 3.6 Billion

EVALUATING YOUR FINANCIAL SITUATION

First-time entrepreneurs frequently use their personal funds to get their business underway. This does not mean that once you are in business, you won't need additional capital—the remaining chapters of this book are a testament to that. Business owners use many techniques to obtain personal loans for business financing, during start-up and beyond. You can borrow from individuals or from institutions, using a loan secured with collateral or an unsecured loan made on a promise or contract. The latter is the most advantageous to you as a borrower because you don't risk losing anything tangible. Your promise to pay is made on the basis of your debt-paying history.

If you are already inundated with debt, you may not be able to get the long-term financing you want, and it won't be a favorable rate even if you can. In this case, you'll have to look at equity financing as an option. The difference between equity financing and a standard loan is that you sacrifice a portion of your business, profits, and possibly some control when you finance with equity. Also, it is more difficult to convince someone to buy part of your business, either as a partner, limited partner, or perhaps as a shareholder of your corporation. Nevertheless, equity money at least allows you to proceed with your business start-up. You can also use it to take you through a growth period when you are expanding a facility, buying a new vehicle or piece of equipment, or perhaps going into a new product line with heavy development costs (see Chapter 7, Expansion Financing). Any long-term situation that will bring in profits over a period of years can qualify for long-term debt, with lower monthly payments and perhaps lower interest rates.

To begin planning your financial requirements, answer a few fundamental questions:

- When are you going to repay the money? (Different situations will also determine what type of money you need, whether equity or individual loans.)
- How much do you need? (The use and scheduling of the financing will depend on the amount that you need.)
- Can you afford the cost of the money? (Lenders charge a wide range of interest rates and fees for the use of their money.)

Lenders generate revenue by charging interest on the principal amount of the loan and fees for the transaction. When interest rates rise to a point where more borrowers can no longer afford to make their loan payments and still make a profit, demand usually starts to dry up. Two good examples of this are the sharp decrease in borrowing during the recession of the early '80s, and the Federal Reserve's severe credit tightening of 1994, which was intended to stave off inflation. Interest can represent a substantial cost, depending upon the interest rate and terms you secure. Even if your rate is low, it is essential for you to develop an accurate profit-and-loss projection, covering at least three years, including the cost of the interest on the money you borrow.

In the beginning, be aware that even if you make a good profit-and-loss projection with strong estimates and forecasted profits, you can still get into trouble if you don't make a good cash flow projection. A cash flow projection will show whether you can truly afford the loan. It subtracts the money you pay out from the money you take in. When the prime rate hit 20 percent in the '80s, there were a lot of vacant desks and empty chairs in escrow offices and lending departments at banks and not a lot of lending. Businesses were forced to curtail their expansion because the cost of borrowing was exorbitant.

Despite the value of cash flow projections, many businesspeople don't make them on a regular basis. They might make a profit-and-loss projection, or a balance sheet, or have them prepared by their bookkeeper or accountant every three months or so to see where they stand, but they often lack a cash flow projection. When raising money, however, you have no choice. Fortunately, these financial tools are not terribly difficult to compose, and are useful to have at any time during the year.

But if you focus on just one financial statement, you do so at your peril. For example, Freddie Laker of Laker Airways focused on the income statement and did not pay enough attention to the cash flow statement. This resulted in the eventual dissolution of the corporation. How can a company earn a profit yet generate a negative cash flow? If the company reinvests by acquiring a lot of equipment, such as airplanes, the capital expenditures may exceed the net income. This resultant negative cash flow may jeopardize the continuation of the business. It is important to view each financial statement as one perspective, and all the statements are necessary to attain the whole picture.

The interest you pay will show on your profit-and-loss statement, but the principal payments will show on your cash flow document. This is usually a large item, and sometimes overlooked when people first make their plans. You can make simple projections yourself or give them to an expert, such as an accountant or a financial consultant. If, every 6 or 12 months, you prepare a written summary of projections, it helps to identify these needs.

Your banker is going to be looking at these projections to make sure that you can repay the loan from the profits of the business. The banker is also going to check the cash flow projection to see that you have enough to cover your own draw for your living expenses, or that you have a separate income. Keep in mind that it may take 12 months or more before you can break even, meaning that income and expenses match up. Of course, some businesses can set up in a location with heavy foot traffic (in a mall for instance) and begin to generate a positive cash flow immediately. Using the advice of suppliers and other industry contacts, you'll want to estimate how soon you can realistically predict sales and expenses in order to estimate when you will break even and start earning a positive cash flow.

You'll also want to add in some extra money when you're making an application for a loan. A good rule of thumb is to take your first 12 months of expenses and add 20 percent to that amount.

There is one more critical financial sheet to develop before beginning the search for start-up financing—the balance sheet. The balance sheet simply shows your total assets and liabilities, and subtracts the two to arrive at your total net worth.

START-UP FINANCING STARTS WITH YOU

At the race track, many bettors place wagers on a particular horse. But those who are well vested in horse racing place their wager based more upon the jockey than the horse. In a similar context, many investors and lenders base their decisions more upon the quality of the management team than the product line. The experienced businessperson knows that sales are only part of the package. The rest—presenting your business and business description—involves your creative skills to give the impression that you have a profitable and stable business. Bankers, investors, and suppliers are all going to be looking to see what kind of person you are. Are you the kind of person who has repaid debts? Do you have a reputation of stability? If you've had trouble along these lines, it doesn't necessarily mean that you can't go into business. But wherever you have a problem—if, for example, you have a ratio out of line in your plan—you should be ready with an explanation for it.

When you raise money, you become a salesperson by default. And just as in any selling situation, you want to be able to answer objections as they arise to avoid objections later when making the close. If you have some unusual element in your business plan worth noting, footnote or comment on it in the plan as a way of handling the objection before it's a question in the lender's mind.

When evaluating your financial situation, take a look at your assets, (see Figure 3–1) both personal and business. If you're tight on cash, ask yourself how you can sell those assets to free up the cash. It doesn't matter whether they are personal or part of the business proper; they're all assets. Make a careful inventory of everything valuable you have. Analyze the situation to see what you might be able to sell. Cite problems in your personal expenditures, places where you might be spending more than you should. Identify where you might be able to cut back. When you show a personal statement to banks and other prospective funding sources, they will want to make sure you can live within the income you generate.

Figure 3–1   Personal Financial Statement

Statement of Financial Condition as of _____ **19,** _____

Individual Information	Coapplicant Information
Name	Name
Home Address	Home Address
· City, State & Zip	City, State & Zip
Name of Employer	Name of Employer
Title/Position	Title/Position
No. of Years with Employer	No. of Years with Employer
Employer Address	Employer Address
City, State & Zip	City, State & Zip
Home Phone Business Phone	Home Phone Business Phone

Source of Income	Totals	Contingent Liabilities	Totals
Salary (applicant)		If guarantor, comaker, or endorser	
Salary (coapplicant)		If you have any legal claims	
Bonuses & Commissions (applicant)		If you have liability for a lease or contract	
Bonuses & Commissions (coapplicant)		If you have outstanding letters of credit	
Income from Rental Property		If you have outstanding surety bonds	
Investment Income		If you have any contested tax liens	
Other Income*		If you listed an amount for any of the above, detail:	
Total Income*			

*Income from alimony, child support, or separate maintenance income need not be revealed if you do not wish to have it considered as a basis for repaying this obligation.

Assets	Totals	Liabilities	Totals
Cash, checking, & savings		Secured loans	
Marketable securities		Unsecured loans	
Nonmarketable securities		Charge account bills	
Real estate owned/home		Personal debts	
Partial interest in real estate equities		Monthly bills	
Automobiles		Real estate mortgages	
Personal property		Unpaid income tax	
Personal loans		Other unpaid taxes and interest	
Cash value—Life insurance		Other debts—Itemize	
Other assets—Itemize			
		Total Liabilities	
		Net Worth	
Total Assets		Total Liabilities & Net Worth	

What Investors Look For

Let's look at some of the characteristics that investors commonly look for in loan applicants. Whether it's a small personal loan or your first bank business loan, the lender will be considering it as if it were a personal loan. Thus, your ability to attract money depends as much on their perception of your character as on the completeness of your paperwork as depicted in Figure 3–1. Some items that investors consider are:

- *Stability.* They're going to check to see how long you've worked at jobs, where you've lived, or how long you've lived in a certain neighborhood. Although none of these items by itself would keep you from getting a loan, investors look at the overall picture, so try to make everything as positive as you can. If there is little evidence of stability, be prepared to answer any objection that may arise. If you've been moving around for one reason or another, or you've changed jobs for better opportunities, prepare a brief, logical explanation.
- *Income.* How well do you live within yours? Some people make a lot of money but have no discipline. They haven't learned to manage money effectively and live within their means. Although lenders may look at the total amount of money you've been making, they're also going to examine how well you've managed it. Obviously, if a person can't manage his or her personal finances, lenders will conclude it's going to be difficult for that person to manage the assets of a growing business.
- *Debt management.* Lenders will check how well you've been able to pay off your debts. What's your track record? If you have a charge account, do you pay it on time? Have you incurred a lot of late-payment penalties? Did you pay your car loan on time? Are you ever late with your rent or mortgage check? How well will you be able to demonstrate that you paid off your past debts? If you have some problems in this area, have an explanation ready to satisfy these people.

You are probably aware that anyone who receives a credit application from you can have your personal credit report accessed by computer almost instantaneously. But did you know you also have access to these records? Take advantage of this capability and arm yourself with the same information. Get a copy of your credit reports from any or all of the major national credit-reporting agencies. TRW (Texas), TransUnion (Ohio), and Equifax (Georgia) are the consumer credit reporting agencies used most frequently (see Appendix C for details). For a nominal charge (free in some cases), the company will give you a complete printout of the same record the lenders order. Check it for errors, in anticipation of any potential questions a lender might raise. Prevailing law requires credit bureaus to provide debtors with such a record whenever they apply for credit. Furthermore, they have to allow you the opportunity to correct any mistakes.

A particular lender may use one credit firm over another for some reason, or they may get two credit reports. It's amazing how different two credit reports can look. Therefore, it's a good idea to check out more than one and clean them up by disputing any erroneous information you find *before* you apply for your loan. The one thing lenders dislike in any loan-proposal process is a surprise. Eliminate the possibility that they will occur in advance of making your loan presentation.

Sometimes these reports can be confusing. If this is so, make an appointment with the credit company to have someone explain the items in question. They may not like the idea of doing this, but the law is very clear on this point. You may be able to go directly to, say, a department store credit office and ask a staff member to help you with a problem you may have with your store account. Let's assume it is an erroneous late payment charge on your account. You can go to the department store and explain that you've paid the money off, and you'd like to have that late-payment comment removed from your record and a note sent to the credit bureau to that effect. Sometimes they will remove the derogatory mark even if it is warranted; in other cases, you simply have to let it "cycle off" your report.

Some former creditors may not cooperate. Say you had a dispute with a plumber: The plumber did a job for you but it wasn't done right, so you didn't promptly pay the $100 charge. Finally, after two or three months of haggling, you pay the plumber, but by this time the plumber has filed a lien for nonpayment. Perhaps the plumber holds a grudge and refuses to send a note acknowledging payment. You have the right to put a statement in your credit file up to 100 words explaining that there was a misunderstanding, which is another way of cleaning up your credit record.

Methods of Raising Money

To understand where you can go to acquire the necessary capital to start, better manage, or expand your venture, you must first become acquainted with the various types of money, how they are generated and in what forms you'll be able to obtain it.

There are two kinds of funding: *internal* and *external*. Internal funding is the most inexpensive way to generate capital because you are relying on your own operation to raise the necessary money. External capital is just what it implies: capital generated outside the realm of the company. Sources for external funding include banks, suppliers, commercial finance companies, investment bankers, and venture capital funds.

When planning to raise money, you should consider internal options before searching for an external source. Not only is it a logical way of proceeding, but it allows you avoid the cost of borrowing as long as possible. Even if you can't generate all your capital requirements internally, at least you'll offset the amount of money required so that only a portion has to be raised through external sources.

There's another plus to using internal funding. Lenders are more apt to take a risk on you and your company if they know that you have an internal commitment to the venture. They will also have more confidence in your management ability when you can show you know how to make the most out of internal resources. But there is also a danger to utilizing internal funding. You may end up investing a considerable portion of your assets into the business, making yourself unattractive to external funding because there is less opportunity for them. Generally speaking, though, entrepreneurs who utilize internal funding before they look externally will experience greater long-term success.

At some point during the growth of your business, you will need to raise capital through external sources. As you evaluate these sources, you should realize that there are several types of capital that can be generated through external funding, and many entrepreneurs utilize a combination of these external sources.

Self-Financing

In most cases, a business is born out of the cash reserves of its owner. Many lenders and investors refrain from risking any money on a proposed business unless the principal owner or owners have a vested interest in it. This is especially true on the small-business level. If you are unwilling to accept the fact that you will have to commit some or all of your funds to start your business, perhaps you should rethink the idea of entrepreneurship.

Many experts espouse the theory, "Why risk your own money when you can use someone else's?" This aforementioned theory of Other People's Money (OPM) has been advocated for years. Certainly, it is an enticing thought, but unrealistic in the world of small business. Why? Because you simply won't find anyone else to fund 100 percent of the business unless you're willing to give up ownership. For lenders or investors to take substantial risk, they're going to ask for something substantial in return. Either the cost of the money is going to be extremely high in terms of interest, or you are going to have to relinquish the majority of equity within the company. Sure, you won't be risking your money, but you will be risking your place in the future of your business. In a backlash to an era of easier credit, many lenders insist on the "Big E," equity. Lenders believe that you should take some direct financial risk to ensure that you will protect their investment.

By utilizing your own money, you risk your own finances but you do not relinquish control of your company. Furthermore, you reduce your debt service, and consequently will look more attractive to external sources because of the confidence you've exhibited in the business by investing your own money.

To determine just how much money you have to invest in a business, evaluate your finances on the credit and debit sides using a personal balance sheet. Begin by listing all your assets and their value in the top portion of the form, including house, car, jewelry, and so on. Next list all your debts in the bottom portion, including credit cards, mortgage, bank notes, personal debts, auto loans, and any others. Compute the ratio between total assets and total liabilities to determine your net worth or degree of indebtedness. Then you are ready to realistically evaluate the needs of the business you are planning to run.

Set up this computation so that you have an assets-to-liabilities ratio; that is, Asset:Liabilities. Line A:Line B. The ratio will look something like 2:1; or, if you are like most people nowadays, 1:2. This is generally referred to as the *acid-test ratio* or *quick ratio,* the indicator of exactly where you will be if you run into some bad luck and you don't do anything to correct your financial position. If your assets exceed your liabilities, you should be able to keep the creditors from knocking on your door.

To assist you in obtaining or regaining control of your personal finances, consider the cash flow statement (Figure 3–2). Many businesspeople compute these monthly. To determine your cash flow, first enter your variable and fixed expenses. Add these to arrive at your total monthly expenses. Now write in your gross income, which should include your payroll check total, your spouse's pay (if applicable), and any extra money you earn (income from an apartment house, stocks, bonds, etc.). Subtract any deductions that appear on the face of the payroll or other checks to arrive at take-home pay. Next, subtract expenses from gross income to get your net income. Finally, subtract appropriate living expenses from net income. On the bottom line, enter remainder. This is your *disposable* or *discretionary income.* Disposable income is money that works for you. It can be used for anything from leisure activities to building a savings or money market account.

By creating a cash flow statement, you are charting your leverage. When the standard monthly expenses are deducted every month, what is left shows you how much more debt you can incur. If you incur any

Figure 3–2 Personal Cash Flow Statement

Statement of Financial Condition as of _____ **19,** _____

Monthly Variable Expenses		Totals	
Grocery purchases: Food, beverages, sundries			
Automobile: Gasoline, repairs, servicing			
Utility bills: Electricity, water, phone, etc.			
Clothing			
Medical, dental, prescription drugs			
Entertainment			
Contingency food			
Other monthly variable expenses—Itemize			
Total Variable Expenses	**A**		

Monthly Fixed Expenses		Totals	
Rent or mortgage payment			
Auto loan: Car 1			
Auto loan: Car 2			
Credit card payment 1			
Credit card payment 2			
Credit card payment 3			
Credit card payment 4			
Major store accounts			
Donations			
Insurance payments			
Home improvement loans—Itemize			
Total Fixed Expenses	**B**		

Total Monthly Expenses (A + B = C) **C**

Monthly Income			
Gross Income	**D**		
Payroll Deductions	**E**		
Net Income (D-E)	**F**		
Disposable Income (F-C)	**G**		

more than that, you are forced to borrow. That is why you must understand cash flow: Your knowledge of it can keep you out of trouble, both before and after you start your business.

Debt Financing

Debt financing offers the widest choice of possibilities for raising money. It is a form of external funding based on receiving a loan from an outside source, repayable over a specified period of time at a specific rate that is usually tied to the going cost of money in the financial markets.

Debt financing sources offer loans that are either secured or unsecured. Security is simply offering some form of collateral as an assurance that the loan will be repaid. If the debtor defaults on the loan, that collateral is forfeited to satisfy the payment of the debt. Most lenders will ask for security of some sort on a loan. Very few will lend you money based on your name or idea alone.

What type of security can you offer a lender when seeking a loan from an outside source? Here are the more common types:

- *Guarantor.* Guarantors sign an agreement with the bank that states they will guarantee the payment of the loan.
- *Endorser.* Same as a guarantor except an endorser may be asked to also post some sort of collateral.
- *Comaker.* Acts as a principal on the loan.
- *Accounts receivable.* The bank will usually advance 65 to 80 percent of the value of the qualified (bona fide creditors) receivables just as soon as the goods are shipped.
- *Equipment.* Lenders will usually accept 60 to 65 percent of the value of capital equipment as collateral for a loan. An exception is restaurant equipment for which the market value drops after purchase to 10 percent of the original cost.
- *Securities.* If your company is publicly held, you can offer stocks and bonds within the company as security for the repayment of a loan.
- *Real estate.* Most lenders will lend up to 90 percent of the assessed value of the real estate, either commercial or private.
- *Savings account.* If you have a savings account or certificate of deposit, you can use these to secure a loan.
- *Chattel mortgage.* Using equipment as collateral for the loan, the lender makes a loan based on something less than the

equipment's present value and holds a mortgage on it until the loan is repaid.

- *Insurance policies.* Usually, loans can be made up to 95 percent of the policy's cash value.
- *Warehouse inventory.* Lenders will usually advance up to only 50 percent of the value of inventory. Some lenders refuse to lend based upon inventory due to the increased turbulence of financial markets. It really depends upon the type of inventory, considering the uniqueness of the product, readily available channels of distribution, its rating on the "fad meter," and so on. A key question is, how easy is it to convert the inventory into cash?
- *Display merchandise.* Similar to warehouse inventory, display merchandise such as furniture, cars, home electronic equipment, and so on can be used to secure loans through a method known as *floor planning.*
- *Leases.* If the lender you're approaching for a loan holds the mortgage on property that you are trying to lease, the lender can simply assign the lease payments to you.

You can also attempt to acquire debt financing through an unsecured loan. In this type of loan, your credit reputation is the only security the lender will be accepting. You may either receive a signature or personal loan for several thousand dollars, or more if you have a good relationship with the bank. But these loans are usually short-term and have very high interest rates.

Keep in mind that most outside lenders are very conservative and probably will not grant you an unsecured loan unless you've done a tremendous amount of business with them in the past and have performed above expectations. Even if you do have this type of relationship with a lender, you may still be asked to post collateral on a loan due to economic conditions or your present financial condition. In addition to secured or unsecured loans, most debt will be subject to a repayment period. As discussed in *Small Business Management Fundamentals*, by Dan Steinhoff and John F. Burgess[1] there are three primary types of repayment terms:

1. *Short-term loan.* Loans for short-term uses, typically paid back within 6 to 18 months.
2. *Intermediate-term loan.* Loans paid back within roughly three years.

   3. *Long-term loan.* Loans paid back from the cash flow of the business in less than five years.

Considered by some to be an internal source because of frequency of use and reliability, debt financing through family and friends is perhaps the entrepreneur's best source. Although most experienced business operators frown upon this source of financing for start-ups or business expansion, it remains as one of the most popular avenues from which to launch a business.

   According to the SBA, over 11 percent of businesses in the United States were started using money borrowed from family and friends. In fact, many new entrepreneurs don't actively seek this money; it is offered by encouraging parents, relatives, or friends.

   One pitfall is that too many entrepreneurs borrow money on a very informal basis from people close to them; the terms of the loan are agreed on verbally and there is no written contract. It is important when borrowing money from relatives or friends, have your attorney draw up legal papers spelling out rates, terms and amounts. Even family and friends are sensitive about the issue of money. If they don't feel you are running your business correctly, they may step in and try to interfere with your operational plans. In some cases, you can't prevent this even with a written contract, where state laws guarantee corporate voting rights to an individual who has invested money in a business. By taking the necessary precautions, however, you can prevent undue complications.

   Credit cards are one of the most overlooked resources for obtaining start-up capital. The downside is that most charge perilously high interest rates; but it is a way to get several thousand dollars quickly without the hassle of dealing with paperwork. Just don't go above your specified credit amount. Recently, several banks and nonbanks have begun to offer very low-cost credit card interest for a defined period of time. This may make it very attractive to use credit cards for start-up purposes.

   Let's assume you have three credit cards with a credit line on each of $3,000. You want to start a small business that you think will require approximately $8,000. You could cash in each card for the full amount and start that business. Within six months, you could probably build up a very good business and approach your local bank for a $10,000 loan at about 10 percent interest, then pay off your credit card balances (which most likely have 20-percent annual rates). After another six months, you could pay off the bank loan of $10,000. Appendix C contains a listing of companies offering lines of credit and business credit cards. Limits on cards designed for business use may reach as high as $200,000 or more. Banks, of course, are the largest source of available debt financing, but they're a less-than-ideal source for the entrepreneur looking for seed money and initial research and development capital, unless your aim is a government-guaranteed loan. Conversely, after you get started, they are one of the best financing sources.

Banks will require both personal and business references from you before they will make any commitments, in addition to character references, a complete business plan outlining your plans, how you're going to start, and how much money you expect to make. They will also ask to see a plan on how the loan is going to be used to fund the business. Above all, they're going to be looking at you as an individual because they're investing in *you*.

When you first start in business, unless you're unusually well-capitalized, you will need to evaluate your personal expenses to determine whether there is any chance of reducing your living costs. You want to show that you have positive cash flow. Banks want to be assured that the money generated by the business will cover your living expenses, that you're not going further into debt. From a financial point of view, they evaluate you and your business as a single entity.

A small-business loan carries an interest rate somewhere above the prime rate, which is the rate that banks charge their most favored customers. Small businesses usually pay 1 to 3 percent above prime. Generally, the borrower is more concerned with just finding a loan than with locking in the lowest interest rate; and being excited about your new business is fine, but that doesn't mean you should agree to pay usurious rates to the first bank that approves a loan for you. Whether it's money up front or money charged you in increments so you don't feel it, paying too much is never wise. Based on what you can qualify for, find a loan with a low interest rate and monthly payments you can afford. If your neighborhood business bank isn't competitive, look elsewhere until you find what you want.

For most small business owners, commercial lenders are the only game in town, because banks tend to shy away from small companies experiencing rapid sales growth, a temporary decline, or a seasonal slump. In addition, firms that are already highly leveraged (a high debt-to-equity ratio) will usually have a hard time getting more bank funding. But the business bank will often step in where other banks fear to tread because they are set up to handle just those situations, and because they know they can get most, if not all, of their defaulted loan back by selling off the collateral pledged against it. Not that liquidation is a desired goal by any means; most business lenders dislike it almost as much as banks do, and they, as you, try to avoid it at all costs.

Small and medium-sized operations are the usual recipients of such loans, although business lenders are generally reluctant to get involved with high-tech companies (too volatile) or services, which obviously don't have the type of assets (except for receivables) suitable for use as collateral. (These are the target of venture capitalists.) For very similar reasons, start-up loans are very rare, and lenders won't loan money on assets that don't exist.

Government Debt Financing

The government has instituted a number of loan programs tailor-made for startups. One is a *direct loan,* by which the SBA loans its funds appropriated by Congress. The other type, the *SBA-guaranteed loan,* doesn't use government money. Instead, it is loaned by the bank or by another financial institution but guaranteed by the SBA for up to 80 percent of the face value of the loan. That said, note that the Small Business Administration rarely makes direct loans. Rather, they guarantee loans through a participation program set up with banks, and make direct loans only to persons with disabilities or to disabled veterans. Other direct loans funded through the SBA are awarded for disaster relief to businesses that are victims of natural catastrophes. But even those that qualify cannot solicit a loan from the SBA if they can legitimately obtain a loan from a bank or private source. There-fore, you must first apply to a bank or alternate lending source; and if you live in a city with a population over 200,000, you must have been turned down by two financial institutions before seeking SBA funds. For a comprehensive discussion of SBA financing opportunities and how to apply, refer to Chapter 4, SBA Loans.

The SBA is, without doubt, the largest single source of federally assisted financing for small business. According to Jack Zwick, author of *A Handbook of Small Business Finance,*[2] there are five major programs generally available to small businesses on a yearly basis:

1. *Farmers Home Administration (FmHA) of the USDA.* Limited to cities or areas with a population of 50,000 or less outside major metropolitan areas, FmHA loans are guaranteed long-term loans backed 90 percent by the FmHA. They can be used as a source of start-up or working capital, or for new equip-ment purchases, refinancing, or expansion (including pur-chase of real estate). Loans for real estate and major construction are also available for up to 30 years. Equipment and machinery can be financed for up to 15 years or their de-preciable life, if shorter. Capital funds can be obtained for six-year terms. There is no limit on the amount you can borrow. Approval depends solely on need and the way you plan to use the money.

2. *Economic Development Administration of the Department of Commerce.* EDA makes loans and guarantees to new and existing businesses in depressed areas—regions that have high unemployment and low-to-medium income levels. Loans may be granted to cover working capital or to purchase fixed assets. Working capital loans extend up to seven years, while loans for fixed assets may extend up to 25 years. The loan applicant is expected to provide 15 percent of the required funding. Interest rates vary according to the prevailing prime rate at the time the loan is granted.

3. *Department of Energy.* DOE loans are geared toward firms developing methods to increase domestic energy efficiency through conservation, alternate energy sources, or new ways of energy utilization. Funding from the DOE does not have to be repaid, and guarantees can run as high as $30 million. For companies operating in geothermal zones, loans can be guaranteed up to $200 million.

4. *Department of Housing and Urban Development (HUD).* HUD has several programs consisting of grants and loans for the construction of commercial and residential building to rehabilitate needy areas in targeted cities. Funds are channeled through local HUD officials in cities and towns. They, in turn, make loans or grants to entrepreneurs to develop properties. In the recent past, over $3 billion in loans and grants were disbursed through HUD for these programs.

5. *Department of the Interior.* The DOI has a historic preservation-grants program through which it makes grants for the restoration of rundown properties that have been declared historic sites by a state agency. Reports indicate there are some 2,000 properties listed as historic locations in the United States, and the list grows each year.

In addition to the five federal programs listed, there are several other important government financing sources you should consider when trying to raise money:

- *State Business and Industrial Development Corporations (SBIDCs).* SBIDCs are capitalized through state governments and are usually interested in making long-term loans from 5 to 20 years for either the expansion of an existing small business or for the purchase of capital equipment. Lender requirements and interests vary from state to state. Some SBIDCs commit funds to very high-risk ventures, while others look for minimal risk.

- *Local Development Companies (LDCs).* LDCs are capitalized through local investment groups. These agencies differ from community to community according to their priorities and interests, but in general will solicit funds from the SBA and bank sources to supply money to local business for the construction or expansion of facilities. The LDC will usually receive a loan guarantee from the SBA—up to $1 million with additional unlimited funds originating from banks. All moneys are directed to the LDC as the loan recipient, not the business applying for the financing. The only drawback to LDCs is that they will finance only up to 10 percent of a project.

- *Export Revolving Line of Credit Program.* This program guarantees up to 90 percent of a bank line of credit to a small business exporter who is eligible according to SBA criteria.

- *Export-Import Bank (EXIMBANK).* This source provides working capital for smaller companies to finance preshipment and foreign marketing operations.

- *The Small Business Innovation Research Program (SBIR).* This program is an opportunity for small businesses to benefit from over $1 billion in federal grants. The SBIR Program (a result of the 1982 Small Business Innovation Development Act) is intended to stir innovative activities among small companies. There is no central SBIR agency; instead, each branch of the federal government sponsors an SBIR program with its own awards. Eligibility for receipt of SBIR funding is extended to any small company capable of demonstrating science or high-tech expertise. The program categorizes small businesses as independently owned companies with 500 or fewer employees. Average recipient companies have had fewer than 35 employees, and 45 percent of Phase I awards have gone to companies with 10 employees or less. In 1993, Congress showed its support for the SBIR programs by appropriating $700 million for its 1993 and 1994 fiscal years. SBIR spokesperson David Speser believes the program has succeeded because much of today's "good technology and new industries are started in the small-business sector."[3] In fact, Speser says many large high-tech corporations are now looking to become subcontractors to small firms with government contracts. The government sponsors three national SBIR conferences each year, allowing small companies to meet with more than 100 government agency officials, high-tech management experts, and corporate representatives.

Equity Financing

Equity financing means you sell off a portion of your business to investors who may or may not actively participate in its management. The main variable involved in equity financing is how much control to give up. During start-up, you will probably have to give up as much as 50 percent of the equity in your business. If you have capital to invest in the company, you can receive a proportionate amount of equity for your funds. However, while the 50/50 rule is fairly common, a lot of entrepreneurs opt for a 51/49 split. Some equity investors have begun to provide capital for a minority share in the business. You can also offset the 50/50 rule by placing an equity value on proprietary knowledge such as patents or specific operating information, negotiate a value for this knowledge, and receive equity for that contribution. The legal form you choose for your business—sole proprietorship, general partnership, limited partnership, corporation, subchapter-S corporation, or limited liability corporation—will have a dramatic effect on the way you will want to divide equity. The following are the most typical legal forms entrepreneurs choose for their ventures.

Sole Proprietorship

A sole proprietorship is a business you start and run by yourself. There is one owner, one equity investor: You. You are the only one responsible for the business.

Partnership

If you form a partnership, you have a general partner, and each of you own the business equally. You're both responsible for running the business and for the liabilities of that business. If it goes bankrupt, you share the consequences equally.

Limited Partnership

In a limited partnership arrangement, your goal is to recruit investors to become partners in your company on a limited basis. Sometimes referred to as syndications, limited partnerships consist of a general partner, who manages the money raised to actively operate the business, and the investors, who are considered the limited partners. Should the venture meet with misfortune, the partners' liability is "limited" to what they have invested. They can lose their original investment in the event of collapse, but they can't be assessed everything as they could if they came into a business as a general partner.

As the general partner, you would assume the obligation of running the venture on a daily basis. Limited partners, by their legally constituted role, serve as passive investors rather than active managers. The advantage for the limited partners is that they invest the money while someone else produces the profits. These profits, other than the amounts needed for business operation and possible reinvestment into the business for expansion, must be divided among the partners. If a business succeeds, they may reap profit distribution far in excess of anything they would be likely to get as conventional stockholders. Along the same lines, by taking advantage of the limited partnership structure, you don't have to give up the equity in your business permanently in order to proceed with a specific project venture.

It is important to know that rules governing limited partnership capitalization vary from state to state and must be strictly observed. In many states, you cannot advertise or offer limited partnership participation publicly without formal "registration" as a securities offering. Where this is the case, you are suddenly facing on a state level many of the same rules, filing procedures, and disclosure headaches that companies going public encounter at the federal (Securities and Exchange Commission) level. This is expensive and time-consuming and is the sort of activity that you should undertake only in conjunction with a securities lawyer.

In many states, you can secure exemption from registration if the offering is limited to a preset number of investors and is not trumpeted to the public. For instance, you could hold a cocktail party at which the potential limited partners of your venture could be approached; but you couldn't advertise in the local newspaper for limited partners to join your venture. Find out what the rules are in your state with respect to forming limited partnerships, and don't try to manipulate them.

Corporation

You can also form a corporation in order to raise equity financing. Partners forming a corporation can divide ownership into shares, selling this private stock to equity investors; responsibilities can be defined in the corporate minutes, and a partner who wants to leave can be accommodated without much legal hassle or dissolution of the business. Stock can be used as collateral (in a partnership it cannot); death of one shareholder doesn't stop the business (in a partnership it sometimes does). And you can enjoy many executive privileges that are difficult to justify in a sole proprietorship or partnership.

Another advantage is that banks are more amenable to loaning to a corporation. Profits can be delayed, capital can be accumulated without taxation, and the corporation can loan money to you personally. To raise additional capital or even start-up capital, the corporation may elect to offer stock within the company to the investing public. In this manner, the company goes from a privately held corporation to a publicly held corporation. The only disadvantage is possible double taxation, because the corporation must pay taxes on its net income, and you must pay taxes on any dividends you may receive from the corporation.

Subchapter-S Corporation

Taking the corporation one step further, and infusing elements of the sole proprietorship and partnerships, is the subchapter-S corporation. This form of operation allows you to take on passive investors who will contribute money to your business for stock within the corporation. Like a limited partnership, a subchapter-S corporation gives you full operational responsibilities while taking on investors within the company.

Unlike limited partnerships, however, a subchapter-S corporation is still a corporation with all the privileges except one: They elect not to be taxed as corporations. Instead, the shareholders of a subchapter-S corporation include in their individual gross incomes their proportionate shares of the corporate profits and losses. Subchapter-S corporations are excellent devices to allow small businesses to avoid double taxation. If your company does produce a substantial profit, forming a subchapter-S corporation would be wise because the profits will be added to your personal income and taxed at an individual rate that may be lower than the regular corporate rate on that income.

To qualify under subchapter-S, the corporation must be a domestic corporation, must not be a member of an affiliated group, must not have more than 35 shareholders (all of whom are either individuals or estates), must not have a nonresident alien as a shareholder, and may have only one class of outstanding stock. Under the new rules, the corporation may now have an unlimited amount of passive income from rents, royalties, and interest.

A passive activity is one in which a taxpayer does not materially participate. Material participation requires involvement in operations on a regular, continuous, substantial basis. Under the 1986 Tax Reform Act, losses and credits from a "passive" business activity can be deducted only against passive income. Passive losses and credits will not be usable against nonpassive income, which includes a compensation and portfolio income. However, rental losses and credits can be used against up to $25,000 of nonpassive income.

Limited Liability Companies

A new business form called the limited liability company (LLC) has sprung up in 38 states. The LLC arose from the desire of business owners to adopt a business structure that permitted them to operate as a traditional partnership. This distributes the income and income tax to the partners (reported on their individual income tax returns), but also protects them from personal liability for the business debts, as with the corporate business form. In the case of the entrepreneur, unless a separate corporation is established, the owner and partners (if any) assume complete liability for all debts of the business. Under the LLC concept, on the other hand, an individual is not responsible for the firm's debt.

The LLC also offers a number of advantages over S corporations. For one, while S corporations can issue only one class of company stock, LLCs can offer several different classes with different rights. In addition, S corporations are limited to a maximum of 35 individual shareholders (who must be U.S. residents), while an unlimited number of individuals, corporations, and partnerships may participate in an LLC.

The LLC also carries significant tax advantages over the limited partnership. For one, unless the partner in a limited partnership assumes an active role, his or her losses are considered "passive," and therefore ineligible as tax deductions against active income. But if the partner does take an active role in the firm's management, he or she becomes liable for the firm's debt. It's a catch-22: The owners of an LLC, on the other hand, do not assume liability for the business's debt, and any losses can be used as tax deductions against active income.

In exchange for these two considerable benefits, however, the owners of LLCs must meet the *transferability restriction test,* which means the ownership interests in the LLC are not transferable without some restrictions. It's this restriction that makes the LLC structure unworkable for major corporations. For corporations to attract large sums of capital, their corporate stock must be easily transferable in the stock exchanges. But this restriction should not pose a problem for typical entrepreneurial businesses, in which ownership transfers take place relatively infrequently.

A number of quirks in current state LLC legislation require tricky maneuvering and plenty of advance planning. For example, LLC legislation in Colorado and Wyoming don't allow for continuity of the business, which means the business is dissolved upon the death, retirement, resignation, or expulsion of an owner. While the same is true for both individual proprietorships and partnerships, you must still plan accordingly.

In Florida, the state's 5.5 percent corporate tax also applies to LLCs. And with state shortfalls in tax revenues and strained budgets, other states may look to LLCs for additional tax revenues, even though similar businesses such as S corporations are typically exempt from state and federal income taxes. Also, since the LLC is a relatively new legal form for businesses, federal and state governments are still looking at ways to tighten the regulations surrounding this business tool. These attempts come from a concern that some investment promoters are using this legal form to evade securities laws. Although most LLCs are legitimate, the Securities and Exchange Commission (SEC) is moving quickly to tighten control of those firms engaged in irregular activity. In addition, LLCs cannot issue an Initial Public Offering (IPO). Still, conversion to another form of corporation can be done fairly easily prior to going public. If this form of business sounds like it would fit your needs, explore new and pending legislation concerning LLCs in your area.

Venture Capitalists

Professional investors, known in the aggregate as venture capitalists, are a ready source of start-up funds, although many of them prefer to invest in new and existing businesses poised for rapid growth. Once reserved for high-growth, high-tech businesses, there is now an abundance of venture capital available for businesses in any field, as long as they promise strong returns. Many of the more than 500 venture capital funds in the United States are controlled by banks, but they operate by completely different rules.

Business Angels

Individual venture capitalists interested in providing seed and start-up financing are commonly referred to as *angels*. According to the Center for Venture Research, part of the Whittemore School of Business and Economics at the University of New Hampshire, they are figures in the "invisible venture capital market" which invests $10 to $20 billion annually in over 30,000 ventures.[4] These informal investors are more likely than institutional ("visible") sources to pour their money into an entrepreneurial business if its prospects for growth are high but perhaps not spectacular. Business angels, unlike other venture capital investors, prefer to invest their money in the operation as early as possible. They understand high risk, and they expect high return. Most are veteran businesspeople looking for an investment they can monitor, which is why they usually invest in a business near them. This is more a preference than a hard and fast rule, and it is always secondary to the desire for a premium return on investment. Though not all angels invest in entrepreneurial ventures, their substantial contribution to the $300 billion "invisible" venture capital market proves their potential as a capital source for your business.[5]

As mentioned, venture capitalists (who are also a topic of discussion in Chapter 7, Expansion Financing) historically have invested in technology-related industries; not new technology necessarily, but applications of existing technology such as computer-related communications, electronics, genetic engineering, and medical/health-related fields. They also make investments in service and distribution businesses and even a few consumer-related companies.

The key to attracting institutional venture funding is to prove your company's potential for growth. You will have a difficult time attracting venture capitalists if your company does not have the potential to grow tremendously in 10 years or less.

Before approaching venture capitalists of any kind, do some research to help you become acquainted with them. Find out if what you require matches their preferred investment strategy, and compare different venture capitalists' preferences. The venture capital directories available today (see the "Resources" section of Appendix C) list the investment preferences of thousands of venture capital funds, one of which may have the money that will fuel your future.

NOTE: Because there is no universal system or standard for rating the trustworthiness of venture capital firms, business angels, and other investment sources, your best defense is information. Too often, entrepreneurs put their faith in a firm that promises to find them the financing that will launch their business toward new frontiers, only to find themselves six months later with an empty wallet and no funding. Research, research, research! Contact the firms, fund managers, angels, and matching services to request background information. Read up on the companies, study their track record, and, if possible, talk with companies that have benefited from their assistance. If you don't like what you find, keep looking.

Once a decision is made to finance your firm, the investor's actual investment is negotiable and can take a variety of forms, ranging from a straight common stock purchase to debentures with conversion features to straight loans. Venture capitalists usually use a combination of investment instruments to structure the deal that will be most beneficial to both parties.

Regardless of whether you are a spectacular success or a catastrophic failure, there will come a time when the venture capitalist will want out—or when you will want to end the relationship. This is the point at which the venture capitalist will realize the appreciated gain (or loss) on investment. This "exit" will have been discussed in some depth at the time you negotiated the original deal. You will either take your company public, repurchase the investor's stock, merge with another firm, or, in some circumstances, liquidate your business.

SBICs

Another type of professional investor, called a small business investment corporation (SBIC), operates under the auspices of the federal government and makes money available to business start-ups. They are private investors, but every dollar they invest is matched with three to four dollars in SBA-guaranteed loans. An SBIC's criteria, however, is just as stringent as a bank's or any other private investor's—perhaps even more so. This is the overwhelming reason why, historically, new businesses have seldom had occasion to use an SBIC.

Under the law, SBICs must invest exclusively in small firms with net worth of less than $6 million and average after-tax earnings (over the past two years) of less than $2 million. Being licensed and regulated by a government agency distinguishes SBICs from other "private" venture capital firms. The advantage of this arrangement to the SBIC comes in the form of leverage. An SBIC that is in compliance with the regulations and that has invested substantially all of its initial private capital can borrow additional investment funds, (a practice known as leveraging) from the Federal Treasury. Beyond that, the operations of an SBIC are not significantly different from those of a private venture capital fund.

MESBICs

An offshoot of the SBIC is the MESBIC, the Minority Enterprise Small Business Investment Company. A MESBIC is privately capitalized. In SBICs, and here, borrowers must have at least $150,000 when they start, and then they're eligible for government-guaranteed loans. If you have an ongoing business but need more capital, check into these investors. They will want a company that looks like it will become very profitable. When they sell in three or four years, they want a three to five times return on their money.

SBDCs

Yet another avenue for financing is Small Business Development Companies (SBDCs). The only difference between these financing entities and SBICs is that their capital comes exclusively from the following private interests:

- Multinational corporations and conglomerates.
- Utilities.
- Firms dealing with infrastructure.
- Private business consortia.

Like SBICs and MESBICs, the SBDCs that operate in this country invest for the long run, which is one reason they like to focus on proven businesses. Don't approach them if you are trying to finance a short-term equipment purchase or need an overnight loan; that's what banks are for.

A cooperative effort between the private sector, the educational community, and federal, state, and local governments, SBDCs offer current and prospective small business owners counseling, training, and technical assistance in all aspects of small business management—most of it free or at low cost. There are 57 SBDCs, one or more in each of the 50 states, the District of Columbia, Puerto Rico, and the Virgin Islands, with more than 700 service locations. Each SBDC has a "lead" organization that sponsors and manages a program and coordinates the services, which are offered through a network of subcenters and satellite locations at colleges, universities, vocational schools, chambers of commerce, and economic development corporations.

In addition to programs unique to their areas, all SBDCs provide training and technical assistance with such business essentials as finance, marketing, organization, human resources, and production. Though the SBDC program is sponsored by the Small Business Administration (SBA), each center has leeway to develop services tailored to the local community and the needs of its individual clients.

Trade Credit for a Start-Up?

A supplier will seldom extend you credit unless you're a regular customer—then it's 30 to 90 days without interest. And if your business is a start-up, getting trade credit is twice as difficult. Suppliers want to make every order C.O.D. until you've established that you can pay bills on time. Still, you can negotiate a trade credit basis with suppliers. Preparing a financial plan is one of the things you can do to facilitate these negotiations.

When visiting a supplier to set up an order, ask to speak directly to the owner of the business if the company is small. If it's a larger business, ask to speak to the chief financial officer or whomever approves credit. Introduce yourself and show the officer your financial plan. Tell the owner or financial officer about your start-up business and explain that you need to get your first orders on credit in order to launch your venture.

The owner or financial officer may give you half the order on credit with balance due upon delivery. Of course, the trick here is to get your goods shipped to you and sell them before you have to pay for them yourself. You could borrow the money to pay for your inventory, but you would have to pay interest on that money. This is one of the most effective ways to reduce the amount of initial working capital you need. The key to this kind of financing, as with all others, is knowing how to reach it and being prepared when you do. (For a complete discussion on the value of trade credit to ongoing operations, see Chapter 5, Bootstrap Financing.)

ALL IN THE FAMILY

Frances Huffman

Some say, "Don't do it!" Others claim it's the only way to go. What are we talking about? The very touchy, potentially volatile prospect of borrowing seed money from friends and family. In many ways, friends and family seem like the logical place for cash-strapped entrepreneurs to go, considering the difficulties in finding outside financing. Banks have tightened their lending practices, Small Business Administration (SBA) loans require personal guarantees many people can't meet, and few outside investors can be convinced to give an unproven product or service a try. If you don't have the money yourself (and who does?), where else can you turn?

Hitting up your inner circle of friends and relatives may seem like the only viable solution to the money hunt. In fact, after personal savings, friends and family are the second most popular source for business start-up capital. After all, friends and family know you're trustworthy and competent, so lending money to you doesn't seem so risky to them.

However, taking money from people you know has its own risks and can threaten the relationship if your business fails and you can't repay the loan. "A bad loan to a family member can result in lots of lingering hostility," warns Bob Calvin, founder and president of Management Dimensions Inc., a Chicago-based management consulting firm. "Family relationships are complicated enough as it is. A bad loan can turn every family encounter into a stressful situation." Mixing money and friendship or love creates a potentially explosive combination. But don't despair: There are ways to navigate the delicate process without stepping on anybody's toes. And if you handle the situation in a professional manner, both you and your friends or family should benefit from the union.

The Family Tree

"In this economy, getting money from outside investors is especially difficult," says inventor Doren Berkovich, who sent queries to 50 investors but received only two replies—both of them saying, "No, thank you." Following those

(Continued)

(Continued)

rejections, Berkovich sought out a long-time friend to fund the $40,000 needed to get his Mouse Chase electronic cat toy invention off the ground. When Berkovich, whose company, Day Dream Enterprises, is located in Thousand Oaks, California, first broached the subject of a loan, his friend was skeptical about lending his hard-earned cash. Berkovich finally quelled his friend's fears by presenting him with a formal business plan and writing a brief business contract explaining all the ramifications of the deal.

According to experts, that's the right thing to do. "Putting everything in writing is mandatory," says Calvin. Telling a friend, "Oh, I'll just pay you back when I can" won't cut it when you're borrowing thousands of dollars. Many budding business owners erroneously assume a personal loan from a friend or relative means you can take your time paying it back. Wrong! "You've got to treat a loan from a [friend or] family member exactly as you would treat a loan from the bank," adds Calvin. "That means setting up a repayment schedule and paying market interest rates."

Some people are willing to put up money to get your business going, but they assume the investment gives them free license to meddle in your affairs. If the person who's lending you money has some business savvy, you may want to include that person as a partner in your business. However, if you're looking for a straight investment as opposed to a partner, make it clear from the start that the loan doesn't entitle the lender to dictate how you run your business. "We let our friends and family know upfront that this was a passive investment," says Jim Ervin, who, along with partners Tom Snyder and Jon Kumnick, raised $200,000 from personal acquaintances to start Safety Floor International, a floor safety and service company in Washington, DC. Ervin says the trio turned to friends and family in 1991 after testing traditional loan avenues—banks, the SBA and private investors—to no avail. "We figured, who better to borrow from than our friends?" says Ervin. "They already know us, they know we have integrity, and they know we'll be successful at whatever we set out to do. It's not like trying to convince a private investor who has never even heard of us that we're worthy of his or her money."

Knowing which people to target was one of the first steps to finding financing for Safety Floor. Ervin and his partners singled out friends and family who had the money to spare. According to Calvin, it's imperative to solicit money only from those who won't be financially strapped if they lend you the money. "No family members (or friends) should invest more than they can afford to lose," Calvin warns. That may seem bleak, but it's sound advice.

Another tip for saving relationships: Don't borrow too much money from one person. That has worked for John Bintz, who's still in the development stages of his Chicago-based ferryboat service, Chi-Mich Transportation. "I figured borrowing a few thousand dollars from lots of friends was better than borrowing a tremendous amount from one person," says Bintz, who expects to hit the waterways sometime this year. The founders of Safety Floor share this philosophy. "We just felt more comfortable borrowing small amounts of money—$5,000 here, $30,000 there—as opposed to hitting up one person for the entire amount," Ervin says. And so far, with 1992 gross sales of $1.5 million, Ervin and his cohorts have been able to pay back the loans without a hitch.

4

SBA LOANS

The Small Business Administration was established as an independent agency in 1953 by the Department of Commerce. Its purpose is to help entrepreneurs form successful small enterprises by securing the required capital to start a business or expand operations. Today, the SBA offers small businesses financial, procurement, management assistance, and advocacy nationwide. Programs are delivered by SBA offices in every state, the District of Columbia, the Virgin Islands, Puerto Rico, and Guam (for a list of SBA Business Information Centers see Appendix C). In addition, the SBA works with thousands of leading educational and training institutions to promote and foster small business development and growth. The Small Business Development Centers (SBDC), the Service Corps of Retired Executives (SCORE) and the Small Business Institutes (SBI) are some of the resource partners that counsel and train thousands of businesses every year.

TYPES OF SBA LOANS

As indicated in the previous chapter, there are basically three types of SBA loans. One is a *direct loan*, by which the SBA lends its own funds, appropriated by Congress. Another is the *SBA-guaranteed loan*, which doesn't use government money; instead, money is loaned by the bank or other financial institutions but is guaranteed by the SBA. The third type is a fairly new addition to the SBA portfolio, called the *MicroLoan* program. It is funded by the SBA and handled by nonprofit organizations to provide start-up businesses with small amounts of capital in order to give them momentum.[1]

Although advertised as one of the three SBA loan types, keep in mind an important point: The SBA rarely makes direct loans. They are reserved to Vietnam-era veterans and, 30-percent disabled veterans from any area, handicapped persons, persons living in economically distressed areas, and 8(a) program participants who are socially and economically disadvantaged persons. In general, recipients of these loans must have had loan requests denied by two conventional lenders for reasons other than credit factors. Other direct loans funded through the SBA go for disaster relief to businesses that have fallen victim to natural catastrophes. Even those who qualify cannot solicit a loan from the SBA if they can legitimately obtain a loan from a bank or private source. Therefore, you must first apply to a bank or alternate lending source. Additionally, if you live in a city with a population over 200,000, you must have been turned down by two financial institutions before seeking SBA funds. The financial assistance required cannot be obtainable on reasonable terms through the public offering or private placing of securities, or through the disposal "at a fair price" of assets not required to conduct business properly or not necessary to potential growth.

If you do apply for an SBA loan, the lead time it takes to process the loan depends on the circumstances involved. It often takes entrepreneurs one year to 18 months before their loans are approved, although a properly prepared application for an SBA loan might be processed in as little as two months, with the applicant receiving the money within one week after a bank willing to participate in a guarantee is found.

But whatever your circumstance, a visit to your local SBA is always helpful. Staff there can, for instance, provide you with a list of banks in your area that are more "small business-friendly," where you have a better chance in receiving a loan. Small local banks are usually more inclined to work with small businesses. Appendix E provides you with a list of such banks.

7(a) Loan Guaranty Program

The 7(a) Loan Guaranty is the SBA's primary loan program and accounts for more than 90 percent of the agency's total loan effort. Under the 7(a) program, loans are made for small businesses expanding or renovating facilities, purchasing machinery and equipment, financing receivables, augmenting working capital, refinancing existing debt (with compelling reasons), financing seasonal lines of credit, constructing commercial buildings, and purchasing land or buildings. Although private lending institutions fund the loans, the SBA guarantees them. The SBA can guarantee as much as 80 percent on loans of up to $100,000 and 75 percent on loans of more than $100,000. In most cases, the maximum loan amount is $750,000 (75 percent of $1 million), although the bank can loan you more than that. Exceptions are made in the International Trade, DELTA, and 504 loan programs, which have higher loan limits.[2]

The guidelines for SBA-guaranteed loans are similar to those for standard bank loans: You must establish your equity, history, management experience, and so on. In addition, your company must qualify as a small business according to SBA size standards, which vary from industry to industry.[3] The SBA charges a fee of 2 percent of the loan amount it guarantees, and banks usually charge a standard battery of fees including a charge for packaging the loan and submitting it to the SBA.

Keep in mind that under a loan guarantee, the SBA itself is not making the loan. It is simply protecting the lending institution against default of the loan. In essence, the SBA is a form of security in a guaranteed loan that reduces the risks perceived by lenders when dealing with small-business loans. The process works like this: You submit a loan application to a lender for initial review. The lender certifies that it could not provide funding on reasonable terms except with an SBA guaranty and forwards a copy of the application and a credit analysis to the nearest SBA. After SBA approval, the lending institution closes the loan and disburses the funds to you, and you make monthly loan payments to the lender. As with any other loan, you are responsible for repaying the full amount of the loan.

The interest rate charged on SBA guaranteed loans is based on the prime rate. The SBA does not set interest rates; it is not a lender. It does, however, regulate the amount of interest that a lender may charge an SBA borrower. If the loan has a term of less than seven years, the rate is prime plus no more than 2.25 percent. If the loan has a term of seven years or more, the SBA allows the lender to charge a margin of as much as 2.75 percent above the prevailing prime rate. For loans under $50,000, rates can be slightly higher.

To secure the loan, you must pledge sufficient assets. Personal guarantees are required from all the principal owners of the business.

As collateral for an SBA guaranteed loan, you can use certain assets as security, including:

- Land or buildings.
- Machinery or equipment.
- Real estate or chattel mortgages.
- Warehouse receipts for marketable merchandise.
- Personal endorsement of a guarantor (a friend who is able and willing to pay off the loan if you fail).
- Accounts receivable.
- Savings accounts.
- Life insurance policies.
- Stocks and bonds.

In general, the SBA looks for good character, management expertise and commitment, sufficient funds to operate the business on a sound financial basis, a feasible business plan, adequate equity or investment in the business, sufficient collateral (although in most cases a loan will not be declined solely on insufficient collateral basis), and the ability to repay the loan. The chief benefits offered by the 7(a) loan are the low down payment required, longer terms than conventional loans (7 to 10 years instead of the usual 3 to 5 years), lower interest rates and higher advance rates. Less cash up front and lower rates (less interest to pay) means better cash flow, which is precisely what you need both during and after the start-up period. Also, there is no prepayment penalty associated with SBA loans, so you can pay off the loan whenever you want without incurring a charge. Businesses that grow more quickly than expected particularly appreciate this feature.

Specialized Loan and Lender Delivery Programs under 7(a)

In addition to the standard loan guaranty, the SBA has two categories of targeted programs under 7(a), those that are designed to meet the specialized needs of borrowers and those that meet the needs of lenders. In general, the same rules, regulations, interest rates, fees, and so on as the regular 7(a) loan guaranty apply.

Programs for Borrowers

CAPLines (former GreenLine Program)

If you are a small business with short-term and cyclical working capital needs, the CAPLines program may interest you. A loan under this program can be for any dollar amount (except for the Small Asset-Based Line, explained later) and the SBA will guarantee 75 percent up to $750,000 (80 percent on loans less than $100,000). Basically, CAPLines are used to finance seasonal working-capital needs; direct costs needed to perform construction, service, and supply contracts; direct costs associated with commercial and residential building construction without a firm commitment to purchase; operating capital by obtaining advances against existing inventory and accounts receivable; or to consolidate short-term debts. The lines of credit have a maturity of up to five years, but a shorter initial maturity may be established. Interest rates are negotiated with the lender, up to 2.25 percent over the prime rate, and the guarantee fee is the same as for any standard 7(a) loan. The primary collateral will be the short-term assets financed by the loan. Types of short-term working capital loan programs under CAPLines include:

Revolving or nonrevolving:

- *Seasonal Line.* Funds the anticipated inventory and accounts receivables for peak seasons and seasonal sales fluctuations.
- *Contract Line.* Finances the direct labor and material costs associated with performing assignable contracts.
- *Builders Line.* For small general contractors or builders constructing or renovating commercial or residential buildings to finance direct labor and material costs with the building project serving as the collateral.

Revolving:

- *Standard Asset-Based Line.* An asset-based line of credit that provides financing for cyclical, growth, recurring, or short-term needs. Repayment comes from converting short-term assets into cash, which is remitted to the lender. Business continually draw, based on existing assets, and repay as their cash cycle dictates. This line is generally used by businesses that provide credit for other businesses. Additional fees may be charged by the lender to cover the continual servicing and monitoring of collaterals required by this loan.
- *Small Asset-Based Line.* An asset-based line of credit up to $200,000. In addition, if the business can consistently show

repayment ability from cash flow for the full amount, some of the stricter servicing requirements of the standard asset-based line are waived.

International Trade Loan Program

The International Trade Loan Program is the option for small businesses that are engaged in international trade, preparing to engage in international trade, or suffer adverse effects by competition from imports. Proceeds may be used for working capital or purchasing land and buildings, building or remodeling facilities, purchasing or reconditioning machinery, or other improvements that will be used within the United States to produce goods or services for export. The SBA will guarantee as much as $1.25 million in combined working-capital and fixed assets loans. Loans for facilities and equipment can have maturities of up to 25 years, but if the working-capital portion of the loan is made according to the provisions of the Export Working Capital Program (next section), it will have a maximum maturity of three years. As for collaterals, only those located in the United States, its territories and possessions are accepted, and the lender must take a first-lien position (or first mortgage) for loans under this program. Personal guarantees and other additional collateral may be required.

Export Working Capital Program

The Export Working Capital Program (EWCP) was developed in response to the needs of exporters seeking short-term working capital. It can be obtained by completing a one-page application form and streamlined documentation, and turnaround is usually within 10 days. The SBA guarantees 75 percent of the principal and interest, up to $750,000 (80 percent on loans of $100,000 or less), and the guaranty may be combined with other loans as long as the total exposure for the SBA does not exceed the $750,000 limit. If the EWCP is combined with an international trade loan, however, the SBA's exposure can go up to $1.25 million. Loan maturities typically either match a single transaction cycle or support a line of credit, generally with a term of 12 months. Unlike other 7(a) programs, you and your lender negotiate interest rates and fees.

DELTA

The Defense Loan and Technical Assistance Program (DELTA) was created to help defense-dependent small firms that are adversely affected by defense cuts. The goal is to help business owners diversify into the commercial market instead of going out of business. The program provides both financial and technical assistance in a joint effort of the SBA and the Department of Defense (DoD), and functions within the general rules of the 7(a) Program and the 504 Certified Development Company Program. Up to $1 billion in gross lending is offered through this program. Individually, however, the maximum gross loan you can get for your company is $1.25 million, with a maximum guaranty of $1 million under 504. To be eligible, your business must meet SBA size standards and have derived at least 25 percent of total company revenues during the preceding fiscal year from DoD contracts, defense-related contracts with the Department of Energy, or subcontracts in support of defense-related prime contracts. Your business must also be adversely impacted by reductions in defense spending; and you have to use the loan to retain jobs of defense workers, be located in an adversely impacted community, and create new economic activity and jobs, or modernize or expand your plant so it can diversify operations while remaining in the national technical and industrial base. In addition to the loan, you may require technical assistance to make the transition to the commercial market, which will be provided through the small business development centers, the Service Corps for Retired Executives, other federal agencies, and other technical and management assistance providers.

SPECIALIZED PROGRAMS

The Minorities and the Women's Prequalification Loan Programs

These programs are for women or minorities who own or want to start a business. They offer loan packaging support and the SBA's commitment, through the form of a letter of prequalification which you can take to a lender, making it easier to secure a loan. To qualify, businesses must be at least 51 percent owned, operated, and managed by people of ethnic or racial minorities, or by women; have average annual sales for the preceding three years that do not exceed $5 million; employ fewer than 100 people, including affiliates; and not be engaged in speculation or investment. An intermediary (nonprofit in the case of the women's program, or both nonprofit and for-profit organizations in the case of the minority program) will help you assemble a package for SBA approval and then locate a lender offering the most competitive rates. Another big advantage of these programs is that once the package is assembled, usually it takes only three days for the SBA to make a decision and issue the letter of prequalification. The maximum amount for these loans is $250,000 with the SBA guaranteeing up to 75 percent (80 percent on loans of $100,000 or less). Under the minority program, some district offices may have other limits. Because these are pilot programs, they are available at a limited number of locations. Check your local SBA for more information.

The LowDoc Loan Program

The SBA has adopted a program similar to the 7(a) program, which makes applying for a loan somewhat easier. Called the LowDoc Loan Program, it combines a simplified application process with a more rapid response from SBA loan officers—two weeks—slashing pages of red tape out of the loan process. The LowDoc loan program streamlines the loan application process for guaranteed loans of less than $100,000.

The LowDoc loan program was created in response to complaints that the SBA's loan application process for smaller loans was needlessly cumbersome for both borrowers and lenders who participate in the SBA's 7(a) General Business Loan Guarantee Program. The process tended to discourage borrowers from applying for and lenders from making loans of less than $100,000. The SBA will guarantee up to 80 percent of the loan amount.

The approval process relies heavily on a lender's experience and judgment of a borrower's credit history and character. The primary considerations are the borrower's willingness and ability to repay debts, as shown by his or her personal and business credit history and past or projected cash flow. No predetermined percentage of equity is required, and lack of full collateral is not necessarily a determining factor.

The application form for loans less than $50,000 consists of a single page. Applications for loans of $50,000 to $100,000 include the same short-form application plus the applicant's income tax returns for the previous three years and personal financial statements from all other guarantors and co-owners of the business. Commercial lenders are likely to require additional paperwork to satisfy their own requirements. Other documents required by legislation, regulation, and executive order are dealt with at the loan closing.

Any small business eligible under the regular 7(a) loan program can apply under LowDoc if its average annual sales for the previous three years were $5 million or less and it employs 100 or fewer individuals, including the owner and partners or principles.

FA$TRAK

FA$TRAK makes capital available to entrepreneurs seeking loans of up to $100,000, without requiring the lender to use the SBA process.

LOWDOC LOAN PROGRAM

The Small Business Administration recently adopted a new program that makes applying for a loan somewhat easier. Called the LowDoc Loan Program, it combines a simplified application process with a more rapid response from SBA loan officers of perhaps two or three days, slashing pages of bureaucracy and red tape out of the loan process.

The LowDoc program was created in response to complaints that the SBA's loan application process for smaller loans was needlessly cumbersome for both borrowers and lenders that participate in SBA's 7(a) General Business Loan Guarantee Program. The process tended to discourage borrowers from applying and lenders from making loans of less than $100,000. LowDoc streamlines the loan application process for guaranteed loans under $100,000. The approval process relies heavily on a lender's experience and judgment of a borrower's credit history and character. The primary considerations are the borrower's willingness and ability to repay debts, as shown by his or her personal and business credit history, and by past or projected cash flow. No predetermined percentage of equity is required, and lack of full collateral is not necessarily a determining factor.

The application form for loans under $50,000 consists of a single page. Applications for loans from $50,000 to $100,000 include that short-form application plus the applicant's income tax returns for the previous three years and personal financial statements from all other guarantors and co-owners of the business. Commercial lenders are likely to require additional paperwork to satisfy their own requirements. Other documents required by legislation, regulation, and executive order are dealt with at the loan closing.

Eligibility

Any small business eligible under the regular 7(a) loan program can apply under LowDoc if its average annual sales for the previous three years is $5,000,000 or less and it employs 100 or fewer individuals, including the owner, partners, or principals.

Lenders simply use their existing documentation and procedures to make and service loans, and the SBA guarantees up to 50 percent of the loan. For a list of FA$TRAK lenders, contact your local SBA office. Like most 7(a) loans, maturities are usually five to seven years for working capital and up to 25 years for real estate equipment. For revolving credits, you may take up to five years after the first disbursement to repay the loan.

The Certified and Preferred Lenders Programs

Certified lenders are those that have been heavily involved in regular SBA loan-guaranty processing and have met certain other criteria. Participants are delegated partial (certified lenders) or full (preferred lenders) authority to approve loans, which results in faster service. Certified lenders account for 10 percent of all SBA business loans, while preferred lenders account for 18 percent. A list of participants in these programs can be obtained from your local SBA office.

504 Certified Development Company (CDC) Program

If you are planning to develop industrial, commercial or retail property, or are in the market for a piece of property or major equipment, a 504 loan is worth investigating. This fixed-rate financing program was developed with the help of certified development companies, nonprofit organizations sponsored by private interests or by state and local governments, which work closely with the SBA to support small business. There are about 290 CDCs nationwide. Start-up business owners usually do not qualify for this type of loan because of the sums involved, but it is beneficial for owners of larger businesses making substantial investments.[4]

Forty percent of the loan (up to $1 million) is an SBA 504 second mortgage debenture funded by CDC. The remaining 60 percent is composed of the borrower's down payment (10 percent minimum) and a first mortgage funded by the participating bank (60 percent less the down payment—at least 50 percent). Terms of 10 or 20 years and margins (fees) from 2 to 3 points are available for the SBA's portion of the loan, which has a fixed rate. You and the bank decide on the rate, term, and margin of the other portion of the loan.

The 504 affords the same benefits as the SBA 7(a) loan: low down payment, longer-than-usual terms, and attractive interest rates. As with all SBA programs, there are specific conditions (profit cap, size standards, job creation, net worth limit, etc.) which must be satisfied in order for a business to be eligible. Contact your local bank or the SBA for details.

The 7(m) MicroLoan Program

For low-cost start-up and other small-business uses, a lot of entrepreneurs have taken advantage of the SBA's newest lending vehicle, the MicroLoan Program. Established in June 1992, it offers loans ranging from $100 to $25,000 to businesses that cannot approach traditional lenders because the amount they need is too small.[5] The money can be used for most of the same purposes as the 7(a) loan (working capital, equipment purchases, fixtures, and leasehold improvements), and as a line of credit. It may not be used to pay existing debts. Completed applications usually are processed by intermediaries in less than one week. This 100-percent guaranteed loan program is currently offered in most states, but because it is still fairly new, it may not be available at your local SBA. In addition, because the MicroLoan program is part of a larger guaranteed loan program offered by participating states, there are different regulations, maximum loan amounts, rates, terms, and fees. To find out what your state or any other has to offer, call your regional SBA office (listed in Appendix D) or talk with the SBA sales manager of a commercial bank in the area in question.

Small Business Investment Company Program

The Small Business Investment Company (SBIC) Program fills the gap between the availability of venture capital and the needs of small businesses that are either starting or growing. Licensed and regulated by the SBA, SBICs are privately owned and managed investment firms that make capital available to small businesses through investments or loans. They use their own funds plus funds obtained at favorable rates with the SBA guaranties or by selling their preferred stock to the SBA. SBICs are for-profit firms whose incentive is to share in the success of a small business. They provide funding to all types of manufacturing and service industries and debt-equity investments and management assistance. Most seek businesses with strong growth potential and consider a wide variety of investment opportunities.

The Surety Bond Program

By law, prime contractors to the federal government must post surety bonds on federal construction projects valued at $100,000 or more. Many state, county, city, and private-sector projects require bonding as well. The SBA can guarantee bid, performance, and payments bonds for contracts up to $1.25 million for small businesses that cannot obtain bonds through regular commercial channels. There are two ways to obtain bonding: Prior Approval, when contractors apply through a surety bonding agent and the guarantee goes to the surety; or Preferred Sureties, which are authorized by the SBA to issue, monitor, and service bonds without prior SBA approval.

TYPES OF LENDERS

There are primarily three types of lenders the SBA uses to fund loans:

1. *Infrequent participant lenders.* Just what the name infers, these are bank and nonbank lending institutions that deal with the SBA on a sporadic basis. Most of the lenders involved with SBA deals fall into this category. An infrequent lender sends the SBA all paperwork involved with any particular loan guarantee situation. The SBA does an independent analysis of the plan and determines whether it will guarantee the loan that the institution is going to give the borrower.

2. *Certified lenders.* These are lending institutions that participate with the SBA on a regular basis and have an SBA-involved staff trained and certified by the agency. Under this program, the lender reviews all the paperwork, decides whether the borrower merits a loan, but the SBA has the final word. Only after the lender has approved the loan does the SBA review the documents, which it must do within three days.

3. *Preferred lenders.* Certified lenders that have graduated to the top of the list based on performance. Under the Preferred Lenders Program, the SBA designates its "best and most reliable lending partners" as preferred lenders, which may make

final decisions regarding loan approval and processing (with final review by the SBA).

Not all banks are eligible for either the Bank Certification Program or Preferred Lenders Program. Indeed, most preferred lenders tend to be major commercial banks that may have specialized SBA divisions. To become certified, each bank must meet four criteria:

1. *Experience.* A minimum of 10 years' SBA lending.
2. *Prudence.* A good record with few loans bought back by the SBA.
3. *Community Lending.* A solid record of loans to local borrowers, especially to minorities and women.
4. *Assistance to small business.* A record of helping local small firms.

Even with eligibility, some certified banks request a regular credit check from the SBA for some of their loans, and there's a reason: If a bank is negligent in approving a loan under the Certified Lending Program, the SBA can deny liability. The Bank Certification Program is not geared toward every type of SBA request; it's primarily designed for stable businesses that have proven track records.

LOAN RESTRICTIONS

Any programs as attractive as those offered by the SBA come with their share of contingencies, restrictions and conditions that must be satisfied in order for you to be considered for any loan funded by or through the SBA, whether you are starting a new business or obtaining capital for an existing one. First of all, the business requesting SBA financing must be independently owned and operated, not dominant in its field, and must meet employment or sales standards developed by the administration. Loans cannot be made to speculative businesses; media-related businesses; businesses engaged in gambling, lending, or investing; recreational or amusement facilities; or nonprofit enterprises.

Furthermore, loans cannot be made to:

- Pay off a creditor who is adequately secured and in a position to sustain loss.
- Provide funds for distribution to the principals of the applicant.
- Replenish funds previously used for such purposes.

- Encourage a monopoly or activity that is inconsistent with the accepted standards of the American system of free competitive enterprise.
- Purchase property that will be held for sale or investment.
- Relocate a business for other than sound business purposes.
- Effect a change of ownership unless it will aid in the sound development of the company or will engage a person hampered or prevented from participating in the free enterprise system because of economic, physical, or social disadvantages.
- Acquire or start another business besides the present one.
- Expand to an additional location.
- Create an absentee-ownership business.
- Refinance debt of any kind.

Be fully prepared to prove to the SBA that your proposed company has the ability to compete and be successful in its particular field. Remember that whether you are seeking a loan for an untried business or an established one, do not underestimate the importance of the category into which the SBA groups it. The success or failure of your application may rest on its SBA-assigned classification. Determine the most fitting discipline, field, or area for your business from the list provided, state this in your application, and be prepared to defend your choice.

As a way of helping you prepare for this question, you should understand how the SBA formulates its guidelines. A key publication to rely on is the *Standard Industrial Classification (SIC) Manual*, published by the Bureau of the Budget in Washington, DC. The SBA also uses published information concerning the nature of similar companies, as well as your description of the proposed business. The SBA will not intentionally work against you, so it is your job to steer the administration in the direction most beneficial to you. Another important point to keep in mind is that to apply for an SBA loan, you have to qualify as a small business according to the SBA Maximum Size Standard. The standard varies for each industry and is based on the average number of employees during the preceding 12 months or on sales averaged over the previous three years.

The standards used by the SBA to judge the size of a business interested in qualifying for a loan vary across industries, but there is a constant: the SBA's basic tenet that the business applying for the loan must be "small" by its definition. Generally, the following guidelines apply, according to William Cohen's *The Entrepreneur and Small Business Problem Solver:*[6]

- *Manufacturing.* Firms engaged in manufacturing a product are constrained by their number of employees. Average employment in the preceding four calendar quarters must not exceed 500. If employment exceeded 500 but not 1,500 for a manufacturing company, the SBA's determination is based on a specific size standard for the particular industry.
- *Wholesaling.* Average employment should be 100 employees.
- *Services.* From $2.5 million to $21.5 million in annual receipts.
- *Retailing.* Annual sales from $5 million to $21 million.
- *Construction.* General construction: Average annual receipts from $13.5 million to $17 million for the three most recently completed fiscal years, depending on the industry. Special Trade: Average annual receipts not to exceed $7 million.
- *Agriculture.* Annual receipts from $0.5 million to $9 million.

Because these qualifications may change at any time, call the SBA to request their most current published information so that you can most accurately gauge your options when you are ready to start actively seeking funds.

SBA LOAN STRUCTURE

Product classification and size are not the only statistics the SBA will require from your business. Whether you are applying for a loan to finance a start-up or fund an existing business, to be successful at applying for a loan, entrepreneurs need to develop a loan proposal with the following elements:

- *A description of the business you plan to establish.* A written description of your existing or proposed business. This may be taken from your business plan (or may be the business plan itself) and should include information on:
  a) Type of organization.
  b) Date of formation.
  c) Location.
  d) Product or service.
  e) Brief history of business.
  f) Proposed future operations.
  g) Service area.
  h) Competition.

     i) Customers.

     j) Suppliers.

     k) Zoning.

- *Your experience and management capabilities.* Provide resumés on each owner and key management personnel.
- *Personal financial statements.* Statements are required of all principal owners (20 percent or more) and guarantors, should not be older than 60 days, and should show all personal assets and liabilities. In addition, attach a copy of last year's federal income tax return (forms for personal financial statements can be obtained at banks).
- *How much money you plan to invest and how much you will need to borrow.*
- *Loan repayment.* A brief written statement indicating how the loan funds will be repaid. Include repayment sources and time required. Make sure to support the information by cash flow schedules, budgets, and other appropriate information.
- *Future operation projections.* Include projections for at least one year or until positive cash flow can be shown. Show how much you expect to take in, what the expenses will be, and the basis of your estimates. Use a profit-and-loss format and explain assumptions used and deviations from trend or industry standards.
- *Financial data (business).* Existing businesses should provide at least the past three years financial statements, profit-and-loss statements, and a reconciliation of net worth. Include agings of accounts payable and accounts receivable and a schedule of term debt. (If the business has been in existence less than three years, provide the preceding for that period.) Proposed new business need only a proforma balance sheet showing sources and uses of both equity and borrowed funds.
- *The collateral you can offer as security for the loan.* Include an estimate of its current market value.
- *Other items as they apply.* Include leases (copies of proposed); franchise agreements, purchase agreements, plans, specifications, cost breakdowns, copies of licenses, letters of reference, letters of intent, contracts, purchase orders, partnership agreements, and articles of incorporation.

Accuracy is of utmost importance. Keep notes on everything that goes into the loan package as backup, in the event you are called upon to explain or prove a figure or statement in any of the documents.

In addition to the list just given, the SBA has the following credit underwriting requirements:

1. You must have a reasonable investment in your business, usually 30 percent to 50 percent of the total project cost for new business ventures and business acquisitions. The percentage varies according to the degree of risk involved. In case of an existing business, the debt-to-equity ratio should not exceed four to one (4:1).

2. You must establish that you have or can obtain the necessary knowledge, experience, or technical expertise to operate and manage the business profitably.

3. You must establish the viability and marketability of your product or service by identifying your market and how you plan to successfully sell to that market.

4. You must establish the ability to repay the loan and provide required owner compensation from the profits of the business. Projection forms are available from banks for this purpose.

5. You must provide collateral sufficient to protect the interest of the government. Normally, loans will not by declined solely because of a lack of collateral if the other four factors described are favorable.

The Personal Financial Statement

This form lists all your assets and liabilities and must be prepared for each major stockholder (having at least 20 percent ownership), partner, officer, and owner of the business. Your financial statement must be current (not more than 60 days preceding the date of your loan application), and it must accurately portray your financial position. The SBA may reject your application if any misrepresentation or inflated entries are found. Obtain copies of SBA Form 413 for preparing your personal balance sheet.

The Financial Plan

Because this is a major element in your application for a loan, this section explains its components in more detail. Every business, large or small, new or old, needs to have a financial plan to guide it. New businesses have the biggest challenge of all. Whether you call this an operating plan, a forecast, or a projection, it must show your potential profit or loss and your cash flow during the first 12 months of operation, as shown in Figure 4–1. Preparing these estimates will probably be the most difficult part of preparing your loan package, and you may want to enlist the services of an accountant to do this for you. You can use SBA Form 1099 for preparing a forecast, or you can have your accountant develop one for you. If your projections show that you will gross more than $250,000 during the first year, then a *proforma balance sheet* should be made as of the end of the first-year forecast.

Prepare a reasonable and realistic projection of your monthly sales, expenses, profits, and cash flow. A reasonable and realistic estimate is one that is based on fact; it is an educated guess, not a pipe dream that cannot be substantiated. The more documented proof you have to back up your estimates, the better your chance of securing the funding you requested. In addition, the exercise of putting all these numbers together will make you more knowledgeable about your business, and this, too, will increase your chances of success.

The first month in your projection should be the month in which your business is fully operational. This could very well be two, three, or more months *after* you receive your loan funds. Some people prefer to begin by estimating their sales. Others prefer to start by estimating expenses. As long as your numbers are solid estimates, you should not worry about how you arrive at them. The point is that you include the following items in your projection:

- *Total sales (Net).* Total sales include both "cash" and "on-account" sales. Net sales are total sales minus returns and refunds. If your business has separate profit-making departments, estimate sales for each department separately.
- *Cost of sales.* Cost of sales should account for the cost of merchandise sold and freight or transportation charges you pay on incoming inventory. If any of your employees will be paid a sales commission, the amount of commissions should be included in your cost of sales.
- *Gross profit.* Gross profit, sometimes called gross margin, is the difference between net sales and cost of sales.

The second half of your operating plan projections deal with expenses. These are costs incurred on a monthly basis in order to operate your company. They are:

- *Salaries.* Your estimated payroll costs. It does not include your own salary compensation.
- *Payroll taxes and benefits.* All state and federal obligations, as well as any company-paid benefits you provide your employees,

Figure 4-1   Financial Plan

	Month 1	Month 2	Month 3	Month 4	Month 5	Month 6	Month 7	Month 8	Month 9	Month 10	Month 11	Month 12	Total
Sales													
Cost of sales													
Gross profit													
Expenses													
Advertising													
Automobile													
Bank discounts													
Depreciation													
Dues/subscriptions													
Insurance													
Interest													
Office supplies													
Payroll taxes													
Professional services													
Rent													
Repairs/maintenance													
Salaries													
Supplies													
Taxes/licenses													
Utilities/phone													
Miscellaneous													
Total expenses													
Profit before taxes													

such as vacation, sick pay, health insurance, or others, should be included in this entry.

- *Outside services.* Services necessary to operate your business on a monthly basis such as janitorial, pest control, and so on.
- *Supplies.* All items purchased for office and operating use in the business (not for resale) are included here. This could include cleansers, paper towels, lightbulbs, cash register tapes, ashtrays, stationery supplies, business cards, printing of forms, as well as pens, pencils, staplers, typewriter ribbons, and postage.
- *Repairs and maintenance.* All repairs to equipment used in the operation of the business, as well as any maintenance contracts or regularly scheduled service work.
- *Advertising.* Budgeted costs for marketing your company, product, or service. These should include any special promotions or grand-opening events.
- *Cars, delivery, and travel.* Any costs incurred by you or your employees for air fare, meals, lodging, vehicle rental, or lease payments; gas and the mileage allowance set forth by the IRS for private or company-owned vehicles.
- *Accounting/legal.* Costs generated to maintain your accounting records, prepare year-end financial statements and tax return, consult with an attorney, or subscribe to a security service.
- *Rent.* Monthly rent, lease, or mortgage payment on the use of operating facilities.
- *Phone.* Monthly costs incurred for all telecommunications services such as basic phone, fax, cellular phone, and so on.
- *Utilities.* Cost of electricity, gas or oil for heating water, garbage collection, and sewer charges, if applicable.
- *Insurance.* Property, product, and liability coverage. Do not forget to include any special coverage needed for your particular business, but do not include life insurance in this category.
- *Taxes and licenses.* All applicable taxes and licensing fees such as business licenses, inventory tax, sales tax, excise tax, and personal property tax (excludes income and payroll tax).
- *Interest.* On business debts only. This does not include the portion of your payment that covers principal repayment of your loan.
- *Depreciation.* The IRS will allow you to deduct a certain percentage of the cost of various fixed assets.
- *Other.* Any miscellaneous expenses that do not appear in the preceding categories.

- *Total expenses.* Total of all the previous expenses.
- *Profit before taxes.* The difference between the gross profit of your business and the total expenses.

In making your projections, understand that sales, profits, and cash are not the same thing. Obviously they are related, but it is not unusual for a business to encounter periodic shortages of cash *even though sales and profits may be booming.* For this reason, it is necessary that you prepare a separate schedule specifically for cash flow. This involves projecting total monthly cash inflow and outflow for a 12-month period. You can do this after you have prepared your projections for sales and expenses.

A *cash flow projection* is necessary to enable you to manage receipts and disbursements so that cash is always available to meet expenses as they become due. In your projection, pay close attention to timing, and take into account the time lag between sales and the collection of receivables, and between expenses and the due dates for their payment. You can prepare your own cash flow statement (see Figure 4–2) or use SBA Form 1100. Although Form 1100 is more detailed, it is no more difficult to prepare your own.

In your cash flow projection, the following items should appear:

- *Cash sales.* A monthly total of all cash and credit card sales.
- *Accounts receivable.* The percentage of sales that have been made on credit accounts that can be collected within a given month.
- *Other.* List all other sources of cash inflow, including family members, stock offerings, and any other loans except start-up funding.
- *Total cash available.* The total money on hand before any disbursements are made.
- *Owner's draw.* The monthly stipend(s) received by the owner(s).
- *Loan principal repayments.* Principal only, excluding any interest payments.
- *Cost of sales.*
- *Total expenses.*
- *Capital expenditures.* All costs associated with the purchase of equipment, fixtures, tools, leasehold improvements, vehicles, and other capital assets in the first month.
- *Reserve for taxes.* A reserve fund for future income tax.
- *Other.* Any miscellaneous disbursements that do not appear in the preceding categories.

Figure 4-2 Cash Flow Projection

	1st month	2nd month	3rd month	4th month	5th month	6th month	7th month	8th month	9th month	10th month	11th month	12th month	Totals
Cash sales													
Receivables													
Other income													
Total income													
Material													
Direct labor													
Overhead													
Marketing & sales													
Brewery operations/R&D													
G&A													
Taxes													
Capital													
Loans													
Total expenses													
Cash flow													
Cumulative cash flow													

- *Total disbursements.*
- *Monthly cash flow.* Total available cash after all disbursements have been met.
- *Cumulative cash flow.* The yearly total on the monthly cash flow.

Capital Requirements

When obtaining an SBA loan to start a new business, or any other kind of loan for that matter, you must be able to account for all the costs of getting your business launched, how much of these costs can be met using your personal funds, and how much will come from your loan. The following statement is an example of how to summarize the use of funds required for your business:

Capital equipment/building improvements	$ 1.2 million
Inventory	$ 3.5 million
Labor	$ 1.8 million
Overhead	$ 8.7 million
Marketing	$ 1.8 million
Research & Development	$ 4 million
G&A	$ 4 million
Miscellaneous	$ .6 million
TOTAL CAPITAL REQUIRED	$18.4 million
Less: Investment by applicant	($ 9.9 million)
TOTAL LOAN REQUESTED	$ 8.5 million

Keep all your notes and worksheets to show how you determined each of the figures on this statement. Obtain written price quotations on all items you plan to purchase for the business. For equipment, you should estimate the amount of money you will need for repair and maintenance as well.

The cost for building improvements should be based on three bids from reliable contractors. For inventory, you should budget enough money to carry you through your opening period and the first few months. Prepare a list of your major suppliers, and for each one obtain information on their prices, delivery schedules, and terms of payment. See the example on page 101.

Estimate your required working capital from your cash flow projection. Your goal is to have enough cash at all times to cover three months' expenses and inventory replenishment. Since it's unlikely that

SAMPLE LIST OF SUPPLIERS (NAMES ARE FICTIONAL)

Adams Specialties
2 Hilltop Pl.
Brisbane, CA 94123
(Cutting and dye equipment)
Terms: 2% 10 days, net 30

Superior Machinery, Inc.
166 Mill Rd.
Los Angeles, CA 90231
(Stamping, imprinting, and folding equipment)
Terms: 2% 10 days, net 30

Silver Distributing Co.
400 University Ave.
Costa Mesa, CA 92345
(Plastics supplier)
Terms: 2% 10 days, net 30

Hi-Test, Inc.
106 Technology Blvd.
San Francisco, CA 94622
(Testing equipment)
Terms: Net 10 days

Associated Wholesalers Inc.
1633 Eastern Ave.
Los Angeles, CA 92122
(High-absorbent padding and tape fasteners)
Terms: 2%, 10 days net 25

your business will generate enough cash flow to meet this target, you will have to make up the shortage with loan funds.

The SBA will expect you, as an owner, to make a considerable investment in the business, preferably 20 percent or more. Your investment can be in any form that benefits the business—cash, furniture, equipment, or other. Prepare a statement indicating what you intend to invest, as the following example demonstrates:

INVESTMENT STATEMENT

The undersigned applicants, John Smith, Roger Smith, and Steve Smith, hereby declare that they will make an investment of the assets listed below in the proposed business to be known as Softie Baby Care, Inc.

Capital equipment/building improvements	$1.2 million
Overhead	$8.7 million
TOTAL INVESTMENT	$9.9 million

(Date)

(Signed)   John Smith

Roger Smith

Steve Smith

You will also need to prepare a brief description of your business. This does not have to be as involved as the one described in Chapter 2, Business Plan, or in Appendix A. You merely need to describe your business and include a paragraph outlining the expected benefits you will receive from the loan. For example:

- Softie Baby Care, Inc. will provide ecology-minded consumers with an environmentally safe disposable diaper that will feature all the elements that are popular among users of disposable diapers, but will include an added benefit—biodegradability. The product, which is patent pending, will target current users of disposable diapers who are deeply concerned about the environment, as well as those consumers using cloth diapers and diaper services. This product will be distributed to wholesalers who will in turn sell to major supermarkets, specialty stores, department stores, and major toy stores.

- The company was incorporated in 1995 in the State of California under the name of Softie Baby Care. The company's CEO, president, and vice president have over 30 years of combined experience within the diaper industry.

- The company has applied for a patent on the primary technology around which the business is built. It enables the plastic within a disposable diaper to break down upon extended exposure to sunlight. Lease agreements are also in place for a 20,000-square-foot facility in a light industrial area of Los Angeles, as well as for major equipment needed to begin production. The company is currently being funded by $3 million from the three principals, with purchase orders for 500,000 units already in hand. Capital will be used to purchase needed equipment and materials for development of the product and initial test marketing.

COLLATERAL

Collateral will be one of the major criteria by which the SBA judges a loan application, therefore you need to prepare an itemized list and accurately describe the collateral you are prepared to offer. Obtain copies of SBA Form 4, Schedule A to do this.

You can get SBA forms from your bank or from the nearest SBA office. We suggest you get three copies of the required forms: one for preparing a draft, one for the final copy, and a spare copy in case you need an extra in a hurry.

The Loan Application

The loan application form is the last document you should fill out. Much of the information on that form is a summary of the data just described and listed in the business plan. If you have prepared this data correctly, it should contain all the information you and the lender will require about the proposed new business or existing business and the financing it needs to begin. There are two sides to the application form. The front side is divided into six sections with instructions for completing the information requested in each included. The sections on the loan application are as follows:

1. *Applicant.* All relevant information about yourself and your business in this section, such as your full legal name, fictitious name statement if applicable, trade name of borrower, street address, employer's ID number, type of business, date business established, number of employees, and bank of business account.
2. *Management.* List the name and home address of each person who will assume responsibility for managing the business.
3. *Use of proceeds.* List all expenditures and estimated costs such as land acquisition; new plant or building construction, building

expansion, or repair; acquisition or capital equipment, inventory, working capital, all debt services (including the SBA), total loan requested, and term of loan.

4. *Summary of collateral.* A summary of the assets you wish to use as collateral for your loan. Assets are grouped under six categories, A through F: A = Land and Building, B = Machinery and Equipment, C = Furniture and Fixtures, D = Accounts Receivables, and F = Other.

5. *Previous government financing.* A description of any government loans you, any principals, or affiliates have requested.

6. *Indebtedness.* All outstanding debts, including installment contracts, personal loans, mortgages payable, and others.

The back side of the form has 17 items that must be provided, including:

1. Personal history statement.
2. Personal balance sheet.
3. Financial statements.
4. Business description.
5. Management team.
6. Cosigners.
7. Equipment list.
8. Description of any bankruptcies or insolvencies.
9. Description of any lawsuits.
10. Any familial relations employed by the SBA.
11. A list of existing or proposed subsidiaries.
12. Statements of any financial interest in any entity you buy from, sell to, or use the services of.
13. A list of franchise agreements, if applicable.
14. Written bids from three contractors for back-up estimates.
15. Declination letters.

As an applicant for an SBA business loan, you may obtain the assistance of any attorney, accountant, appraiser, or other representative to aid in the preparation and presentation of the application. Such representation is not mandatory, but if a loan is approved, the services of an attorney may be necessary for the preparation of closing documents, title abstracts, and more. The SBA allows payment of reasonable fees or other compensation for services performed by consultants engaged to assist the applicant.

FED FUNDS

Erika Kotite

The Small Business Administration (SBA) was started in 1953 to "help small businesses start, grow, and prosper." Included in that pledge was a loan program to make low-interest, long-term loans available to businesses that would otherwise have a hard time finding capital. Today, the SBA has a $5-billion loan fund that is distributed both as direct loans and through guarantees made on loans issued through local banks.

In its 40 years, the SBA loan program has effectively helped nearly 1 million small-business owners get the money they need to develop products, hire employees, purchase equipment, and make building improvements. Many borrowers get SBA funding after they've been rejected by other lending institutions. And those rejections are rampant: Since the beginning of 1991, business loans by banks have dropped about 8 percent. These days, few banks make loans to anyone who doesn't have substantial collateral and a long track record. The SBA focuses less on the business owner's collateral and more on his or her "repayment ability." "We want to see a careful cash flow projection showing how the loan will be paid back," says Mary Brennan Lukens, associate deputy administrator for business development at the SBA in Washington, DC.

But while your chances of receiving an SBA loan are greater than that of getting a conventional business loan, it's a mistake to take SBA loans for granted. Not everybody is entitled to a loan simply by asking for one. "You're not borrowing lightly," says Cristi Cristich, president and owner of Cristek Interconnects Inc., an electronic connector manufacturer in Anaheim, California. "The SBA's terms are more favorable [than a bank's], but they still require personal guarantees."

The SBA makes several different types of loans. Understanding the different programs before you start your search and preparing your applications properly puts you that much closer to getting the money you need.

Dividing the Pie

Most people think of SBA loans as money going straight from the government's coffers into an entrepreneur's hands. While this is true in some cases, it happens rarely. Direct loans account for only a tiny percentage of the SBA loan program; less than 0.5 percent of 1992's total $5-billion pool. Direct loans never exceed $150,000, and they are given only to applicants unable to secure either a bank loan or an SBA-guaranteed loan.

By far, the SBA's most active lending arena is the 7(a) Guaranteed Loan Program. Based on a working partnership with local banks and other lending institutions, the 7(a) program guarantees 75 percent, or up to $500,000, of small-business loans issued by a qualified lender. The small-business owner gains significant advantages from this private/public partnership—longer terms, for one thing. According to Phil Gentry, deputy district director and chief of finance at the SBA district office in Portland, Oregon, at least 50 percent of all bank business loans are for less than one year. By contrast, an SBA loan's maximum maturity is 25 years; the average maturity for most working capital SBA loans is between five and seven years. What does this mean? "You can borrow more," says Cristich, who notes that because payments are amortized over a longer period of time, they are smaller and more manageable.

Another advantage is that applying for an SBA-guaranteed loan helps build the relationship between banker and entrepreneur. Take the case of Jennifer Norrid, president and owner of PC Support Inc., a desktop computer consulting company in Albuquerque, New Mexico. When Norrid applied for her first SBA loan in 1986, PC Support was already a $200,000 business with an impressive list of loyal clients. Yet four banks turned down her loan application.

Norrid finally approached a bank that was a certified SBA lender, and worked closely with one of the loan officers, who told her she needed at least $15,000 in cash collateral. She didn't have it, but managed to get two friends to buy certificates of deposit (CDs) at the bank and allow her to use them as collateral. By using the CDs and emphasizing Norrid's sterling client references, the banker was able to lend her $48,000. "Without the SBA program, I wouldn't have been able to develop my business," says Norrid.

5

BOOTSTRAP FINANCING

Most of the current literature on the subject of raising money deals with the more glamorous and exciting stages of business operation—start-up and expansion. Between these relatively short-lived events lies the real work: the day-to-day operation of the business. The other events may grab all the attention, but this is the true critical period, when your actions ultimately determine whether you are going to succeed or fail. Each year, new businesses emerge after having managed to secure the money to fund their start-up, but a lot disappear each year for the opposite reason, because they are unable to find the funding necessary to continue operating. The outcomes are different but the reason is the same: Money is the linchpin throughout the business cycle, and your ability or inability to raise it goes a long way toward deciding your entrepreneurial future.

Bootstrap financing—using your own resources to create opportunities for your business—is one of the most popular forms of internal funding because it relies on your ability to utilize all your resources to free additional capital to launch a venture, meet operational needs, or expand your business. A long time ago, before the government was guaranteeing loans, bootstrap financing was the major way new businesses got started. It has since evolved into a financing tactic used chiefly to meet operational demands. As Small Business Investment Companies (SBICs), which are partially funded by the SBA, have become more conservative in their lending policies, and with the SBA itself having earned the reputation as the "lender of last resort," many entrepreneurs have become acquainted once again with this proven method. Instead of looking outward immediately, they are turning inward for solutions.

When raising capital for ongoing operations is the goal, bootstrap financing is one of the most cost-effective routes for entrepreneurs to explore. It utilizes resources and opportunities within their own companies, which they free up simply by managing their finances better. Bootstrap methods can help you get out of a financial crunch without the help of others, or fund expansion plans that would otherwise require a visit to the bank or an extensive application process with the SBA. You finance your growth with your current earnings and assets.

There are distinct advantages to the various methods of bootstrap financing:

- Your business will be worth more because you borrow less and, therefore, don't have to sacrifice your equity position.
- You don't have to pay interest on borrowed money.
- Coming from a stronger position (with less debt), you look more desirable to external lenders and investors when the time comes to raise money for expansion or other business events.
- You can be creative in finding ways to raise profits, without having to look to external sources.

Business in the United States has been affected by the credit crunch of the late '80s and '90s. Money simply isn't as easy to procure, which has led business owners to become more resourceful. This chapter discusses the most popular and effective forms of bootstrap financing being used by today's successful entrepreneurs.

TRADE CREDIT

The foremost source of operating capital is *trade credit*. Normally, a supplier will extend credit to you once you've become a regular customer. The typical time spans used by creditors are 30, 60, and 90 days, interest-free. For example, suppose a supplier ships something to you and the bill is due in 30 days but you have trade credit or terms. Your terms might be net 60 days from the receipt of goods, in which case you would have 30 extra days to pay for the items.

When starting out, as explained in Chapter 3, Start-Up Financing, suppliers are not going to give you trade credit. They're going to want to make every order C.O.D. (cash/check on delivery) until you've established that you can pay your bills on time. While this is a fairly normal practice, you're going to have to negotiate a trade credit basis with suppliers in order to raise money during the start-up period. A properly prepared financial plan will help you tremendously in these negotiations.

Businesses may give you half the order on credit, with the balance due upon delivery. Of course, the trick is to have goods shipped to you and sell them before you have to pay for them yourself. You could borrow the money to pay for your inventory, but you would have to pay interest on that money. This is what makes trade credit one of the most important ways to reduce the amount of working capital you need, especially if you are running or want to run a retail operation. Despite the urge to use trade credit on a continual and consistent basis, you should consider it as a source of capital to meet relatively small, short-term needs. Do not look at it as a long-term solution. By doing so, you may find your business heavily committed to those suppliers who accept extended credit terms. As a result, the business may no longer have ready access to other, more competitive suppliers who might offer lower prices, a superior product, or more reliable deliveries.

The Cost of Trade Credit

Depending on the terms available from your suppliers, the cost of trade credit can be quite high. Assume you make a purchase from a supplier who decides to extend credit to you. The terms the supplier offers you are 2-percent cash discount within 10 days and a net date of 30 days. Essentially, the supplier is saying that if you pay within 10 days, the purchase price will be discounted by 2 percent. On the other hand, by forfeiting the 2 percent discount, you are able to use your money for 20 more days, and it will cost you only that 2 percent discount. On an annualized basis, this is actually costing you 36 percent of the total cost of the items you are purchasing from the supplier (360 days ÷ 20 days = 18 times per year without discount; 18 times × 2% discount = 36% discount missed).[1]

Cash discounts aren't the only factor to consider. There are also late-payment or delinquency penalties should you extend payment beyond the agreed-upon terms. These usually run between 1 and 2 percent on a monthly basis. If you miss your net payment date for an entire year, that can cost you as much as 12 to 24 percent in penalty interest.

Effective use of trade credit requires intelligent planning to avoid unnecessary costs through forfeiture of cash discounts or the incidence of delinquency penalties. Every business should take full advantage of the trade credit available to them, without incurring additional costs, in order to reduce the need for capital from other sources.

FACTORING

This financing method involves actually selling your accounts receivable to a buyer, such as a commercial finance company, as a means to raise capital. A "factor" buys accounts receivable, usually at a discount rate that ranges between 1 and 15 percent. The factor then becomes the creditor and assumes the task of collecting the receivables as well as doing what would have been your paperwork. Factoring can be performed on a nonnotification basis, which means your customers are never made aware that their accounts have been sold.

There are pros and cons to factoring. Many financial experts believe that you should not attempt factoring unless you cannot acquire the necessary capital from other sources. However, it is no secret that factoring can be a very good financial tool to utilize despite its potential drawbacks. If you take into account the costs associated with maintaining accounts receivable, such as bookkeeping, collections, and credit verifications, and compare those expenses against the discount rate you'll have to apply when selling them, sometimes it even pays to utilize this financing method. After all, even if the factor takes on only part of the paperwork chores involved in maintaining accounts receivable, your internal costs will shrink significantly. Most of the time, the factor will assume full responsibility for the paperwork.

In addition to reduced internal costs, factoring also frees up money that would otherwise be tied to receivables, especially for businesses that sell to other businesses or to the government where there are often prolonged delays in payment that factoring could easily offset. You can then turn around and use the money to generate profit through other avenues of the company. This is just more evidence that factoring is a very useful tool for raising money and keeping cash flow going. According to Mace Edwards, publisher of the *Edwards Directory of American Factors* in Newton, Massachusetts, factoring firms financed at least $62 billion in receivables in 1993, up from $46 billion in 1987. Much of that capital went to small business.[2]

CUSTOMERS

Your customers are another source of bootstrap financing, and there are several different ways to profit from your association with them.

One way to obtain financing is by having them write you a letter of credit. Suppose you're starting a business to manufacture industrial-grade cloth bags. A large corporation has placed an order with your firm to supply them a steady flow of cloth bags. The major supplier of the material used in production is located in India. You obtain a letter of credit from your customer when you place the order, and purchase the material for the bags using the letter as security. This way, you don't put up a penny to buy the material.

You may find opportunities for customer financing through other contacts. If you are a contractor doing some damage restoration on some interior walls of a customer's home, for instance, having them buy the materials for the job will increase your cash flow. Another way to handle the situation is to ask for a down payment from the customer as a way to cover materials and labor costs. Otherwise, you are actually helping them finance the work. Having customers pick up the initial job costs is one simple way they can act as a source of financing.

REAL ESTATE

Another bootstrap financing source is real estate, and there are several ways to take advantage whether you own property or not. The first is to simply lease your facility, which reduces start-up costs because the expense to get into a lease is not usually as high as the outright purchase of the property. Also, when negotiating a lease, you may be able to arrange payments that correspond to seasonal peaks or growth patterns. Unlike a purchase, however, a lease is neither an investment nor an asset. At the end of the lease, you are left with nothing but the decision to renegotiate or walk away. This is the main reason some business owners prefer purchasing to leasing.

If you enter into a business that requires you to purchase a facility, your start-up costs increase, but financing the structure over a period of 30 years or more lets you spread out the repayment of the debt. In this case as well, the loan on the facility can be structured to make optimum use of your planned growth or seasonal peaks. For instance, you can arrange a graduated payment mortgage or adjustable-rate mortgage that initially has very small monthly payments at first with an increasing monthly cost over the life of the loan. The logic here is that you give your business time to grow. Eventually, you can refinance the loan when time and interest rates permit. Another advantage to the outright purchase of a facility is continuing appreciation of the property (usually) and the decrease of your principal amount to create a valuable asset known as *equity*. The longer you make payments on a loan, the lower the loan's principal balance becomes, and the greater the difference between the value and the amount owed (which is your equity). Lenders will often loan up to 75 or 80 percent of the property's value once it has been appraised.

This applies to any private real estate you might own. If you need a certain amount of money that you can't get any other way, you may have to borrow against the equity in your home or sell it altogether. If your home is appreciating in value, real estate is a useful asset that opens up new possibilities for you. If it is depreciating, it won't be quite as attractive.

EQUIPMENT SUPPLIERS

If you spend a lot of money on equipment, you may find yourself without enough working capital to keep your business going month to month. Instead of paying out cash for your equipment, the manufacturers of the equipment can loan you the money; that is, they sell the equipment over a period of time. In this way, equipment suppliers are a source of bootstrap financing.

Two types of credit contracts are commonly used to finance equipment purchases:

1. *The conditional sales contract.* The purchaser does not receive title to the equipment until it is fully paid for.
2. *The chattel-mortgage contract.* The equipment becomes the property of the purchaser on delivery, but the seller holds a mortgage claim against it until the amount specified in the contract is paid.

By using your equipment suppliers to finance the purchase of equipment you need, you reduce the amount of money required up front. There are also lenders willing to finance 60 to 80 percent of the equipment value. The difference represents the borrower's down payment on a new purchase. The loan is repaid in monthly installments, usually over one to five years, or the usable life of that piece of equipment.

LEASING

Another bootstrap financing option is to lease equipment instead of purchasing it. Generally, if you are able to shop around and get the best kind of leasing arrangement, it's much better to lease. Leasing a photocopier, for example, rather than paying $3,000 cash for it, or leasing a car or van to avoid paying out $8,000, helps you the same way leasing a facility does—it preserves your cash flow.

Businesses have used lease arrangements for decades. It is common for businesses to lease real property for a retail facility, office space, production plant, farm lands, and so on. Although many people do not consider leasing a true form of financing, it has characteristics that make it similar to ownership:

- The lessor owns the property for a specific term at a predetermined cost paid in installments.

- The lessor is responsible for all costs associated with the ownership of the leased property such as property taxes, insurance, and so on.

- As the owner, the lessor either benefits from the capital appreciation of the property or loses from any depreciation in value.

- Finally, the lessor enjoys all the tax benefits of owning the property such as depreciation, interest, property taxes, and more.

As mentioned, there are certain inherent advantages to leasing:

- *Minimum cash outlay.* Through leasing, the use of an asset is acquired without a large initial capital outlay, freeing capital for other uses.

- *No down payment.* Whereas a loan usually requires anywhere from 10 to 25 percent down, leases are financed 100 percent.

- *No equipment obsolescence.* Provides an opportunity to use new or updated equipment all of the time by exchanging the equipment at the end of the lease term.

- *Built-in maintenance.* Depending on the terms of the lease, maintenance of the equipment can be included, thereby reducing your working capital expenses.

- *Tax advantages.* These often include the deductibility of the lease as an operating expense, as well as an investment tax credit.

- *Lower payments and longer term period than loans.* Because leases are more flexible, they can be spread over a longer period than a loan, thus reducing the monthly payments, making them lower than a loan.

- *Expert advice available from lessor.* This is especially true if the lessor is the manufacturer.

- *Protection of assets.* In the event of bankruptcy, the lessor has less of a chance of claiming your assets than creditors'.

Because of the question of cash flow, it is usually better from a dollars-and-cents standpoint to lease rather than buy. There are many ways that a lease can be modified to increase your cash position:

- A down payment lower than 10 percent or no down payment at all.
- Maintenance costs that are built into the lease package, thereby reducing your working capital expenses. If you needed employees or a repair person to do maintenance on purchased equipment, it would cost you more than if you had leased.
- Assignment of all executory costs such as insurance, property taxes, and so on. While this will initially increase your cash flow, from a tax standpoint, it will reduce the amount of taxable income the business generates.
- Extension of the lease term to cover the entire economic life of the property; or use of the property can be guaranteed for as long as you wish to use it.
- A purchase option can be added to the lease allowing you to buy the property after the lease period has ended. A fixed purchase price can also be added to the option provision.
- Lease payments can be structured to accommodate seasonal variations in the business or tied to indexes that track interest to create an adjustable lease.

If purchasing will not jeopardize your cash flow, it may be your most beneficial financing method because it gives you assets that are vitally important to a young business. If you are unsure how long you will stay at a given location or use certain pieces of equipment, leasing may be what you need.

MANAGING CASH FLOW

Bootstrap financing really begins and ends with your attention to good financial management so your company can generate the funds it needs. Be careful and informed when it comes time to buy. Make sure that you don't go top-dollar when it's not necessary, and that you aren't in an overly expensive office or location unless it's really going to pay off (a lot of professional services subscribe to the "fancy office equals big business" philosophy). If a new desk is not crucial and you have an opportunity to buy a used desk, then by all means do so. This is the meaning behind bootstrap financing: It requires you to spend money or *avoid* spending money carefully to reduce the amount of money you need.

Also, keep a close watch on operating expenses. If interest rates are high, it won't take too many unpaid bills to wipe out your profits. At an 11 to 12 percent interest rate, carrying an unpaid $10,000 is costing you plenty. Tight, competitive profit margins mean more money can be lost trying to collect bills than was earned in the first place.

Product-oriented businesses can protect their cash flow by starting each production order off on the right track. Implement a four-step payment plan. Negotiate terms and conditions that require payments when *you* want them. Profitable cash flow will happen when you establish and execute timely cash flow concepts on every order. Many firms overlook these critical factors:

1. Identifying a billable event—other than delivery.
2. Setting payment due dates.
3. Establishing penalties for late payment.
4. Determining place of payment.

The result: great sales but no cash.

You need a negotiation plan, so be prepared to consider these steps before accepting an order. It should be prepared and followed with the same care used to document your production process. Time invested in obtaining favorable cash flow terms and conditions can mean added profit and higher returns on your investment. Never forget the fact that your cash flow will never get any better than what is defined in the negotiation process. Take steps to get the best available payment terms.

The first step for product-based businesses is to bill before delivery. There are three ways you can issue an invoice before you ship the final product:

1. *Milestone billing* is a fairly common practice where heavy up-front investment is required for a new product or job. In this case, the completion of a certain event or milestone (placing a subcontract, passing a critical design review, completing a set of test/equipment/tools, or receiving a large amount of material) is given a billing value. This authorizes you to issue an invoice when the event occurs—often long before completion of a deliverable item.
2. A second way is to establish *progress billings*, which are fairly common in the defense and aerospace industries. Progress

billings allow you to invoice costs, as incurred, on a routine bi-monthly or monthly basis. In this way, your customer finances your inventory. The advantage is that while a job is in process, your investment is reduced. In effect, you recover your costs before you deliver anything. (In this case, your customer does have a lien against the inventory.)

3. A third way is to utilize *subline item billings,* which are common in the construction industry. This billing term recognizes the times when an entire item cannot be completed, but principal elements of it are. Examples of subitems are the foundation, plumbing, frame, and roof. Each could be subitems of an apartment complex. The advantage here is that an invoice can be issued as each major subelement is completed, thus speeding cash flow.

The second step, setting payment due dates, is important because it defines *when* you will be paid. Why take an order if you don't make an effort to assure payment? Bear in mind that extending credit to customers has a real cost to you. Be sure your contract (and price) provides for that cost. Poor credit risks should be sold C.O.D. Discounts can be offered but tied to the shipment date, customer acceptance date, your invoice date, or a calendar date. The point is, once the payment date is established in your contract (purchase order, etc.) you have a legally enforceable document.

The third step, establishing penalties for late payment, will help get timely payment. What happens today if a customer pays you 30 days late? Do you collect interest, or are you just happy to get paid? If your terms and conditions require a penalty for late payment, you improve your chances for timely payment—and based on contract terms, you have legal remedies available to you to collect interest from delinquent accounts.

The fourth step, determining place of payment, can make a two-to five-day difference in cash receipts. Firms that sell throughout the United States use geographically dispersed deposit lock boxes. Each order requires payment to the lock box closest to the customer. Other firms require payment directly to their bank. This makes the money available for use faster. These firms let their accounting department figure out who paid what after the deposit, rather than delaying it while they do their thing.

You can negotiate profitable cash flow to save collection time and effort. You must place extra emphasis on payment provisions if you want to *keep* the profit you work hard to earn.

6

CREDIT

"In God we trust. All others pay cash." You see this slogan in professional offices and retail outlets all over the country. It conveys the very real apprehension entrepreneurs must overcome when making decisions concerning credit. Businesses in every industry rely to some degree on credit for their success. Entrepreneurs need it to finance their growth, and their customers need it to finance purchases. For both parties, credit sustains them during the cash droughts in a business cycle. Whatever your line of work—manufacturing, wholesaling, retailing, or service—you have an automatic auxiliary business you may not know about: loaning money. Any time a business extends credit, either to consumers or other businesses, its money is being used interest-free.

Chapter 3, Start-Up Financing, discussed ways of using trade credit in the preliminary growth stage to acquire inventory and supplies. The most common use of credit, however, is for ongoing operations. Credit is used in the course of doing business every day, everywhere, and in every industry. Consumers buy on credit; businesses pay for goods and services with credit to keep their supply on par with market demand. Without it, businesses would be forced to operate according to their cash supply, causing shortages and surpluses that would inevitably defeat any hopes of sustained growth and development. This chapter explores both sides of the credit management issue, from extending it to earning it, and details how businesses can use it consistently as a method of raising money to support their day-to-day operations.

Maintaining tight control of credit, the kind you extend and the kind you seek from others, is the only way to operate profitably. However, since, essentially, you're trying to control the human factor (which often proves futile), you face certain inherent hazards. How will you know whether the customer is as good a credit risk as you are? How can you tell whether credit will actually increase your sales? Will it cost a lot to sell on credit?

TRADE CREDIT: TIPS AND TRAPS

How would you like an interest-free business loan without the hassle of credit checks and filling out papers? Sound too good to be true? Well, businesses do it every day using *payables financing*. In a nutshell, this means that businesses, big and small, can use trade credit (sometimes called commercial credit) to keep their businesses going. Just as consumer credit is the fine art of keeping someone from using your money carelessly, trade credit is the fine art of using other people's money.

Although almost 90 percent of American businesses raise money through trade credit, generally in the form of *invoices* or *promises to pay*, most of the information on trade credit available to small businesses is written in a style that would test a Harvard MBA. Also, often it is based on ideal situations, portraying a company big enough to have credit managers, collections departments, and payables divisions.

Most entrepreneurs don't have this luxury. If you are a hands-on owner, you are generally involved in opening and closing your doors, handling employee problems, making inventory decisions, solving advertising problems, and filling out forms. Credit manager is just one of the many hats you wear daily, which is why it needs to be clear-cut and easily understandable.

Your Credit Policy

The biggest problem most small businesses face with their credit policies is that they have none. Credit decisions—whether asking for credit or granting credit—are generally made on the spur of the moment, relying on a gut feeling. But sharp businesspeople realize that credit is one of the most important aspects of business financing. It must be managed according to a prescribed plan, and that plan must have two definite aspects: what you will do as a borrower, and what you will do as a lender.

The first step in determining your long-range credit policy is to get a fix on the exact status of your credit rating. Just as you turn to consumer credit bureaus to get a picture of the customer, so other businesses can turn to financial rating services to get a picture of you. Dun & Bradstreet is just one major company that produces reports on businesses. These reports give a detailed picture of your operation, including types of credit, payment history, size of operation, capitalization, net worth, and so on. Your listing with credit-reporting companies is of utmost importance in determining your policies. Ask these agencies for copies of their reports on you. If you are not listed, take steps to become so. Their books are the bible of the trade-credit business, so you have to be listed in them to successfully use trade credit to make your business grow.

Once you have a record of the exact public appraisal of your credit rating, you will be able to plan your long-range strategy with accurate data. If there is inaccurate information in these reports, you must have it investigated, and make sure that your side of the story is included in future credit reports.

ATTRIBUTES OF A GOOD CREDIT SYSTEM

When designing your credit policy, you can get overwhelmed by all the elements you have to consider. As a rule of thumb, keep in mind that a good credit system is:

- Clear, fast, and consistent.
- Does not invade a customer's privacy.
- Inexpensive (credit analysis and decision making is centralized).
- Based upon prior experience, taking into account characteristic of good, questionable, and bad accounts.

Tip: As you go along in your operations, try to determine a correlation between customers characteristics and future uncollectibility.

Source: Shim, J., and Siegel, J., *The Vest-Pocket CFO*, Prentice-Hall, Englewood Cliffs, NJ, 1995.

Establishing Your Credit Policies

There are two general questions to ask yourself: To whom should credit be given, and how much credit should be given? To answer these questions, consider the following factors:

- *Competitive position.* Organizations in monopolistic markets have considerably more flexibility in setting credit policies than others facing more aggressive competition. But as we all know, real monopolies are rare. Most companies experience such a position only during very short periods, after they have introduced radically new products and before their competitors have had time to introduce "me-too" products. A company in such as position may be tempted to take advantage of the situation; however, restricting credit too much could damage customer relations with long-lasting effects. When making this decision, analyze your company's competitive position and use credit to your benefit. Sometimes it may give you a competitive advantage against a competitor.

Another way to look at your system is to put yourself in the position of a bank or other source of lending money. The same set of guidelines that they use in extending credit to you should be used by you to extend credit to customers. The guidelines are known as the Five Cs of credit. They are:

- *Character.* Refers to the customer's integrity and willingness to repay the financial obligation.
- *Capacity.* Addresses the customer's cash flow and ability to repay the debt.
- *Capital.* The customer's financial net worth. A wealthy customer will be more desirable even if his or her cash flows are relatively low.
- *Collateral.* Refers to the resale value of the product in the event repossession becomes necessary.
- *Conditions.* Refers to national or international economic, industrial, and firm-specific prospects during the time period of the credit.

Source: Bygrave, William, *The Portable MBA in Entrepreneurship*, John Wiley & Sons, Inc., 1997.

- *Elasticity of demand.* Economic factors play an important part in credit policy. If demand for a product is inelastic—that is, if an increase in price or restriction in the terms of credit will produce a relative small drop in demand with the result that net sales revenues actually increase—then there is some potential flexibility in the terms of sale. Remember, though, that this flexibility will be for the whole industry, so you will probably have to accept the general industry practice.
- *Length of company's order backlog and whether the company is working at full output capacity.* The key here is that a company operating below full capacity or below its optimum output may well be tempted to offer unusually generous credit terms to stimulate demand. The problem then is whether the cost of the additional funds tied up in accounts receivable will be more than offset by the additional sales and reduced operating costs. On the other hand, a company working at full capacity, with its product back ordered, is in a position to tighten up on its credit policies to reduce its investment in receivables.

Types of Trade Credit

Basically, there are two types of trade credit:

1. *Promises.* Also known as promises to pay, they are of two kinds: invoices and promissory notes. Any time you order goods and don't want to lay out the cash at that time, you get them on an invoice. If the amount of goods is high-priced, you may, on occasion, be asked to sign a promissory note guaranteeing payment.
2. *Orders.* Also known as orders to pay, they differ from promises in that you sign a document specifying the rate of payment, the dates of payment, and the method of transaction. Once an order to pay is accepted, it becomes known as a trade acceptance. This term allows the company that is granting you credit to use your trade acceptance as a guaranteed source of receivables income. This practice generally occurs when the amount of cash is considerable, usually over $10,000.

When you order goods, you will probably receive them on an invoice. This simply means that the supplier has checked your credit, believes you to be a good risk, and lets you have the goods. Many small businesses slip up at this point by not specifying their terms when ordering.

One major term to always ask for is "ROG as of the 25th." This means you want the billing date to start upon receipt of goods (ROG). The reason you ask for the 25th is that most American businesses consider the 24th to be the end of the billing and shipping month, a custom solidified over the years.

Say you order a line of T-shirts on June 8 and you receive them on the 15th. If you had not specified ROG, your billing obligation would be the 8th instead of the 15th. If you specified "as of the 25th," and this was accepted, then you would not be billed until the 25th or later. When you are billed, your net payment would not be due for 30 days, or July 25. The effect of this technique is that you get the T-shirts to sell for 45 days, interest-free.

It makes sense to request shipping terms. Many business owners ignore the money-saving aspect of "FOB" terms. This abbreviation stands for "Free on Board" and simply designates who pays the freight. If you request in your order "FOB destination," the supplier pays the freight. If you don't specify this, chances are you'll be paying it.

FOB terms are always negotiable. Remember, most suppliers want your business and will make exceptions. This is a point worth haggling over. The money-saving initials to include in your order are "ROG as of the 25th," and "FOB destination."

Spell Out Credit Terms

Spell out credit terms *exactly* so there's no chance for confusion. Most businesses will ask for "ROG as of the 25th, FOB destination," then turn around and reject or renegotiate any orders coming in like that. Their view is that they should not let anyone else use their money even though they want to use that of others!

Make sure that all the credit you grant is "EOM," otherwise known as "end of the month." This is generally written up as "net 15 EOM," meaning you expect the customer receiving your goods to pay you by the 15th of the following month. If you ship radios out on June 20, using this phrase will guarantee payment by July 15. In other words, you've cut the maximum time someone else can use your money down to 25 days. To see just how important this aspect is, consider this: If you carry someone for three months, you have lost 10 percent of your net profit. Carrying them for four months results in a loss of 14 percent, and five months brings the loss to 19 percent. Generally, if a bill is not paid in five years, you can write it off as a total loss.

To eliminate this potential loss of business revenue, you must spell out your credit terms exactly and stick to your guns. If someone else is using your money, you want to cut your risk to a minimum.

Expensive Discounts

Often a customer will ask if there is a cash discount for fast payment. Although this is a standard practice, you should decide for yourself whether to allow this. It is an expensive proposition. If you give a customer terms of "2 percent 10, net 30," then that customer can deduct 2 percent from the cost of goods if they pay you within 10 days. If you go along with this, then you are letting the customer use your money for a very low interest rate.

In effect, the customer is paying you only $2 interest for the use of $98, based on a $100 order. On the other hand, quick-paying customers will boost your cash flow and cut down on your bookkeeping chores, so weigh both sides of the issue. If a customer applies for credit and your research tells you that his or her credit history is bad but the business picture looks bright, then you will move from "promises to pay" into the realm of "orders to pay."

You have the customer sign a promissory note stating that, on a certain date, a specified amount of cash is due. Businesses will sign these documents because they know you have recourse with this kind of document. If all else fails, you can have your bank draft an order to pay, which is then transferred to the other business's bank. Businesses don't like this to happen because it tips off the bank that the customer isn't paying his or her bills.

ESTABLISHING CREDIT

When you start your credit policy, you want to establish a good line of credit with suppliers. Make sure to pay according to the terms of the agreement during your first six months of operation. Because of the unpredictability of the mail, you always have room to maneuver. The check has to be dated the day the payment is due. If it is dated after that, your creditor will correctly assume you have not met your obligation.

Once you establish your credit line, you can begin using other businesses' money. The key to doing this is to make sure that you keep in touch with your creditors. If, for example, you are going to be late in paying, let them know ahead of time. If you can't make full payment on the first month, make a partial payment. If you are going to have to be carried for a longer period of time, make sure that the creditors always know. The availability of trade credit helps you reduce the amount of cash you have to borrow from other institutions. Since there is no interest charged for such credit, this amounts to free money. To be a successful entrepreneur, you must make yourself aware of the intricacies of

IS YOUR FIRM CREDITWORTHY?

It is worth remembering that your ability to obtain money when you need it is as necessary to the operation of your business as is a good location, the right equipment, reliable sources of supplies and materials, or an adequate labor force. Before a bank or any other lending agency decides to lend you money, the loan officer must feel that your firm's credit is worthy of the investment. By all odds, the character of the borrower comes first. Next is your ability to manage your business, what you are going to do with the money, when you plan to pay back, and so forth. Ask yourself: What sort of person are you? Would you lend yourself money?

trade credit. A visit to your local banker can be a big help here. Make sure you establish a definite policy for your trade-credit operations.

The soundest business practice is to pay all your bills in a timely manner. But should conditions prohibit this, as is often the case with entrepreneurial ventures, you can safely use trade credit to help you survive the rough times.

COLLECTIONS

The moment you decide to extend credit to customers—whether to consumers or to other businesses—you automatically inherit another occupation, that of bill collector. Most entrepreneurs realize that bad debts cost money, but few realize exactly how much. If your business averages 7 percent net profit after taxes, and you have $100 in bad receivables, you have to gross $1,429 more to make up for it!

Bill collecting requires a combination of scientific procedure, good management, and regular control. There are dozens of laws spelling out what you can and cannot do when going after money that's owed you. The first step is to set up a clear, well-ordered collection policy. There are basically two possible policies: the "100 percenters" and the "pay when you canners." The "100 percenters" have a firm, rigid collection policy that shoots for everything owed on the exact due date. The "pay when you can" school uses a more flexible approach, taking into consideration the many possible reasons for slow paying.

Your policy should fall somewhere between these two extremes. If you are dealing with perishable products like food, you need a strict policy. If you are dealing with products that have a long life, then you can have a more relaxed policy. You should decide up front what kinds of collection procedures to use, the time period of a collection, and the various approaches you will use. The most important step is to think your policy through, then make sure all of your employees know exactly what it is. This will save you time in the long run since you won't have to be called in to solve every collection problem.

A full 80 percent of collection and payment problems revolve around invoicing difficulties. Costly mistakes on invoices occur in several areas. The major errors are wrong addresses, wrong person billed, payment terms not spelled out, and due dates not clearly specified.

The invoice you send out (see Figure 6–1) should always be typed or computer-generated. Illegible handwriting accounts for many of the errors. It should be written in terms understandable by everyone, especially your customers.

If you invoice a customer on an irregular basis, always have the payment terms spelled out. If you do regular business with a customer, keep a *statement of account* that you send out monthly. A statement of account is simply a recap of all the invoices sent to a customer during a given month. This statement should list each invoice by number, date shipped, and amount due. Whether using a computerized or a manual system, be sure to stay organized and know how your system works. In a manual system, many businesspeople lump all the invoices together, then spend time at the end of the month sorting them out, which presents several problems. If you are a one- or two-person operation, there's a chance of losing an invoice. If you wait until the end of the month, you may also face other end-of-the-month bookkeeping problems and be tempted to put off the invoicing. Remember that if you don't promptly bill your customers, they will be using your money interest-free. The rule: Stay up to date with them.

When you prepare an invoice (and are not using computerized filings), immediately file it in a special folder clearly marked with the customer's name. This folder should have a ledger sheet attached so that when you file the original invoice, it can easily be checked.

Aging Receivables

There are many different techniques for setting up an aging system. You can either automate by purchasing appropriate accounting software with this function, or you can set up your own manual system, with code letters, different colored folders, and so on. The key is to make sure that anyone in your business can tell, at a glance, what the status of any account is at any given time.

Figure 6–1 Invoice

Bill to: _____   Date: _____

_____   Invoice No.: _____

_____   Salesperson: _____

_____

P.O. No.	Quantity	Description	Price	Discount	Total
				Subtotal	
				Sales Tax	
				Total	

Statement of Account

Payments	
Balance	
Current Charges	
New Balance	

Current	30 Days	60 Days	90+ Days

The best operators have their accountants provide them with recaps of receivables on a monthly basis, so that they can structure their collection efforts in a logical, orderly way. A regular analysis of your receivables is a must for any business. Good receivables can quickly turn into overdue ones, and from there into collection problems, and then into losses, while you're preoccupied with other aspects of running your business.

If you have a customer's history in front of you, you will be able to immediately spot any problems you're likely to have. If a customer traditionally pays 10 days after a due date, that person is probably taking advantage of an implied grace period. You would see this reflected on their payment ledger and know that it isn't cause for worry.

On the other hand, if a customer has traditionally been prompt with payments and is suddenly overdue, you have a problem. Problems with overdue accounts seldom go away by themselves. The further behind you let a customer get, the greater the risk that you will never collect. If a bill isn't paid when it's due, it's costing you money. Even levying a 1 percent surcharge doesn't begin to compensate for the staff hours and costs you face when trying to collect. Adding a service charge can serve as a warning to the slow payer. It lets the customer know you aren't going to allow your business to be treated in this manner. If the customer continues to do so, he or she is going to have to pay more. Although the service charge may not improve your profit situation, it may help prod the slow-paying customer.

Before proceeding with firm collection procedures, however, you owe it to your customer to determine why he or she is slow to pay. The customer could be confused, negligent, delinquent for reasons beyond their control, seasonally delinquent, chronically slow, or they simply cannot pay. Each situation must be dealt with differently.

Confused customers have lost their invoices, are unclear about the terms, or do not want to pay because the balance is too small. Usually, this type of delinquent account will pay once these confusions are cleared up. Such accounts should be sent a form note that is pleasant and to the point.

A negligent customer has the money and the intention to pay, but needs reminding that the bill is past due. Often companies instruct their employees not to process bills until past-due notices are sent. To speed up payment of these accounts, mail the past-due notices early. You must keep on top of negligent accounts because they can quickly become delinquent and cost you money.

Not-at-fault delinquent customers have faced some sort of disaster—fire, flood, earthquake, loss of key employee(s), and so on. If this is the situation, we recommend that you don't press for payment and let the customers know that you will carry the account for a reasonable time until they are back on their feet.

Seasonally delinquent accounts will fall behind during the slow seasons. When their income is reduced, they still have fixed expenses to meet, and you must make allowances for this. Check to see if other suppliers are getting paid. If they are, proceed with your collections.

THE COLLECTION PROCESS

The collection process is a step-by-step procedure that starts with friendly reminders, followed by firm requests, then demands for payment, and, finally, threats of legal action. Each step has proven techniques that will pay off. The important thing to remember is to organize your approach and then follow through.

The most effective pattern is to begin with written reminders, followed by collection letters, backed up by phone calls. Most operators prepare and print a series of collection form letters that are mailed regularly, generally 10 days apart.

As an entrepreneur, you have many jobs to do each day. If you run your business by yourself, your first reaction probably is, "I can't take time out to write collection letters; I don't even have a secretary." That's a valid problem, but collection letters can be effective in a planned form. The first step in your letter campaign is to send another copy of the bill to the customer along with a handwritten note on the bill reading, "In case you forgot," or "past due." This reminds customers without questioning their creditworthiness, and gives them the benefit of the doubt. The tone of the letters should move gradually from friendly persuasion to firm demands.

Personalized Letters

With accounts that are three months old, you will have to adopt a slightly tougher policy. This is an area where form letters aren't as effective as personalized letters. Seasoned veterans use a number of standard techniques to elicit responses.

First and most important, be brief. Letters that are long and complicated go to the bottom of the stack, especially if the recipient is loaded with work. Think how you act when you get your morning mail. If a letter looks as if it's going to take a while to study, you set it aside. Also, make sure the letter is clear. When your reader can't tell right away what your letter is about, it too gets put aside. We're not suggesting that you start off with, "Pay up or we'll break your knees," but you should get to the topic at hand quickly.

Along with brief and clear, be accurate. Nothing destroys the effectiveness of a collection appeal faster than being wrong. The letter must have the correct invoice (or statement) number, date, and amount. It should also accurately reflect the status of the account on the date it was written.

Using the Phone

With the cost of business letters spiraling, many collection pros are turning to the telephone. If you decide to do this, here are the steps you should take. First, make sure you review the situation thoroughly before calling. Have all the facts and figures at hand. Then, make sure you speak in a warm, cordial, yet firm voice. Finally, be sure to listen. Nothing makes phone techniques fail more quickly than a caller who is not listening.

Following is a list of excuses commonly used by debtors. Included are suggestions on how to react to each excuse, which may or may not be applicable to a particular account.

1. *"I paid the bill."* Ask the debtor to send you a copy of the canceled check, money-order receipt, or any other receipt that can prove payment.
2. *"I never got a bill."* Ask the debtor to tell you their residence address in order to verify the one on your records.
3. *"Business is slow right now."* Ask the debtor the place of employment and type of business. If self-employed, ask the name of the company. Also find out when business is expected to pick up.
4. *"I sent it yesterday."* Find out who mailed the payment, the time of day it was mailed, and where it was mailed. Find out if it was a personal check or money order. If it was a money order, ask where it was purchased and the receipt number.
5. *"The insurance company was supposed to pay for this."* Ask the debtor the name of the insurance company. Find out if the debtor has a group or individual policy. If it is a group policy, get the name of the employer and the name of the insured employee, which may be different from that of the employee. In addition, you may need to know the name of the insurance agency where the policy was purchased. Further, ask the debtor for the policy number and any other identifying or

claim number. Investigate why the insurance company did not pay.

6. *"I am out of work."* Ask for the last place of employment and how long the debtor has been unemployed. Find out the type of employment and if the debtor expects to be working soon. Have the debtor call you at least once every two weeks to advise you of any change in his or her financial situation.

7. *"I did not get what I ordered."* Ask the debtor what was wrong with the merchandise. If the debtor claims that the right number of items was not received, they were the wrong kind of goods, or part of the merchandise was damaged, ask for payment for the part of the order that was correct and then try to reach an agreement on the disputed portion.

8. *"My signature was forged."* Ask the debtor to come to your office and write a statement proclaiming that the signature was forged and have him or her sign it. Be sure the debtor brings identification with a signature on it. If he or she lives too far to travel to your office, ask for a letter stating that the signature was forged and be sure it is signed and notarized. If the debtor has a driver's license, ask for a photostat copy showing the signature.

9. *"The balance is wrong."* If you cannot resolve the dispute at the time, advise the debtor that you will send an itemized statement and a copy of the payment record. Check the debtor's mailing address to be sure it is correct. Send the statement by registered mail, return receipt requested.

If a customer still hasn't paid after collection letters and phone calls, then we suggest that you turn the account over to a collection agency. Most agencies won't accept bills for amounts less than $50, so some operators wait until they have several overdue accounts before turning them over to a collection agency.

As soon as you start offering credit, familiarize yourself with the reputable collection agencies in your community. In 1991, according to the U.S. Census Bureau, there were 6,580 "credit reporting and collection establishments" in the country.[1] Credit agencies differ in operations and levels of success, so test several of them before you commit yourself. You may want to find out if they are affiliated with a reputable national organization, such as the American Collectors' Association (ACA), or the American Commercial Collectors Association (ACCA).

Small Claims Court

An alternative to the collection agencies is to file a complaint with a small claims court. This is a simple procedure that forces a hearing between you and your debtor and generally results in a judgment in the creditor's favor. In many states, debts up to $1,000 can be handled in this manner, but policies differ from state to state. Check with appropriate local government agencies to determine the best way to handle any small-claims accounts.

Laws on Collection

Like most consumer-oriented legislation, laws on credit and collection tend to be complex in their wording. The following is a brief summary of the main points of some of the most important laws:

- *The Robinson Patman Act (1936).* This act makes it illegal to discriminate among customers on the basis of price if it would injure competition among sellers. This means that cash discounts for customers who pay promptly are legal. Discounts for customers who buy from another company are illegal.
- *The Assignment of Claims Act (1940).* This act permits the assignment of proceeds from contracts to institutions solely involved in banking or financial activity. In effect, this allows businesses to replenish their supply of operating capital immediately on shipment of a product and opens the door to receivables financing.
- *Uniform Commercial Code (1972; frequent revisions).* This provides the basis for all commercial transactions. Of particular interest to you as an entrepreneur are Articles 4 (bank deposits and collections) and 9 (secured transactions, sales of accounts, and chattel paper).
- *The Consumer Credit Protection Act (1968).* This is popularly known as the Truth in Lending Act and protects consumers from unfair credit practices. Although it currently applies only to consumers, it is predicted that it will carry over to commercial dealings as well.
- *The Fair Credit Billing Act (1975).* This act regulates the methods and procedures firms may use in billing credit card accounts and other revolving accounts with a finance charge.
- *The Fair Credit Reporting Act (1970; added to the Truth in Lending Act).* This regulates consumer credit information in regard to

the confidentiality, accuracy, relevancy, and proper utilization of customers' credit histories.

- *The Equal Credit Opportunity Act (1977).* Prohibits discrimination on the basis of sex or marital status in granting credit.
- *The Fair Debt Collection Act (1978).* This eliminates abusive collection practices by debt collectors.
- *Postal regulations.* This legislation requires that no words, illustrations, or codes identifying an addressee as delinquent in payment of a debt may appear on the outside of an envelope or postcard where they might be seen by a third party.
- *Internal Revenue Service.* The IRS governs writing off bad debts.
- *State regulations.* Each state has its own laws regarding collection processes. Discuss these with legal counsel before setting up your long-range collection program.

Organization

All collection procedures are, by nature, after the fact. If you have been thorough in your credit checking and have kept on top of each account, then your collection problems should be minimal.

Millions of dollars are lost each year by creditors. A portion of this money could have been recovered with the use of thorough, well-managed collection systems. Granting credit to your customers is a proven way of building sales volume. Following collection procedures like those included in this book are proven ways of making sure that sales volume is profitable. A good credit and collections policy will remove many of your headaches.

BEATING THE ODDS

Paul Hughes

Bad credit: It's discouraging, debilitating, and depressing . . . and you're worried it might keep you from starting a business. But there's good news: Entrepreneurship may be closer than you think. First, as a start-up business owner, it's only your personal credit that's in question. Your business credit is completely separate, and if you've never owned a business before, it's a clean slate. If you make sure all information about your personal credit is accurate, and you arrange to satisfy past financial obligations and prepare a solid (and we mean solid) business plan to ensure you meet all future obligations, bad credit doesn't have to hamper your start-up business dreams. What you've done matters, but what you do from here on matters more.

First Steps

Start by getting copies of your personal credit report. Perhaps you're not in such dire straits after all. To find out, you need to review the same information creditors see. Credit grantors nationwide, including banks, credit card companies, retailers, and other card and credit issuers, contract with credit reporting agencies to create and maintain credit histories on millions of American consumers. The three largest credit reporting agencies are TRW in Orange, California; Equifax in Atlanta, Georgia; and Trans Union Corp. in Chicago, Illinois.

Request your credit report in writing from each of these companies. TRW provides consumers one free report per person, per calendar year; additional reports cost about $8, depending on the state you live in. Reports from Equifax and Trans Union are $8 each. If you have recently been denied credit, each agency will provide a free report.

In addition to these three agencies, many of the more than 800 local credit bureaus maintain relationships with the top three, sharing information and following the same compiling and reporting procedures. Most start-up entrepreneurs don't need to contact them, but very small vendors or suppliers in rural areas may check their credit through these agencies rather than the "big three." If you think this might apply to you, check your credit with the agencies nearest you; you can find them by contacting Associated Credit Bureaus Inc. (ACB), the Washington, DC-based trade association for the credit reporting industry.

Norm Magnuson, ACB's director of public affairs, says the association also works to educate consumers on consumer credit issues, and is a valuable source of information. Once you get your report, check for errors, omissions, and old information. Each reporting agency gives you recourse if you believe the report is incorrect. It's through this process that you may be able to remedy credit blemishes before you start your

(Continued)

(Continued)

business. Creditors want precise information; if you can provide it, they may be more willing to work with you.

What to Do?

Even with a spotty credit record, all is not lost, says Tim Dolan, manager of marketing communications for TRW. "If you have a bad credit history, acknowledge it to potential lenders and suppliers," says Dolan. "If you're upfront with them, they're more likely to find terms that will work for [you]." However, if you have bad credit, suppliers may tighten payment terms or require a fixed payment schedule. "They may also increase interest charges and/or charge higher penalties if you fail to meet their terms," says Dolan. "And some suppliers request disclosure of your financial performance on a regular basis."

Kent Stone, national manager of customer relations for Dun & Bradstreet in Bethlehem, Pennsylvania, cautions that there are no set rules for what vendors will do when faced with your bad credit. "Each vendor has different credit guidelines and his or her own criteria," Stone says. "Some may want cash-only arrangements; others may require the first order to be C.O.D.; and they might want to see references." Despite special arrangements, Stone says, most vendors are willing to work with you. "It's in their interest to see a company or individual succeed," he says, because that means more business for them.

Another way to quell lenders' fears, says Dolan, is to impress them with your business acumen. Show that old mistakes won't be replicated, and such shortcomings will matter less. That means having "a strong business plan," says Dolan, "including [sections on] operations, finance, sales, and marketing."

Like Dolan, Stone advises being completely upfront about your past credit situation. "Come forward with what occurred," he says. Hiding past problems is a bad idea, says Stone: "If a company gets a hint of something they [weren't aware of], it makes them leery. The more vendors know and understand your company, the more willing they are to work with you."

Taking Care of Business

An essential aspect of starting a business if you have bad credit is to satisfy past creditors as well as future ones.

Contact each creditor, making arrangements—and commitments—to fulfill your financial obligations. This, too, will increase your credibility with suppliers and vendors. The National Foundation for Consumer Credit in Silver Spring, Maryland, can help. While the foundation is not a resource for business advice, it helps consumers with debt management. There are 857 branches, called Consumer Credit Counseling Services, that educate and counsel people with financial difficulties.

Your local counseling service can help you arrange an extended repayment plan with creditors. You just need to show regular income and agree to cancel all outstanding, unsecured credit accounts. You write one check a month to the service, which pays your creditors. Often, past creditors will waive finance fees and other charges so the full amount goes to pay off the outstanding balance.

Although the foundation deals with credit only on the consumer level, that is where your past problems are likely to be. Most of your past creditors will be willing to cooperate with the foundation, which has an excellent reputation among credit grantors, and future creditors may view your involvement with the foundation as a sign of responsibility.

Paying the Price

Once you've done your best to mollify vendors and settle past obligations, you still have to finance your venture. A key reason for business failure is insufficient initial funds, so you'll want to have enough capital before you begin.

Your credit situation probably rules out funding from banks. Independent finance companies are a possibility, but the interest rates are often quite high. The solution may be a secured credit card. Secured credit cards are standard Visa and MasterCards offered by banks, with one key difference: The credit line depends on a savings deposit you maintain with the issuing bank. Most banks offer a credit line of 100 percent of your deposit; some go as high as 150 or even 250 percent.

Although this method requires you to put up cash, the benefits are numerous. Secured savings deposits sometimes pay better rates than local passbook savings accounts; a secured credit card is a way to build positive credit information; and a credit card lends credibility to your business and

(Continued)

(Continued)

helps you track expenditures. Also, although Consumer Credit Counseling Services recommend against it, a secured line of credit won't preclude you from working with them. Finally, banks issuing the cards review accounts periodically, and you could become a "regular" cardholder. Herndon, Virginia-based Bank-card Holders of America is a nonprofit organization that gives consumers information on understanding and using credit to their advantage. The group offers more than 20 different booklets on credit, priced from $1 to $5, as well as a list of banks that issue secured credit cards.

Apart from secured credit cards, most of your business dealings will probably have to be in cash, financed by savings, loans from family and friends, or, once you are established, business revenues.

Up and Running

You've made a good start at cleaning up your personal credit. But once you begin operations, it's equally important to establish good business credit. Here's how:

> Pay all bills on time. Consider paying them before they're due or paying more than you owe. Payments even a few days early or a few dollars over will be remembered by vendors.

> Establish a business credit file with a reporting agency such as Dun & Bradstreet.

Although D&B does not report consumer credit, you are now a business owner, and you need a business credit file. Write or call the company as soon as you begin operations.

"Initially there won't be much information in your file," says D&B's Kent Stone, "but each day, as you deal with more companies, the file will grow." D&B maintains information on banking relationships, vendor payment histories, and any liens against your company. Creating and maintaining a file is free, as are copies of your file. The files are updated once a year.

Bad credit is a hurdle you have to clear, but hurdles are part of business ownership. Credit is just one facet of the task. Be prepared for the rest, and bad credit won't be so difficult to beat after all.

7

EXPANSION FINANCING

It's a dilemma common to businesses large and small: They reach a point in their evolution where they need additional capital to expand, yet haven't made the provisions to secure it. They wait until they absolutely need the money, and by then desperation becomes a factor. This is just more evidence to support the claim that preparation is critical for success in every facet of business. Expansion capital often comes at a high price, either in the form of carrying an abnormally high interest rate or forcing you to give up a substantial amount of your equity. Both of these costs can shrink your return on the investment of time and money you've made in your business. The cost of acquiring expansion funds is at least one explanation why financing sources are so plentiful (ethics is another issue). Lending money has always been a profitable business and perhaps always will be, but it doesn't mean you have to pay through the nose for it. Armed with information, you can make intelligent decisions about how much money you need and where to find it.

WHEN DO YOU NEED EXPANSION CAPITAL?

There's a major misconception among entrepreneurs that expansion capital is required *only* when the firm reaches a level of profitability and production that requires additional personnel, equipment, or facility expansion. Certainly, increases in the volume of production indicate a growth in sales volume, a rise in costs associated with production, and a need to expand capacity, if necessary. All of this requires additional capital to fuel the continued growth, but that still doesn't really address the question of when you need expansion capital.

Why? Profitability is a measure of the company's performance in relation to sales, cost of sales, and overhead, all of which are included in a monthly income statement that charts the business's performance. However, while the income statement portrays the performance of the company, it doesn't denote the timing differences in cash flow.

Why is cash flow important? Cash flow is an endless cycle that companies experience over their existence. It is the actual investment in additional material to continue production (usually referred to as *cost of sales*), the outlay of capital to meet all payables and overhead, and the collection of receivables, all of which occur at different times during the cash flow cycle.

In order to meet demand, production materials have to be purchased at a predetermined time based on your inventory control system in order to replenish your existing inventory of finished goods so that customer demand can be met. Usually, within 30 days after ordering your goods, payment will have to be made. Depending on your production cycle, your inventory of finished goods may or may not have been replenished at that point (refer back to Chapter 6, Credit). Regardless of that fact, however, you still have to sell the product, which could take some time, and then you have to collect if the purchase was not made in cash. If you invoice someone, you will have placed an account on your books as a receivable.

Based on the preceding scenario, you will have paid for the production of the product long before you collect any cash for it from a sale. In the meantime, you still have to meet overhead. If you're not careful, that could lead to the dreaded "cash flow crunch." As you can see, the need for expansion capital originates long before you start experiencing increased sales. To make a sale, first and foremost, your operations have to have the resources available to them to create the product. Without enough product in inventory to sell, it would be very unlikely that you'll experience any increase in sales. The only way to make sure you have enough product present is to plan and evaluate your financial position in relation to projected growth, both in sales and operations requirements.

Prepare

When financing your expansion efforts, heed the advice of entrepreneurs who came before you and plan ahead. Revise your business plan on a yearly basis (even more frequently if possible), and generate marketing plans to complement your business plan. These strategic planning tools not only help you define goals and objectives, they also provide you with a time frame upon which to build your financial projections.

Armed with this knowledge, you'll be able to determine the amount of expansion capital necessary and the general period of time when you'll need it. That, combined with proper financial control techniques, will allow you to be prepared when you need to go knocking on doors for additional capital. It will also allow you to shop for a loan *before* you need it, instead of when you need it. By giving yourself the luxury to shop the type of financing available and the terms being offered, you will be able to arrange a better deal for yourself—and you won't have to take whatever is available.

Expansion Plans

Many times entrepreneurs get so wrapped up with the actual operations of the business, during which they are producing a product and selling it, they fail to adequately plan for the future. For the owner, president, or CEO, planning accounts for 80 percent of their time. Of course, that is in an ideal situation, something a small business rarely faces, but it provides you with an idea of how important planning is to a business, and who ultimately bears the responsibility for determining strategy.

Planning the overall strategy and goals of the company should be done on an annual basis and should be a combined effort of the executive management team. It is not uncommon for large companies to hold off-site meetings where the entire executive group can gather and chart the company's strategy for the upcoming year and beyond. For smaller companies, where the executive management team may consist of the owner and a few key people, the idea is still the same, just on a smaller level.

The main goal of an annual meeting is to do the following:

1. *Set goals.* Both long-term and short-term goals should be defined. These goals can center around any number of business factors such as market share, sales, profit, geographic expansion, product expansion, and others. One objective or several can be set, depending on an analysis of external as well as internal forces.

2. *Review company performance.* Year-end financial statements should be generated to provide a profile of the company's profitability, cash position, liquidity, and net worth. These

When nothing else works, or when you feel that the "normal way of doing things" isn't exactly your way, think outside the box and find your own sources of financing your business. Here are 10 creative ways to get cash when you need it.

1. *Sell your assets.* If you sell your Cadillac for 12 grand and lease a Ford Escort for $189 a month with no money down, you've acquired cheap capital! You also have a cheap car, too; but, hey, who said being an entrepreneur was glamorous? Look around for things you can sell: antiques, pool tables, boats, collections, and so on. A lot of this stuff can go to make way for your business.

2. *Borrow against the cash value of your life insurance.* Write the American Council of Life Insurance in Washington, DC, saying you want a policy loan. Most companies will lend up to 90 percent of the policy's cash value, and your policy stays intact as long as you keep paying the premiums. If you die while there is a loan on the policy, though, it's very likely the benefits will be diminished.

3. *Go online.* Yes, you might have guessed this one. Check out online services that offer entrepreneurs the chance to hold their hat out online, where interested investors from around the country take a look. Business Opportunities Online Inc., a San Diego-based company, is one of the businesses offering you this service. America Online, CompuServe, or Prodigy also have small business or entrepreneur forums that can give you that lead you've been waiting for.

4. *Find a corporate partner.* Strategic alliances make perfect sense if you can answer these three questions posed by Graeme Howard, an investment banker and vice chairman of Datatec Industries Inc., a Fairfield, New Jersey, information technology company: "Can you give and take?"; "Does the company you are going to work with have any experience in partnering?"; and "Can you write down what you are seeking from the partnership arrangement?" If you answered yes to these questions, start to look for your potential partner by contacting the executive director of the trade association in the industry you are targeting to get leads.

5. *Create limited partnerships.* Lou Bucelli and Tim Crouse, cofounders of CME Conference Video Inc. in Mt. Laurel, New Jersey, are the creators of this idea. It is like a partnership program, except that you find a partner to

finance only a specific program, as it is done in some of Hollywood's biggest productions.

6. *Apply for a Small Business Innovation Research (SBIR) grant.* The federal government is one of the biggest buyers of technology. If this is your forte, you may have hit the jackpot. Participants in the SBIR grant program include the departments of agriculture, commerce, defense, education, energy, health and human services, transportation and environmental protection, NASA, the Nuclear Regulatory Commission, and the National Science Foundation.

7. *Apply for a Small Company Offering Registration (SCOR) financing.* The beauty of this program is that it allows companies to raise equity capital without the lengthy, costly, and difficult Securities and Exchange Commission Regulations. With SCOR, companies can sell small amounts of stock to lots of investors—a major advantage over most private placement deals, which are sold in large chunks to accredited investors.

8. *Consider a reverse merger.* A reverse merger occurs when you merge into a blind pool or public shell (a defunct company with no assets or line of business). It introduces a whole new group of shareholders to your company, and there are some reporting requirements and ongoing legal and accounting fees you incur; the good news is that a lot of shells and blind pools have a dollop of cash in them, and if you can manage to close a deal, you can get your hands on it. As a public company, it will be significantly easier to sell shares privately since investors can see that if the company is successful, there is a way for them to cash out.

9. *Try factoring.* This means selling your receivables to a factor (a third party) for cash. The factor then collects the money from your creditors. This can advance 75 to 90 percent of the receivables' face value, which may be really good if you are desperate for cash. Check the *Edwards Directory of American Factors* published by the Edwards Research Group, Inc. in Newton, Massachusetts, for information on about 200 factoring companies.

10. *Apply for an Export-Import Bank of the United States working capital guaranty.* The only requirement is that your products be for export. Your local SBA can give you more details on this.

Adapted from "Found Money" by David R. Evanson, *Entrepreneur Magazine*, April 1995.

can easily be found through an income statement, cash flow statement, and balance sheet, three documents emphasized throughout this book.

3. *Evaluate operation requirements.* In order to meet the goals of the business, determine the requirements in terms of operations. This includes all phases of the business: marketing, production, administration, and research and development. In order to plan, you need to know what the requirements will be in terms of advertising, sales, equipment investment, factory expansion, administrative support, and so on. Without this information, attaining your goals will be impossible.

4. *Create a budget.* Goals, performance of the business, and operational requirements have to be translated into budgets for planning purposes. These budgets are produced in the form of the familiar income statement, balance sheet, and cash flow statement.

As a result of this annual meeting, the various strategic plans will be updated. These include the business plan and marketing plan. It is essential that the business strategy be formalized into some type of written plan. It not only organizes your strategy and projections into a formal presentation that can be presented to your managers and any investors, but it also illustrates projected growth, cash requirements, and capital investment needs. It tells you when you'll need money and how much, which is measured against profit and revenues. With this type of information, you will know whether expansion can be financed from within or through outside sources.

The business plan is developed from a thorough market analysis and internal analysis. It is structured in the following manner:

- *Business description.* Defines the purpose of the business.
- *Marketing strategies.* Defines the scope of the market and stipulates pricing, distribution, and sales strategies in addition to sales potential.
- *Competitive analysis.* Defines the impact of the competition, their key assets and skills, their competitive advantages, their strategies, and any entry barriers that may be present.
- *Design and development plans.* Outlines the requirements to bring a product to market, which is crucial if you are expanding your product line or introducing a new version of an old product.
- *Operations and management plans.* Defines the management team and describes the resources required to operate the business in terms of personnel, materials, and equipment.

- *Financial components.* Defines budgets through financial projections from the income statement, cash flow statement, and balance sheet.

Using your business or marketing plan as a foundation, you can refine your budget; determine time frames when additional capital, personnel, and equipment are required; and form strategies to account for increased working capital and capital expansion. This is important to your expansion plans because costs are identified, time frames stipulated, financial strengths defined, and borrowing capacity illustrated. (See Chapter 2, Business Plan, for a sample cash flow projection, balance sheet, and income statement.)

Aside from its value as a strategic tool, the business and marketing plans also provide you with the type of information lenders and investors look for when evaluating whether to extend a loan or invest in a business, which is important when you approach outside financing sources to secure expansion capital.

Cash Flow Reality

It is clear that proper cash flow is important. Within the scope of planning, it becomes a crucial barometer that measures not only when you will need additional capital, but also the amount at that given time.

Before you form a cash flow budget, you should already have developed several key tables:

- The sales/revenue table.
- Development expense table.
- Cost-of-goods table.
- Capital requirements table.
- Operating expense table.

From these tables, you'll be able to form your various financial statements, including your cash flow projection. However, while the other tables from which you'll draw information quantify the amounts you'll need for expansion (to meet the revenue projections), the cash flow projection places that information in conjunction with the revenue and cost cycles associated with the business.

For instance, if the revenue table projects a 60-percent growth in sales over the coming year, that will necessitate investment in new equipment to handle the additional volume, obsolescence of current equipment, hiring additional personnel to manage the workload, and financing increased working capital required to operate the business. The cost-of-goods table, capital requirement table, and operating expense table formed in the business plan will provide a breakdown of costs to meet the 60-percent growth projected in the revenue table. The next thing you need to do is infuse that information into the cash flow cycle.

Based on past performance, first break down projected sales over the next year according to the percentage of business volume generated in each month. Divide each month's sales according to cash sales and credit sales. Cash sales can be logged into the cash flow statement in the same month they are generated. Credit sales are a different matter. These sales don't refer to credit card sales, which we'll treat as cash, but rather to invoiced sales that are tied to agreed-upon terms. Refer to your accounts receivable records and determine your average collection period. If it is 30 days, then sales made by credit can't be logged into cash until 35 to 40 days after they are made. (Although the collection period is 30 days, you still have to deposit the money and draw upon another bank to receive payment.)

The next line item on a cash flow statement is other income, which refers to any revenue derived from investments, interest on loans that have been extended, and the liquidation of any assets. Total income is the sum of cash sales, receivables, and other income. The first month of your cash budget will usually consist of cash sales, other income, plus any receivables from the previous budget that have aged to a point of collection during the first month of the current budget.

Also tied to the breakdown of sales are cost-of-goods and direct labor. In order to sell the product, it first has to be produced. Since you already have sales broken down by months, you need to determine the cost in material and labor to produce those sales. Refer to your cost-of-goods table in your business plan. Determine the cost of direct labor (for the year) to produce your product. Divide that number by the percentage breakdown of sales. Direct labor can be logged into cash flow during the same month it is accrued.

The cost of materials, on the other hand, is a little different. You need to include the material cost in cash flow within a time frame that will allow you to convert raw material to finished goods in order to fulfill the sale. Therefore, if it requires 60 days to convert raw material to finished goods, and your payable period is 30 days after delivery, then insert the cost of goods under material in cash flow 30 days before sales are logged.

Working capital can be derived from the operating expense table. All personnel and overhead costs are tied to sales (see Chapter 2, Business Plan). You can determine your working capital and payroll requirements by dividing marketing and sales, general and administrative, and overhead expenses by the total projected operating expenses by the percentage breakdown of sales for each month, and applying that amount to the appropriate line items in the cash flow statement.

As for capital equipment, there are two realms of thought. The first is to purchase and install the needed equipment at a point during the year where additional volume will warrant the expenditure, thereby assuring sufficient cash flow to handle the additional debt service or the outright purchase of the equipment. The second method is to have the equipment purchased and installed at the beginning of the business year or quarter closest to the time when you will require the equipment, allowing for training time and a debugging period when any problems the equipment has can be worked out before placing it into full production. Which avenue you choose is dependent upon the strength of your cash flow. If you can handle the additional drain of servicing more debt or purchasing the equipment entirely without the benefit of increased sales, then the latter method would be beneficial. If your cash flow is extremely tight, then choose the former method. Either way, the infusion of capital equipment costs will be logged into cash flow under capital.

In addition to the costs just listed, you also need to include any long-term debts currently being serviced in the cash flow budget under loans and, of course, your tax obligations. Both of these items should be readily obtainable from loan schedules and tax charts used to project these costs. Once all of these costs have been logged into the cash flow budget, add all of them together to produce your total expenses. Total expenses are subtracted from total income. The result is your cash flow, which will either be a surplus or a deficit. If it is a deficit, you need to determine what the minimum cash balance is that you wish to maintain. Calculate the difference between the minimum cash balance and the cash flow deficit. This will result in total amount required for financing purposes. This will also equal the ending cash balance that needs to be added to cumulative cash flow (the total of current cash flow and cash flow from the previous period). Keep in mind when forming a cash flow budget that any amounts financed within a given month need to be included in the cash flow under a projected repayment schedule. You should consult your accountant or financial officer when developing this repayment schedule.

Evaluating Your Business's Financial Position

Of course, not everything is subject to the cash flow statement. It is an important tool when charting the approximate period when infusion of capital will need to be made and the amounts required to maintain a comfortable cash flow situation. One thing it doesn't tell you, though, is your capacity to borrow money. This is often determined by the profitability of the business and its net worth.

By analyzing your income statement and balance sheet, you'll be able to determine your borrowing capacity. This involves the use of financial ratios, specifically, measure of liquidity. The first measure of liquidity you can perform is the *current ratio,* which measures your ratio of assets to liabilities. This ratio provides lenders with a quick look at the business's ability to meet its obligation within a short-term period. If you have strong assets compared to your liabilities, your capacity for additional financing is fairly good. To calculate a current ratio, divide your current assets by your current liabilities, both of which can be found on your balance sheet. Current assets are cash and other assets such as receivables and inventory that will be converted into cash within the upcoming year, whereas current liabilities are those obligations that need to be paid within a year. For a current ratio, generally a two-to-one is more than appropriate.

Another measure of liquidity is the *quick ratio.* Like the current ratio, this measure of liquidity gauges all your liquid assets against current liabilities. Liquid assets refer not only to current assets but all those assets that can be easily converted into current assets. For most businesses, a quick ratio of two or more is very sufficient for borrowing needs.

Another common measure to determine borrowing capacity is *net profit on sales.* This measure determines the percentage of profit the firm experiences compared to sales. To find out what your net profit is on sales, divide net profit before taxes, which can be found in your income statement, by net sales. The result is the profitability of your business. Compare this against industry averages and current interest rates to determine your strength.

All these measures of liquidity are indicators of any short-term financing needs you might have. If you already have low current and quick ratios, taking on additional short-term loans will further weaken your ability to meet your obligations within the upcoming year because the loan would be a current liability. On the other hand, by taking out a long-term loan, you would improve your liquidity because only the portion of the loan that is due and payable during the first year would be applied to current liabilities; the remaining portion would be a current asset.

Generally, a business should be as profitable as the amount of money that can be earned from interest or dividends in securities. If your profitability is strong, the amount of money investors will be willing to place within your business will be equally strong.

The last measure is the *debt-to-equity ratio.* This ratio measures the total liabilities to the total equity within the business. This is done by

VENCAP (VENTURE CAPITAL)

Anne Gene Callot

Acquiring money for your business in the information age has never been easier or more convenient. In the quest for venture capital, a number of financial organizations that can assist you with money for investing in business organizations and online services offer excellent starting points. The Investment Exchange in Calgary, Alberta, Canada, and The Capital Network, Inc. in Austin, Texas, use their own electronic technology to computer-match investors with opportunities. Capital Search Marketing in San Diego, California, guides entrepreneurs to appropriate investors and helps them devise presentations and marketing plans. The National Association of Investment Companies (NAIC) in Washington, DC, offers financial resources for investment in minority businesses. The NAIC also founded the Entrepreneurial Growth and Investment Institute, a nonprofit foundation researching new capital sources for minority entrepreneurs and managers. Resources at the Foundation Center can help nonprofit organizations locate start-up capital.

On the information superhighway, CompuServe offers a slew of business resources that you can access, which will lead you directly to firms and individuals specializing in venture capital. Your best bets on this network include the Finance/Accounting Section of Entrepreneur's Small Business Forum, Iquest Business Management InfoCenter, and the Investors Forum. Prodigy also offers an opportunity to get financial consulting on its Small Business Bulletin Board. America Online offers a personal finance business unit that allows business owners to tap into a variety of personal money-management and investment services. Other, smaller, online computer networks are also beginning to offer venture capital resources.

No matter where you log on to find venture capital, you'll need to assess your financial needs. The more growth potential your business has, the better the chance you'll have of attracting funding. If you're a technology-related business specializing in any of the many computer, electronics, engineering, or health fields, your chances are even better. Trends suggest that businesses in these growth-producing industries gather more venture capital than others. Use caution, though, since you will need to assure the potential investment firm with adequate knowledge of your industry and show how you intend to stay afloat. The key is to properly match your needs with what the venture capitalist has to offer, so that both parties may benefit.

dividing total liabilities by total equity. Most businesses try to stay at a ratio of one-to-one or below. It is not a good idea to leverage your business so much that it cannot maneuver when the unexpected hits. Also, if you are already loaded with debt, you may not be able to get the long-term financing you want, at least not at a favorable rate. Then you'll have to look at equity financing as an option. The difference between equity financing and a regular loan is, of course, that you're giving up a piece of your business, profits, and possibly some control. You may also find it more difficult to find someone to buy part of your business, either as a partner, limited partner, or perhaps as a shareholder of your corporation.

EXPANSION CAPITAL

There are three types of financing sources: short-term financing, intermediate-term financing, and long-term financing. When applying for money, it is important to evaluate your needs so you can look for the type of financing that is most appropriate.

Short-term financing is usually used to meet seasonal and temporary fluctuations in funds, provide working capital, finance current assets such as receivables and inventories, or furnish interim financing for a long-term project or capital asset until long-term financing may be issued. Before deciding on how much short-term financing you need, consider the company's cash flow on a monthly and even weekly basis, taking into account economic conditions, timing of receipts and payments, and season. In comparison to long-term financing, short-term financing terms are easier to arrange, are less costly, and have greater flexibility. The drawbacks are that interest rates fluctuate more often, refinancing is usually needed, and there is the risk of inability to pay. Sources that may be tapped are trade credit, bank loans, bankers' acceptances, finance company loans, commercial paper, receivable financing, and inventory financing.

Intermediate-term financing is primarily obtained from banks and lessors. Loans of this type mature in more than one year and are suitable when short-term unsecured loans are not, such as when a business is bought, capital asset are purchased, and long-term debt is required. If a company wants to issue long-term debt or equity securities but market conditions are unfavorable, it may take an intermediate loan to bridge the gap until long-term financing can be arranged on favorable terms. A firm may employ extendible debt when there is a continuing financing need. This reduces the time and cost of many debt issuances. Because of the longer maturity, interest rates on intermediate-loans are usually more than on short-term loans. In addition, collateral and possible restrictive

---

Factors Influencing Selection of a Financing Source

- Cost, including interest rate, and front-end fees.
- Prepayment penalties.
- Impact on financial ratios.
- Effect on credit rating.
- Risk.
- Restrictions such as minimum working capital.
- Flexibility.
- Anticipated money-market conditions (such as future interest rates) and availability of future financing.
- Inflation rate.
- Profitability and liquidity positions.
- Stability and maturity of operations.
- Tax rate.

Source: Shim, J., and Siegel, J., *The Vest-Pocket CFO,* Prentice-Hall, Englewood Cliffs, NJ, 1995.

---

convenants are required, as opposed to none for commercial paper and unsecured short-term bank loans; budgets and financial statements may have to be routinely submitted to the lender; and "sweeteners" such as stock warrants or a share of the profits are sometimes asked for by the bank. On the other hand, intermediate financing offers the following advantages: flexibility, in that the terms may be changed as the company's financing requirements change; confidentiality of financial information because there is no public issuance; faster procedures when compared to a public offering; avoidance of the possible nonrenewal of a short-term loan; absence of public flotation costs.

Finally, long-term financing is for more than five years; and it is important that you are familiar with the what, why, and how of equity financing (issuing preferred stock and common stock) and long-term debt financing (primarily issuing bonds). This type of finance is often used to fund long-lived assets like a plant or construction projects. Just keep in mind that a financing policy should be in response to the overall strategic direction of the company.

SOURCES OF EXPANSION CAPITAL

Once you've established the need for additional capital, you need to determine which source or sources of financing would be the most appropriate for you. In Coopers & Lybrand's July/August 1994 issue of *Growing Your Business,* 66 percent of fast-growth companies reported that at the initial growth stage they were funded predominantly by external sources: bank loans, investors, and alliances.[1] Owner funding—entrepreneurs putting up their own money—accounted for less than 1 percent of the businesses in the initial growth stage. This is down from 17 percent owner-funded growth at the critical break-even or "survival" stage and 73 percent owner-funded growth at their start-up. These investors are a primary source of financing, and they *do not* invest carelessly. That's why charting your goals is so vital, both in the short term and the long run, as well as performing the proper market analyses, and drawing up your business and marketing plans. By doing this, not only will you know how much you need and when, but you will have a good idea of the type of financing that would be most appropriate. Also, by being thoroughly prepared, you will have a lot more flexibility and credibility when you go shopping for additional capital.

From investors' point of view, nothing could be more important than the strength and credibility of the business they intend to support with financing. They will want every bit of financial, operational, and development information available so they can make an informed decision. It doesn't matter whether you are applying for a short-term working capital loan or offering stock to the public, you'll need to present that information.

So be prepared. The sources for expansion capital are numerous and can be utilized very productively by entrepreneurs who understand their impact and relationship to the overall needs of the business. In the upcoming sections, we will highlight several sources of expansion capital, all of which can be grouped into the following categories:

1. *Bootstrap financing.* Relies on the creative use and control of internal resources to meet short-term operational and growth requirements (refer back to Chapter 5, Bootstrap Financing).

2. *Debt financing.* Offers the widest choice of financing possibilities. Loans are extended by an outside agency at prescribed terms and interest rates (same method as debt financing for start-ups).

3. *Equity financing.* Under this type of arrangement, a percentage of the business is forfeited to the investor for infusion of capital (same method as equity financing for start-ups). Venture capital is the most widely recognized form of equity financing.

Bootstrap Methods for Expansion

When thinking of capital for expansion or short-term operational needs, consider bootstrap financing. As discussed in Chapter 5, this method is probably one of the best and most inexpensive routes an entrepreneur can explore when raising capital for an existing business. It utilizes untapped opportunities that can be found within your own company simply by managing your finances better. Bootstrap financing is a way to pull yourself up without the help of others. You are the one financing your growth by your current earnings and assets.

There are a lot of different methods involved in bootstrap financing, and this is going to be very advantageous to you. Not only will you be able to finance your expansion or working capital internally, you will also have a business that will be worth more because less money has been borrowed and no equity positions have to be relinquished. It's also going to help you because you're not going to have to pay the high cost of borrowed money. This will make you look more desirable to external lenders and investors when the time does come to raise money through these routes. Bootstrap financing enables you to reduce the amount of money that you're going to have to borrow, thereby increasing your profits.

Five possible sources of bootstrap financing for expansion purposes are:

1. Trade credit.
2. Customers (letters of credit).
3. Factoring (selling accounts receivable to a buyer to raise capital).
4. Real estate.
5. Equipment suppliers.

If you have already tapped these sources and have to look beyond your own financial boundaries for assistance, using debt is the next logical choice.

Debt Financing

Chances are, if your business has built a good track record, has a solid customer foundation and a strong financial position, banks and other traditional debt financing institutions will want to talk to you about your additional capital requirements. After all, you're their perfect customer. You already have a solid business, you will generally have good assets with which to secure loans, and the capacity to incur additional debt.

For growth and expansion purposes, debt financing is a strong consideration from your point of view as well. It provides an infusion of capital based on your needs, a time frame suitable for repayment of the loan, and it doesn't require any surrender of equity within the company. It is a straightforward business transaction in which money is loaned to the business at a prescribed user's fee, or interest rate, over a designated period of time, and usually secured by some form of collateral that is forfeited unless the loan is repaid when it matures.

There are several forms of collateral used to secure loans, and the type you'll need greatly depends on the kind of loan you'll require. There are generally three types of loans available through debt financing sources for growth and expansion purposes:

1. *Working capital loans.* Usually short-term, working capital loans are generally tied to the business cycle of a company. They can be secured or unsecured loans, and are used to increase working capital to fund the purchase of inventory, meet overhead, and increase the number of sales made on credit. Collateral used for working capital loans includes receivables and inventory.

2. *Term loans.* These are generally medium- to long-term loans used to finance the purchase of capital equipment, facility expansion, increase working capital, or acquire another business. Term loans aren't tied to the cyclical nature of a business, but on projections of higher earnings and larger profit margins by the business. A specialized type of term loan is the capital loan, a long-term loan used for fixed-asset acquisitions, and which is secured by the equipment purchased.

3. *Interim loans.* On rare occasions, you may be able to finance a short-term interim loan. These are loans made as a bridge until repayment by either the borrower or from another creditor.

As mentioned in Chapter 3, Start-Up Financing, you need to offer some type of security that the loan will be repaid when seeking any of the loans just discussed. Security is posted in the form of collateral, which can take a variety of forms:

- Guarantor.
- Endorsers.
- Comaker.
- Accounts receivable.

- Equipment.
- Securities.
- Real estate.
- Savings account.
- Chattel mortgage.
- Insurance policies.
- Warehouse inventory.
- Display merchandise.
- Leases.

Of course, a loan can also be unsecured, in which case your credit standing is the lender's only security. Unsecured loans, either *signature* or *personal*, are usually arranged with the bank to provide a revolving line of credit to the business on a continuous basis in order to meet short-term needs usually tied to the business cycle of the company. There are generally a few stipulations associated with this type of debt financing. They require that the principal amount be paid off periodically and that a compensating balance, usually 10 percent of the outstanding balance, be held by the bank in a non-interest bearing account.

Repayment periods for most debts vary according to the amount borrowed, the financial wherewithal of the applicant and the term they desire. With venture capital, as with other forms of expansion financing, the repayment is a function of the growth of the business. To review, there are primarily three types of repayment terms:

1. Short-term.
2. Intermediate-term.
3. Long-term.

Chapter 3, Start-Up Financing, talked about debt financing opportunities when putting together a business, but what about the external funds available for expansion financing? Banks still represent the most widely used source, despite their reputation for being conservative. They are ideal sources for debt financing once your business has established a good track record, which means they primarily like to fund ongoing operations and expansion efforts. By and large, banks will require a complete loan proposal or a revised business plan (see Chapter 2, Business Plan). A typical loan proposal consists of:

- Cover sheet.
- Cover letter.
- Table of contents.

- The purpose and amount of the loan.
- Business description.
- Market analysis.
- Operations/management outline.
- Financial components.
- Possible collateral.
- Personal financials.
- Notes.

Be realistic and honest with bankers. They need any and all information about you and your business from you directly, not from somebody else. This will improve significantly your chances of receiving a loan.

When looking for expansion funds, *commercial lenders* are a popular avenue to pursue. Banks tend to steer clear of small companies experiencing rapid sales growth for fear of a parallel decline. Firms that are already highly leveraged will also have a hard time getting additional bank funding. In that case, commercial lenders will often step in because they are set up to handle these situations and they know they can get most, if not all, of a defaulted loan back by selling off the collateral pledged against the note.

The Small Business Administration (SBA) helps small businesses obtain loans for expansion purposes in addition to their myriad of other small-business assistance programs, and also offers management assistance. As with start-up financing, there are two types of SBA loans available for expansion: guaranteed loans and direct loans. Even those who qualify for either a direct or guaranteed loan cannot solicit a loan from the SBA if they can legitimately obtain a loan from a bank or private source. Therefore, you must first apply to a bank or alternate lending source; and, again, if you live in a city with a population over 200,000, you must have been turned down by two financial institutions before seeking funds. Refer back to Chapter 4, SBA Loans, for a review of rates, terms, and conditions.

The SBA's Economic Opportunity Loan (EOL) program also makes funds available to small-business concerns owned by, or to be established by, persons with low incomes seeking expansion financing. As mentioned, Economic Opportunity Loans for veterans receive in-depth management assistance counseling, special workshops and training, prompt processing of loan applications, maximum loan maturity, solutions to a lack of collateral, a flexible approach to the standard repayment schedule, and specialists designated as veterans' loan officers. Both types of handicapped assistance loans, HAL-1 and HAL-2, are also available for financing growth plans as well as start-ups and ongoing operations. In fact, most of the same loans the SBA makes for start-ups are also available to businesses in their stage of initial growth. To find out how to apply for an SBA loan, refer back to Chapter 4.

As explained in Chapter 3, the SBA is without a doubt the largest source of federally assisted financing for small businesses. Here is an abbreviated list of additional programs available to entrepreneurs in search of growth financing:

- Department of Energy.
- Economic Development Administration of the Department of Commerce (EDA).
- Farmers Home Administration of the USDA.
- Department of Housing and Urban Development (HUD).
- Department of the Interior.

The government programs and agencies listed in previous chapters previously as start-up financing and working-capital sources also make funds available for expansion financing. They are:

- Export-Import Bank (EXIMBANK).
- Export Revolving Line of Credit Program.
- Local Development Companies (LDCs).
- Small Business Innovation Research Program (SBIR).
- State Business and Industrial Development Corporations (SBIDCs).

Equity Financing

Through equity financing, you can raise money through private, public, or professional sources that specialize in supporting the growth plans of businesses in your industry. The advent of high technology and the increasing sophistication of entrepreneurs fueled the growth of venture capital funding. Today there are an estimated 720,000 private, public, and professional venture capital investors in the United States, making 489,000 informal venture investments with a mean per-investment dollar value of $66,700. These figures suggest an annual equity capital total of over $33 billion. The investors are part of the "invisible" venture capital market, which is much larger and richer than the visible venture capital market consisting of venture capital funds.[2] That doesn't take into account selling equity in the business through private and public placement of securities, which records another $2.3 billion each year.

As you can see, equity financing is not a minor factor in the world of expansion financing any longer. There are a lot of players and options from which to choose. The idea is to find the right type of equity financing for your business. As explained in Chapter 3, the legal form of your business will have a direct and significant impact on raising equity capital.

Here is a brief recap:

- As a *sole proprietor* and partner, you play a central role in running the business, responsible for the liabilities and responsibilities of that business. If it goes bankrupt, you share that equally.
- *Limited partnerships* recruit investors to become business partners on a limited basis, based on their infusion of equity funds. In a limited partnership, sometimes referred to as a *syndication*, you manage the money raised to actively operate the business, while the investors become limited partners. Should the venture meet with misfortune, the partners' liabilities are limited to what they have invested. Limited partners, by their legally constituted role, serve as passive investors rather than active managers.
- Partners forming a *corporation*, meanwhile, can divide ownership into shares and sell private stock to equity investors. Also, a partner who wants to leave can be accommodated without dissolution of the business. To raise additional capital, the corporation may elect to offer stock within the company to the investing public (see Chapter 8, Public Offerings). In this manner, the company has gone from a privately held corporation to a publicly held corporation.
- The *subchapter-S corporation* allows passive investors who will contribute money to the business for stock within the corporation. Like a limited partnership, a subchapter-S corporation offers full operational responsibilities while taking on investors within the company.

VENTURE CAPITAL

Venture capital is the best-known form of equity financing. As the name implies, it is used to finance relatively new, unproved ideas that are high-risk, high-return businesses. Venture capitalists expect two things from the companies they finance: high returns and a method of exit. Since venture capitalists hit the jackpot with only a small percentage of

THE NEED FOR A CASH BUDGET

The cash budget is the most effective tool for planning the cash requirements and resources of your business. With it you plan your financial operations—the cash you expect to take in and pay out. Your goal in budgeting is to maintain a satisfactory cash position for any contingency. When used to project the cash flow of the business, the cash budget will provide efficient use of cash by timing cash disbursements to coincide with cash receipts. These actions may reduce the need for borrowing temporary additional working capital. Determine periods for repayment of borrowings. Establish the practicality of taking or not taking discounts. Determine periods of surplus cash for investment or purchase of inventory and equipment. Indicate the adequacy or need for additional permanent working capital in the business.

Source: Small Business Administration.

the companies they back, they must go into each deal with the possibility of a return of 5 to 10 times their investment in three to five years if the business is successful. This may mean that they will own anywhere from 25 to 70 percent or more of your business. Each situation is different, and the amount of equity the venture capitalist will hold depends on the stage of the business's development at the time of the investment, the risk perceived, the amount of capital required, as well as the background of the entrepreneur.

What kinds of businesses do venture capitalists invest in? That depends on the particular investor or fund manager. Individual private venture capitalists, also known as *angels*, prefer to invest in industries with which they are familiar. The reason for this is simple: Even though angels will not actively participate in the day-to-day management of the business, they do want a voice within the strategic planning phase of the business in order to reduce the risk faced by the business and to optimize the profits.

On the other hand, private venture capital partnerships and industrial venture capitalists like to invest primarily in technology-related industries (not new technology necessarily, but applications of existing technology). The major areas of investment for venture capitalists are usually in computer-related communications, electronics, genetic engineering, and medical/health-related fields. There are, however, a number of investments in service and distribution businesses and even a few in consumer-related companies.

In addition to the type of business invested in, venture capitalists often define their investments by life cycle: seed, start-up, second-stage, bridge, and leveraged buyout. Some venture capitalists prefer to invest in firms only during the early stages of seed and start-up where the risk is highest and the potential for a high return is also the best. Other venture capital firms will deal only with second-stage financing for expansion purposes or bridge financing where they supply capital for growth until the company goes public. Finally, there are those venture capital companies that concentrate solely on supplying funds for management-led buyouts.

Generally, venture capitalists like to finance firms during the early stages and second stages when growth is very rapid, then cash out of the venture once it is established. As the owner of the business, that is one thing you must be aware of. At some point down the line, the venture capitalist will want out, usually when the risk-reward quotient moderates and the possibility for a high return on investment is no longer present. This "exit" will have been discussed in some depth at the time you negotiated the original deal. You will either take your company public, repurchase the investor's stock, merge with another firm or, in some circumstances, liquidate your business.

Chapter 3 explained that the key to attracting venture capital is the potential growth prospects for the business. Some venture capitalists tie this to earning power. If your business does not have the potential to grow rapidly in five to seven years, you are going to have a difficult time raising money through venture capitalists. Other investors look more at the return on investment. If investors have an opportunity to earn 5 to 10 times their investment in three to five years, they will look very closely at the business.

There are several venture funding sources you can pursue for expansion capital, some of which were described in Chapter 3 and some of which appear here for the first time:

1. *Private venture capital partnerships.* Perhaps the largest source of risk capital, private venture capital partnerships generally look for businesses that have the capability of generating a 30-percent return on investment annually. They like to actively participate in the planning and management phases of the businesses they finance, and have very large capital bases, up to $500 million, to invest in all stages.

2. *Industrial venture capital pools.* Financing from this arena is very limited. There are only about 75 large industrial companies that have formed their own investment pools of risk capital. Their

strategies usually center around funding promising firms that might succeed and make a good acquisition later. They usually prefer high-tech firms or companies that are utilizing current technology in a unique manner.

3. *Investment banking firms.* These are firms that traditionally provide expansion capital by selling stock within a company to public and private equity investors. Some also have formed their own venture capital divisions to provide risk capital for expansion and early-stage financing.

4. *Individual private investors.* Also known as angels, these investors range from friends and family who have only a few thousand dollars to invest to financially secure individuals who have built their own successful businesses and are willing to invest some of their money, sometimes up to a million dollars in a venture, and their experience with businesses of all sizes and at different stages of growth.

5. *Small Business Investment Corporations (SBICs).* Licensed and regulated by the SBA, SBICs are private investors that receive three to four dollars in SBA-guaranteed loans for every dollar they invest. Under the law, SBICs must invest exclusively in small firms with net worth less than $6 million and averaged after-tax earnings (over the past two years) of less than $2 million. They are also restricted in the amount of private equity capital for each funding with a minimum of $500,000 and a maximum of $10 million. Being licensed and regulated by a government agency distinguishes SBICs from other "private" venture capital firms, but other than that, they are not significantly different from other private venture firms.

6. *Minority Enterprise Small Business Investment Companies (MESBICs).* Like SBICs, MESBICs are privately capitalized investment agencies licensed and regulated by the SBA. They are designed to aid minority-owned and minority-managed firms by providing equity funds from private and public capital. As with the SBIC, MESBICs are restricted in the amount of their private funding—currently a minimum of $1 million. If your business has already gotten started but needs more capital, then check into these investors. They will want a business that looks like it will become very profitable.

7. *Small Business Development Companies (SBDCs).* Similar to SBICs, SBDCs are capitalized entirely by private sources such as banks, corporations, utility companies, transportation firms, and the like. Like SBICs and MESBICs, SBDCs make investment commitments on a long-term basis.

Before approaching any of these venture capital firms, do your homework and find out whether your interests and needs match their preferred investment strategy and what strengths the venture capitalist possesses that may help you in building your business. There are a number of directories available that list the investment preferences of venture capitalists.

Once you have narrowed the field to approximately 10 companies, the best way to contact them is through an introduction from a third party—another entrepreneur, a lawyer, a CPA, a banker, or anyone who knows you and the venture capitalist well enough to get his or her attention.

The first meeting with the venture capitalist is very important. Your business plan, your appearance, your conduct, what you say and how you say it are all critical. Be prepared. You will be asked many questions about your business plan.

Once a decision is made to finance your firm, the actual investment by the venture capitalist is negotiable and can take one of a variety of forms. These range from a straight common stock purchase to debentures with conversion features to straight loans. Venture capitalists usually use a combination of investment instruments to structure the deal that will be most beneficial to both parties.

If you cannot secure capital through other equity financing options, you may want to give some thought to going public. On the plus side is the infusion of massive amounts of new capital into the business. Because a successful public offering increases a business's net worth and standing in the business community, it enables the corporation to borrow additional funds on more favorable terms. Having publicly traded shares can also make acquisition of other firms considerably easier (those firms might prefer stock to a cash payment for tax reasons) and improve the position of previous shareholders, both in terms of liquidity and in the dollar value of their holdings.

There are drawbacks, however. For starters, there's the expense: Industry insiders estimate that it costs a firm about 15 percent of its total offering to make the move. For small offerings (between $1 million and $3 million) that means the client would spend at least $250,000. There are also reporting requirements—always a factor in any securities issue but multiplied in a public offering. All companies that want to sell stock to the public must supply those potential investors with detailed information about the corporation on a continuing basis. Those reports include audited financial statements, discussions of the company's plans and transactions, and even information concerning the fiscal relationships between directors, managers, shareholders, and the firm. This is an expensive and time-consuming process, not to mention the feeling it creates of living in a fishbowl. If you're the kind of person who likes to keep your business dealings private, this might not be a viable option. Finally, there is the potential for losing control of the business to large shareholders, particularly if the firm keeps diluting the value of the original holdings with additional stock offerings.

There are still other consequences of going public. Perhaps the most important is that corporate insiders can't take personal advantage of information to which they have access but the public doesn't. For example, management can't use its advance knowledge of an impending deal to make a killing in the company's stock. The law also requires that all transactions between a firm and its fiduciaries—its officers, directors, shareholders—be fair and reasonable to the corporation. That means, for instance, that a director cannot buy land he or she knows the corporation needs and wants for its business. (Initial public stock offerings are covered in the next chapter, Public Offerings.)

SPREADING THE WEALTH

Erika Kotite

Many of today's hottest high-tech companies were nourished by venture capital: Apple Computer, Microsoft, Intel, Data General, and more. In fact, the venture capital industry was virtually launched on the success of computers, software, and other high-tech developments that exploded in the late 1970s and early 1980s.

So how was a magazine about babies able to get the attention of Patricof & Co. Ventures Inc., a $1.5 billion international venture capital firm? Or what about a Massachusetts company that came up with a brand-new way to fry food? These are not exactly the kind of Silicon Valley success stories we're accustomed to. Still, they're the kind with enough potential to tempt today's venture capitalists, who are more careful than ever about where they invest their money. "Diversification is prudent," says Patricia Cloherty, president of New York City-based Patricof & Co. "These days you'll find most investment portfolios have a blend [of businesses]." Food service, retail, consumer goods, telecommunications, industrial products, environmental products and services, media, and publishing are just some of the industries sharing the venture capital pie with high-tech companies. Indeed, many contend the high-tech industry is not (and never has been) a sure bet for investors. And while the tendency to

(Continued)

(Continued)

spread funds over many industries is good news for entrepreneurs outside the high-tech world, the same selection criteria apply: a good business idea, a strong management
team, and the potential to make lots of money in a relatively
short period of time.

New Horizons

Venture capitalists are not abandoning high technology. According to Venture Economics, a research firm in Boston,
software and services attract the most venture capital funding—$562 million in 1992—with medical and health-care-
related businesses close behind at $442 million. These
industries' potential for rapid growth, high returns, and
products that have a protected market share are still powerful magnets for venture capitalists. But a growing number of
venture capital firms are either branching out into other
areas or specializing in other, less crowded industries.

First Analysis Corp. in Chicago, for example, devotes
half its $200 million investment fund pool to environmental
companies. "Why fish in a crowded pond?" says company
president Oliver Nicklin, who estimates only 1 percent of all
venture capital goes to environmental companies. Adds Bret
Maxwell, managing director, "We started specializing in the
environmental industry early, around 1985, so we could become experts." Like high technology, environmental products
and services are complex and change quickly. Also, the added
burden of complying with federal, state, and local regulations
regarding hazardous waste, air pollution, and disposal methods causes many venture capitalists to shy away. The experience and expertise of the partners at First Analysis, however,
allow them to spot opportunity where others just see trouble.
One of those opportunities was the GNI Group Inc., a Deer
Park, Texas, company founded in 1971 to sell radioactive devices. When it decided to switch over to hazardous waste disposal in the mid-1980s, the company asked First Analysis to
provide research coverage—that is, to follow the company's
progress and relate it to potential investors. But First Analysis
was so impressed, it decided to invest in the company itself.

"We had a strong balance sheet already," recalls Carl
Rush, president and CEO of the GNI Group. "But the money
was available, and at the time, we [needed] their strategic

planning expertise." With management and financial help from First Analysis, the GNI Group has grown into a $25 million disposal, reclamation, and waste minimization company. "It wouldn't have been easy without them," says Rush.

Some venture capitalists branching out into new industries look at the idea more than the business structure, but most agree the quality of management is one of the key factors in the decision to invest. "We look for the direct relevance of the management team's skills to the task at hand," says Cloherty. If the skills are not there, the venture capitalist will find an individual or a team who has them.

That's what Cloherty and venture capital company CW Group did in 1986 when they helped publishing executive Rich Huttner form Parenting Unlimited Inc. to acquire *Baby Talk* magazine. Patricof & Co. was looking for someone to head the new venture when Huttner, in search of a new project, contacted the company. The venture capitalists knew immediately they'd found a perfect match. "It was a sleepy, dowdy magazine that had potential," Huttner says. With new management, Patricof & Co. was confident the magazine could revamp its look and expand its circulation. Under Huttner's direction, the company expanded into four magazines—*Baby Talk, Baby on the Way, Basics,* and *Ready for Baby*—and attracted the attention of Time Warner, which bought the company in 1991.

Patricof & Co.'s portfolio includes publishing companies, health care firms, specialty retailers, mail order houses, and electronics firms. "We focus on [companies that will deliver] mid-level returns," Cloherty says. "High-tech may have great returns, but there's a corresponding high risk involved."

Specialty of the Day

While most venture capital companies spread their resources over several industries, others specialize in one area. For instance, a group of investors in Minneapolis started the Food Fund in 1990 strictly to fund companies involved in (you guessed it) the business of feeding people. John Trucano, managing general partner, put together a who's who of food-service giants and a total of $3.85 million in initial investment funds to start the firm. Why food? "Snapple [beverages] and Starbucks [coffee stores] are two of the best-performing

(Continued)

(Continued)

companies right now," says Trucano. "That doesn't go unnoticed by professional investors."

All of the Food Fund's investors have extensive experience in food service—one founded a large bakery chain, another spent eight years with General Mills, and another founded Golden Valley Microwave Foods, which grew to a $200 million publicly traded company. They were attracted by the fact that they could remain in the food-service arena. "They saw it as a fun [opportunity]," Trucano says.

Don't get him wrong: The Food Fund is serious business, too. It has invested in nine companies so far, including a gourmet cookie company, an aseptic packaging manufacturer (for shelf-stable dairy products), and a pasta chips maker. In all of them, Trucano and his partners recognized a spark they hope to fan into a full-blown success.

Motion Technology Inc., a manufacturer of self-ontained frying systems, is the only company the Food Fund has invested in outside the Minnesota/Iowa area; it's located in Natick, Massachusetts. But its unique device for deep-frying foods without needing ventilation or ducts convinced Trucano to go outside his geographic area. "All the Boston firms were too busy with high-tech companies [to bother with them]," says Trucano.

Arthur Harrison, Motion Technology's president, saw an article on the Food Fund and decided to pay the firm a visit when he was at a Minneapolis trade show. "We were intrigued by the fact that they focused on food service," he says. Harrison's company, which had raised its first-stage financing through family and friends, needed about $600,000 to expand its product line and begin national advertising. "We didn't even try the banks," Harrison says. "They aren't available to you unless you are well-established or affiliated with a big-name company."

Before investing, the Food Fund examined Motion Technology closely—its product, facilities, and business plan. The venture capitalists attended trade shows, where they asked the company lots of questions. What they saw impressed them: Motion Technology had a unique product with appeal to a broad spectrum of customers. "They already had more orders than they could fill," Trucano remembers. Now, with an $800,000 infusion of capital, Harrison projects 1993 sales will triple from 1992's. Motion Technology benefited not only from the money, but also from the food-service expertise of some of the biggest names in the business, who, with their contacts, helped the company develop strong leads in production and sales.

Risky Business

Not all venture capital stories have such happy endings. Any venture capital funding is a risk for the investor, and it's the fundings that end in failure that tighten the reins on capital, making it more difficult for you to acquire.

One of Cloherty's deals was a company that developed a technology for making eyeglasses more cheaply. But the recession and technology problems forced it into a Chapter 11 reorganization. "Most companies don't fail and go out of business," she explains. "They just don't realize their potential."

To lessen their risk, most venture capital firms like to stick closely to the areas in which they have a solid background. That means you need to thoroughly research companies to find those that best match your business. But once you find a firm that seems like the perfect match, your job isn't over. Specialty venture capitalists still want solid proof of a viable, growing business: a product or service that has its own solid market, and a management team that's committed to developing the company to its greatest potential as well as being willing to sell or go public when the time comes.

The Food Fund won't take just any kind of food business; for example, it stays away from restaurants because of their high failure rate, and because Trucano feels "we have no added value to give them." Nicklin and Maxwell at First Analysis look for ongoing revenues, usually of at least $1 million, with a product or service already on the market. "We don't [have] any value to add to start-ups," Maxwell explains. Instead, they advise start-up environmental businesses to check out research and development grants from federal and state programs, or from private individuals in similar industries.

Nobody ever said getting venture capital was easy, even if you find a firm with expertise in your industry. But if your company is poised for growth and a deal comes through, you'll find the extra help from people who really know your business could be as valuable as the money itself.

8

PUBLIC OFFERINGS

As your business grows, it needs money to fuel its operation and sustain its level of development. It passes through different stages of growth, feeding upon the investment you provide and, in turn, producing output (your product or service) and profit.

For many entrepreneurs, the ultimate sign of successful growth and the best way to raise a lot of money is by "going public." Selling stock in your company can be an excellent way to obtain a lot of capital, although it is often a long, complex, and expensive process. This chapter provides a fundamental explanation of the costs and benefits associated with public offerings.

ADVANTAGES AND DISADVANTAGES OF TAKING YOUR COMPANY PUBLIC

Raising capital to achieve a higher level of growth is the main reason why companies go public. Selling shares of stock can bring in large sums of money. Companies that go public usually expect to sell shares worth about $1 million to $10 million. They can use this money to pay off debt, buy new facilities, materials, or equipment, and so on. They also raise their net worth, which is not only good in itself, but also helps the business to obtain loans. Publicly traded stock also allows the business owners to "cash in" their equity in the business. Owners of businesses generally hold a large number of shares in their companies. They can sell part of their stock either during the initial public offering (IPO) of stock or at a later time.

In addition to providing these direct financial advantages, trading company stock publicly brings other, less obvious advantages as well. If you sell stock, you can offer stock options as benefits to your employees, or even give them shares of stock outright. In this way, you not only make your benefits package more attractive by offering stock, you also give employees an added reason to work toward the company's success. The more profitable the company is, the more their stock will be worth. Operating as a publicly traded company can also give your business and your employees added prestige. The operations of publicly traded businesses are highly visible to the media and the public, and news of good performance can travel fast. Favorable news regarding your business not only enhances its reputation; it can also inspire investors to buy more of your stock.

Going public, however, also has a number of disadvantages, and they are major considerations. First of all, when your company goes public, your operations really do become *public*. Most businesspeople value their privacy, and attempt to keep information regarding their operations as confidential as possible. But if you go public, you will have to reveal quite a bit of information regarding your operations. The Securities and Exchange Commission (SEC), a government agency that regulates the offering and sale of public stock, requires all public firms to disclose certain bits of information to potential investors, so that they can make intelligent investment decisions. You will be required to disclose your company's sales and profits, as well as the salaries and prerequisites paid to top executives, among other items. If any of your customers account for very large percentages of your gross sales, you may have to reveal who those customers are. Not only will you have to reveal this information when you submit your IPO; you must continue reporting it in quarterly or annual reports after you go public.

You will also need to spend a great deal of money in bringing your IPO to market. You will require the services of a number of professionals, including lawyers and accountants, to start trading stock in your business. You will also need to work with clerical staff to produce various documents, such as your prospectus, which will most likely go through several drafts, and which we will discuss in more detail later. Once you have produced a final, approved prospectus, you will need to have this document printed by a financial printer, who should be experienced in printing prospectuses in the appropriate format. You will then have to mail prospectuses to thousands of potential investors. You will also have to have stock certificates printed. In addition to these costs, you will have to pay various filing fees to the SEC, to the National Association of Securities Dealers (NASD), and to the states in which you plan to offer securities. These fees can run in the tens of thousands of dollars. You will also need to hire and pay underwriters, who will bring your stock to market. Their fees will typically eat up a percentage of the selling price of your stock. Altogether, expect an IPO to cost a few hundred thousand dollars. In addition to these one-time expenses, you will have to prepare and print new quarterly or annual reports updating stockholders on the condition of your business. You might also need to hire new permanent employees, such as chief financial officers or other executives when you decide to go public, if your current executives do not have sufficient experience running public businesses. You might also decide to hire an employee to maintain public or stockholder relations. Although going public can bring a great deal of money into your business, it can also take a significant sum out of it.

Another disadvantage of going public is that you risk being sued by your stockholders. People buy stock expecting that its value will rise. Of course, it does not always do so. A number of factors affect the value of a given stock on any given day. In some cases, businesses make fraudulent claims about their financial health and future prospects when they go public, deceiving investors into believing that they are sound investments. When investors discover that the business is poorly managed, or is financially unhealthy, they generally begin selling stock, causing the value of the stock to fall. In such cases, investors will sue the company issuing the stock, hoping to recoup the money they have lost. Not all such lawsuits, however, are well founded. In many cases, investors will attempt to bring suit against companies that operate honestly and competently, but whose sales or profits are decreasing. Be aware that, by going public, you increase the risks of having a lawsuit brought against you.

Still another disadvantage to going public is that you run the risk of losing control of your business. A public business not only needs to run efficiently and profitably for its own good; it also needs to satisfy its stockholders. If stockholders feel that a company is not profitable or if they are otherwise unhappy with it, they will sell their stock. As more stockholders sell a given company's stock, that stock tends to lose its value. Because companies need to retain existing stockholders to attract new ones, and to preserve their reputation, public companies are generally quite concerned with keeping their stockholders happy. This renders them vulnerable to the stockholders' demands. Stockholders may want the business to change certain ways of doing business; if it doesn't, they can threaten the business with selling off their shares. In some cases, you might find yourself not running the business the way you want to, but the way the stockholders want you to.

You can also lose control of the company in a more dramatic manner. Each share of stock represents a share in the ownership (or equity) of the business. As you start out, you will maintain ownership of the majority of the stock in your company. The remainder will be spread among a number of individual and institutional stockholders. In some cases, however, you may come to sell off a majority of the company's stock. A large percentage of this outstanding stock (or stock that the company does not own) could fall into the hands of a single individual or institution, who could then become the new owner of the business. Such a majority stockholder could take over the business, changing it drastically, although this situation rarely occurs in small businesses. When such *hostile takeovers* do occur, they usually strike large, multimillion-dollar businesses. You can also defend yourself against such takeovers by writing defensive clauses into your IPO charter.

PREPARING A PUBLIC OFFERING

Going public is a very big step, but the process will be easier for you if you prepare for it properly. Good preparation will also make your company more attractive to investors. It will be easier to go public if you simply follow good business practices. By collecting timely and thorough financial data on your company and filing it properly, you will have this information handy when you need to supply it to the government in the process of going public. Conversely, if you require accountants to go through years' worth of poorly maintained or even nonexistent records, you will have to spend thousands of dollars you might have saved.

You also need to take a good, objective look at your employees, especially your top executives. Do they have experience managing a public company? Although they may be excellent at what they do, will they be able to maintain their current workloads and handle the new tasks associated with public firms? Will they be able to attract investors and cultivate relationships with them? If not, you may need to replace your current officers.

You also need to look at your sales and growth pattern. Investors want to buy stock in businesses that have a high potential for growth. One of the best indicators of this potential is current growth. If your company's sales have remained stagnant or have declined, investors will not be too keen to buy shares in your firm. If you can show a history of growth, however, and demonstrate how added funds from a public offering can help your business continue to grow, you will have a better chance of attracting investors.

THE PROCESS OF GOING PUBLIC

Finding an Underwriter

Once you have decided to go public, you will need to attract an investment banking firm that will act as an underwriter, to sell your stock to a variety of institutions (mutual funds, retirement funds, and so on) and individuals. In many cases, one firm acts as the managing underwriter and forms a syndicate of similar firms that will also market the offering. In some cases, an IPO might have two managing underwriters, one of whom will be the lead managing underwriter. Because you and your current personnel may be inexperienced in approaching underwriters, you should probably hire a consultant to help you do so.

You might choose to work with a national, regional, or local underwriter; your syndicate may consist of underwriters of all three types. Large, national underwriters tend to be better known and more prestigious than the other types. If you can attract such an underwriter, potential investors are more likely to view your stock as a sound investment.

Look for an underwriter that has experience in handling offerings of the same size as yours, and that has worked with other firms in your field. You will need to contact underwriters and explain your offering to them. Tell them what your business does, how long it has been in operation, what your sales and profits are, how much money you intend to raise by going public, and so on. If the underwriter is interested in handling your offering, you will need to send a detailed information package to it. From there, you may proceed to a meeting with the underwriter. You might need to meet with several underwriters before you find one that is interested in handling your offering, and with whom you want to work.

Underwriters generally sell stock under two types of arrangements. If they sell it on a *firm commitment* basis, they agree to buy all of the shares offered at a set price and resell them. If they cannot sell all of the shares, they keep unsold shares until they can sell them. Underwriters also sell stock on a *best efforts* basis. In this case, the underwriter does not take any responsibility for any unsold stock. There are several best efforts arrangements, but none of them obligates the underwriter to buy any unsold stock. Look for an underwriter who will sell your stock on a firm commitment basis.

When you settle on an underwriter, you will have to decide the underwriter's commission, which usually ranges from 7 to 10 percent of the stock sold. Although this will be the underwriter's main source of compensation, you may have to pay certain other fees. The underwriter may also ask (or require) you to give it a certain number of shares before you make the public offering, or to give it the option to buy shares at a certain fixed price in the future. You and the underwriter will also have to decide the selling price of the stock before you go public.

Planning the Registration

Once you have finalized all agreements with your underwriter and the lawyers and accountants with whom you will work to bring your offering to market, you should call a meeting to bring all of these parties together. Decide exactly which tasks need to be accomplished, and who will accomplish them, to bring the offering to market on time and in compliance with all applicable regulations. It is important to bring your entire IPO team together, because their work will be interrelated. And set schedules for all of the different tasks that need to be completed. After this meeting, regularly check on everyone's progress, and try to keep everything moving as smoothly as possible.

The Registration Statement

The registration statement consists of two parts: the prospectus and supplemental information. You need to file both parts with the SEC. You will distribute the prospectus to the public and to other potential investors. The SEC will keep the supplemental information on file, where members of the public will have access to it; companies registering IPOs generally do not need to distribute this information to the public.

The prospectus contains detailed information about your business and your offering. It will tell potential investors what kind of business you run, what your market is, who your competitors are, what your sales and profits are and what experience your officers have. You must also indicate how many shares of stock you are selling and what you plan to do with the money you raise by selling them. If your business represents an unusually high risk, you need to inform potential investors of that fact. You also need to describe how you plan to pay dividends. If the company is involved in legal proceedings that have a bearing on the offering, you must let investors know. You also need to include a number of financial statements in the prospectus. The supplemental information includes certain other financial documents, a copy of the underwriting agreement pertaining to your offering, and a listing of expenses related to the offering.

Your prospectus is a sales tool in that, ideally, the information it contains will spur investors to buy shares in your business. At the same time, it must contain enough information to give them a complete picture of the activities, financial status, and projected growth of your company to enable them to make a sound decision.

The prospectus is not a simple document to assemble. You, your accountants, your lawyers, your underwriter, and their lawyers will probably need to meet several times before you can produce a satisfactory prospectus.

Finally, in addition to the preceding information, you will need to fill out the appropriate SEC form(s) for your offering. Depending on the size of the offering and on what type of business you operate, this might be a Form S-1, S-18, SB-1, or SB-2.

The Waiting Period

Once you have filed all of your documents with the SEC, it will take a few weeks to review them. The SEC will most likely have a few questions regarding your offering, and you should do your best to answer them quickly. The faster you can address the SEC's comments, the faster the SEC can approve your offering.

While the SEC reviews your prospectus, you can make copies of it and distribute it to potential investors, through your underwriter and marketing syndicate. You must, however, print a notice in red ink on the cover, indicating that you have filed the offering with the SEC, but it has not yet been approved. You also need to write that you will not sell any shares until the offering has been approved, nor will you take any orders for shares. This preliminary version of the prospectus is known as the *red herring*. You can also present your company to potential investors at formal meetings and presentations during the waiting period.

In addition to applying for federal authorization to sell your stock, you must comply with state regulations as well. Most states have their own laws affecting the sales of securities, and you need to abide by any applicable laws in those states where you plan to offer shares. If you or your underwriter have not already filed the appropriate forms for meeting these various state regulations, do so during the waiting period.

Revising the Prospectus and Selling Stock

After you have received and responded to the SEC's comments, you might need to revise your prospectus to comply with the SEC's requests. In fact, you will probably go through more than one draft even when you are producing the first version of the prospectus. When you produce the final prospectus, you need to agree on the selling price of the stock with your underwriter. Although the underwriter will have been working with you up to this point, this is when the underwriter finally and formally agrees to sell your securities. Once you and the underwriter have executed the underwriting agreement, the underwriter will begin selling your stock. After you have done so, you will be ready to go public.

Closing

The underwriter will generally sell shares in your firm for about five business days after the offering becomes effective. After that period, the sales are "closed," and the underwriter will give you a check for the income produced by the sale of the stock, after deducting the agreed-upon percentage or discount. In exchange for the check, you will provide the underwriter with stock certificates for all of the stock sold.

OPERATING AS A PUBLIC COMPANY

Once you become public, you have to meet a number of requirements that apply specifically to public companies. You will need to file a number of forms with the SEC:

- *Form S-R.* This form lists which funds you have received in exchange for stock, and describes how you have used them.
- *Form 10-Q.* This form summarizes the performance of the company on a quarterly basis.
- *Form 10-K.* This form summarizes the company's performance on an annual basis.
- *Form 8-K.* Use this form to report certain significant events in the life of the company.

In addition to filing these forms, it is also important to maintain good relations with your current shareholders, and with the public at large. You want to remain attractive to investors, both to keep your current shareholders and to attract new ones in case you ever decide to sell more stock.

ADDITIONAL METHODS OF GOING PUBLIC

In addition to the traditional IPO, you may choose to go public in a number of fairly new ways. You may, for instance, choose to underwrite your own offering. Although you will act as the underwriter for the offering, you will need to work with a local or regional underwriter who will help you market your stock. Underwriting your own offering is in some ways riskier than entering a traditional relationship with an underwriter. Large underwriters are highly experienced in making companies public, and are familiar with all of the applicable federal and state regulations. Because you probably will not have this knowledge, and because the smaller underwriters with whom you will work may also be less familiar with these legal requirements than larger underwriters, you run a greater risk of failing to meet all of the applicable regulations.

In about 38 states, you can also use Form U-7 to raise funds. This form is also known as the SCOR or Small Corporate Offering Registration form and the ULOR or Uniform Limited Offering Registration form. Businesses can use this form to raise about $1 million. It reduces the documentation companies need to file, and it cuts legal and accounting costs as well.

This chapter introduced the traditional process of going public, and outlined two additional methods for raising capital. But going public is a complex procedure, and you should consult the SEC and at least one professional consultant or underwriter. They can help you make the decision to go public and on the method of going public that would be best for your company.

9

INTERNET FINANCING

HISTORY OF THE INTERNET

The Internet is the world's largest computer network. Founded in 1969 by the U.S. Government's Advanced Research Projects Agency (ARPA) to facilitate communication between high-tech research sites, the Internet now spans the globe and has become the primary clearinghouse for electronic messages and file transfers for both research and commercial use.

The Internet is both an internetworking standard and a coop clearing house like the STAR system is for bank ATM machines. Organizations connect to the Internet through network service providers. The network is owned by its constituent members, including telecommunications companies like Sprint, AT&T, and MCI, as well as network service providers like BBN, CERFnet, ElectriCiti, and other major corporations and universities.

Getting access to the Internet introduces a new financing dimension whose inherent potential has not yet begun to be realized. It provides you with three revolutionary aspects of your ability to communicate with other participants. First, the Internet provides automatic methods of grouping and indexing resources, a feature lacking in paper-based documents outside of a library; second, it provides a connection to vast archives of documents and programs, and has specialized programs with which to search and retrieve documents and articles; and third, and most important, it gives you access to millions of other people.

THE NET HITS THE BIG TIME

The opportunities on the Internet are booming and a lot of companies are tacking on that. On September 27, 1996, for instance, General Motors Acceptance Corp. (GMAC) started marketing $500 million in bonds through Chicago Corp. What makes this otherwise mundane bond issue noteworthy is that it is being done solely on the Internet. A Web-based bulletin board, dubbed Direct Access Notes and run by the regional investment bank, allows investors to download the medium-term notes' prospectus and use an interactive bond calculator. The 60 brokerages that are selling the bonds can view a GMAC multimedia road show via the Web. As for investors, they still must purchase the bonds through one of these brokerages.

GMAC says the Internet is ideal for pitching bonds issued by well-known companies to retail customers who don't normally get a crack at such offerings. In time, individual investors could buy bonds on Chicago Corp's Web site, take part in financial discussions, or even buy and sell stock directly from each other. David Walker, the GMAC director who spearheaded the Internet offering, says they could eventually raise $2 or $3 billion this way. "We're getting a new marketplace and additional funding."

That a powerhouse such as GMAC pursued its sizable deal on the Internet speaks volumes for how the Internet is altering the way businesses reach investors and raise money. So far, most of the pioneering has been on the retail-investor side. Some 800,000 individual investors buy and sell stocks on the Web through a handful of Internet discount brokers such as Accutrade, Inc. and Lombard Brokerage Inc. But now, the Internet action is moving toward Wall Street's most lucrative business: the underwriting and distribution of securities for Corporate America. "A huge revolution has been occurring over the past 12 months of capital-raising on the Internet," says Stephen M. H. Wallman, a commissioner on the Securities & Exchange Commission. By revolutionary standards, though, this one is still in its infancy. GMAC is believed to be the only company of any size to turn to the Web to raise money. Virtually all of the activity has been among tiny companies, such as Spring Street Brewery and Logos Research Systems, Inc. They have bypassed underwriters and brokerages to sell do-it-yourself initial public offerings directly to the public over the Internet. Further, entrepreneurs plan to launch virtual stock exchanges and online investment banks that they believe will reach retail and institutional investors more efficiently and cheaply. One start-up, Albuquerque-based Ben Ezra, Weinstein & Co., is developing software to help companies draft their own prospectuses. The technology craze is even starting to fire up more mainstream companies.

San Francisco-based investment bank Hambrecht & Quist is creating an entirely new business, a brokerless electronic division that will use the Internet to sell individual stocks, mutual funds, and IPOs at the same rates given to its well-moneyed institutional clients. How can it do it? The company is counting on volume. To market its new Internet services, it is targeting employees at companies such as Boeing Co. and Silicon Graphics, Inc., for which it already manages stock-options programs. Starting on January 1, 1997, it offered these employees an electronic library and referrals for investment advice. Employees who meet certain criteria will also get a crack at coveted IPOs and other issues sold by Hambrecht & Quist's flagship business. "Our new market is middle America," says CEO Daniel H. Case III. "We'll be the Price Club of electronic financial services."

ELECTRONIC FINANCIAL SERVICES

E Trade Group Inc., a public Internet discount broker that already offers retail customers Internet trading, is taking a different track. It plans to enter the venture-capital market and underwrite Internet IPOs that it will market to its 90,000 active customers. E Trade is waiting for regulatory approval on both fronts. "We have a boot-your-broker campaign," says CEO Christos M. Cotsakos. "Next is 'boot your banker.'" The fledgling Direct Stock Market, based in Santa Monica, California, is also waiting for SEC approval to start trading the stock of companies that do Internet IPOs on a bulletin board market. "We're going to create a fourth market for sub-NASDAQ stocks," declares Clay Womack, president of Direct Stock Market.

Wit Capital, a New York-based start-up, may be the most ambitious of all. Founder Andrew Klein, who raised $1.6 million through a Web-based IPO for his Spring Street microbrewery, recently hired an expert from the New York Stock Exchange to build an Internet stock exchange that is slated to use an auction-based system to match buyers and sellers. He also plans to become a discount broker and predicts that syndicates of online discount brokers will distribute Internet IPOs in the next six to eight months. "I'm not predicting that you're going to see a whole severing of [corporate] relations with Wall Street," says

Klein, a former securities lawyer. "But if the issuer has an alternative or complementary way to reach out to investors, then the power of those institutions diminishes."

The Web's uses will be limited until the legal and regulatory environment is resolved. The SEC is only beginning to grapple with how to control this burgeoning financial universe, while law enforcers are focusing on how to keep fraud from running rampant. Meanwhile, Wall Street should start to rethink the way it does business. A distant threat today, the Internet is here to stay and can really change the way people do business.

Appendix A

SAMPLE BUSINESS PLAN—BACKBAY BREWING COMPANY

EXECUTIVE SUMMARY

Backbay Brewing Company is a small microbrewery incorporated in 1993 in the state of California. It was formed with the intent to provide beer drinkers of discerning taste with a premium lager beer called Diamond Tap, which will feature a robust flavor while maintaining the high effervescence for which lagers are known. The company's CEO, president, and vice president have over 30 years of combined experience in the beer-brewing industry. Backbay Brewing Company will target beer drinkers in California who have an affinity for quality beer—drinkers of microbrewed beers as well as mass-produced domestic premium beers and imports. These beer drinkers are typically classified as "good" beer drinkers, and are generally more inclined to give microbrewed beer a try. In order to reach this market, Backbay Brewing Company will be sold through wholesalers to bars, taverns, and other drinking establishments as well liquor stores, convenience stores, and major supermarkets. With projected net sales of $2.5 million in its third year, the business will generate pretax net profits of 27 percent. Given this return, investment within the company is very attractive. Backbay Brewing Company will require a total of $1.5 million over two stages to start the business.

1. The first stage will require $1.1 million for product, market, and operational development.
2. The second stage of financing will consist of $400,000 for implementation and working capital until breakeven is reached.

First-stage capital will be used to purchase needed equipment and materials to develop the product and to market it initially. Second-stage financing will be required for the implementation of the company's marketing strategies. In order to obtain its capital requirements, the company is willing to relinquish 25-percent equity to first- and second-stage investors.

The company has registered its recipe for Diamond Tap as a *trade secret* with our patent attorney, Robert Pack, of Newport Beach, California. Lease agreements are also in place for a 15,000-square-foot facility in a light industrial area of Irvine, as well as major equipment needed to begin production. Currently, the company is being funded by $250,000 from the three principals, with purchase orders for 30,200 six-packs, 49,480 22-ounce bottles and 45 kegs already in hand.

THE BUSINESS DESCRIPTION

In the mid-1980s, the American consciousness was tapped by a startling realization: Beer is supposed to have flavor. Europeans had been savoring ale, porter, pilsner, and stout for centuries. But in the United States, such stuff was a revelation. Small breweries sprouted tentatively here and there, and one by one, American beer drinkers sat down with unfamiliar brews from unknown sources—Anchor Steam, Redhook, Sierra Nevada, Bigfoot Ale. As they sipped, they were quietly converted. American "microbrews" became the beer aficionado's small stash of secret joy.

Ten years later, it's a beer bath. In 1992, specialty brews accounted for more than 1 million barrels of beer, according to the Institute for Brewing Studies, a division of the Association of Brewers, with the industry growing at annual clip of 40 percent. That's not really surprising. The beer industry is a $35-billion-a-year business, with Americans consuming an average of 22.7 gallons of beer annually; and California is one of the top regional markets in terms of beer consumption with approximately 11 percent of total malt beverage sales.

While major brewers still account for most of the beer production in the United States, small microbreweries (production plants that turn out 15,000 barrels or fewer per year for the wholesale market) is where most of the growth is occurring. In fact, microbreweries are at the forefront of the beer revolution.

Recognizing the tremendous growth opportunities in this industry and the continued demand for good quality beer, Backbay Brewing Company was formed in 1993 to develop a premium lager beer that would appeal to beer drinkers who enjoy a full-bodied beer (current drinkers of microbrewed beer and those of mass-produced premium domestic and import beer) and are willing to pay extra to get a superior-tasting product. Backbay Brewing Company has perfected a recipe for its premium lager beer called Diamond Tap, and is ready to proceed with the next step, which is development of a finished product in sufficient quantity to meet projected market demand. Priced competitively with other premium microbrewed beers, Diamond Tap will be sold through wholesalers for distribution to bars, taverns, liquor stores, convenience stores, and supermarkets in the state of California, which meets the state's regulatory requirements of three-tiered distribution. The pricing structure for Diamond Tap will provide for a retail price of $6.99 per six-pack, $2.20 per 22-ounce bottle, and $195 per keg, the three products in which Backbay Brewing plans to package Diamond Tap.

During the first three years of operation that this plan covers, Backbay Brewing Company projects that we will be able to obtain 2.8 percent of the microbrewed beer market in California by adhering to the following strategies:

- The first year of business, our goal will be to concentrate on marketing and distribution to raise awareness among consumers and retailers alike. Projected sales goals for the first year at an average wholesale cost of $3.85 for a six-pack, $1.20 for a 22-ounce bottle, and $105 for a keg is projected at $2.1 million from 10,000 barrels, which is a 2.4-percent market share. To reach this goal, it will be necessary to increase our marketing staff by 10 percent and our production staff by 3 percent.
- The second year, our goals will be to reinvest profits to increase our marketing and production staff. With these elements in place, our goal is to increase sales from the first year by 7 percent, resulting in $2.3 million in sales and a 2.5 percent market share.
- The third year, our goals are to increase our marketing and production staff in order to handle an increase in sales by 12 percent to $2.5 million, which will enable us to reach our objective of a 2.8 percent market share.

MARKET STRATEGIES

Current drinkers of microbrewed beers, as well as mass-produced domestic premiums and imports, are the largest market for Diamond Tap premium lager. However, there are segments within this primary group of customers that are targeted by each group of competitors against which Diamond Tap will be marketed. Positioned as a premium microbrewed lager for beer drinkers of discerning taste, Diamond will compete directly with other microbreweries producing a premium lager beer and with significant distribution in California, such as Alpine Village Hofbrau Lager from Alpine Village Hofbrau, Cable Car Lager from Thousand Oaks Brewing Company, Calistoga Lager from the Napa Valley Brewing Company, Cherokee Choice Lager from the Okie Girl Brewery, Eureka Lager from the Los Angeles Brewing Company, Loggers Lager from Boulder Creek Brewing Company, Nevada City Brew (Dark & Gold) from Nevada City Brewing Company, and Truckee Lager from the Truckee Brewing Company.

Market Definition

Americans love their beer! In fact, beer is a $35-billion industry in America with over 85 million beer drinkers consuming an average of 22.7 gallons of beer (per capita) annually according to *Modern Brewery Age*. Overall industry sales, however, have remained flat over the past few years with 31-gallon barrels produced rising from 184,478,000 in 1990 to 188,985,000 currently, a growth of 2.7 percent. While the industry has remained flat, sales of microbrewed beers have skyrocketed, with shipments of 31-gallon barrels rising from 300,000 in 1990 to 1 million currently, a growth of 233 percent.

That increase illustrates the strength of the microbrewery market; however, it isn't the extent of the target market. Drinkers of import beers will also be a key market that Backbay Brewing plans to target in its marketing efforts. According to *Modern Brewery Age*, sales of import beer have decreased since 1990 when this segment accounted for 8,783,000 31-gallon barrels. Currently, imports account for 8,322,884 31-gallon barrels, a 5.2 percent decrease. While this segment has decreased, it is critical to show the total target market for Diamond Tap Premium Lager, which is 9,322,884 31-gallon barrels. California accounts for 12 percent of the total market, according to the *Brewers Almanac*. Using this number as a barometer, the total microbrew and import market in the state of California would be 1,118,746 31-gallon barrels. Industry sales breakdowns are shown in Figure A–1. The growth of microbrewed beer sales is shown.

Figure A–1 U.S. Beer Industry Sales Breakdown

Source: Modern Brewery Age.

The increase in the microbrewery market as opposed to the decrease in the import market reflects several trends in the beer brewery business:

1. Beer drinkers are tiring of bland, mass-produced beers and want a good, quality beer with a distinct, full-bodied taste.
2. Many beer drinkers are pursuing a healthier lifestyle and prefer microbrewed beers because they are typically brewed without preservatives and unnatural additives.
3. Beer drinkers are searching for beer that is fresh, and microbrewed beers aren't pasteurized.

Beyond these factors lies the enormous impact of the baby boomer generation. Many have reached or are reaching their peak earning potentials, and they are changing their attitudes and spending patterns to reflect their affluence. This has not only led to a boom in microbrewed beers as the majority of baby boomers seek out high-quality gourmet products, but has also fueled the growth of premium wines, gourmet coffees, bread, and other products.

From the total U.S. population of 252.7 million, 40.6 percent, or 102.7 million, are considered baby boomers, those individuals between the ages of 30 and 49, according to the U.S. Bureau of the Census. In the state of California, there are 12.3 million baby boomers, and of those, it is estimated that 33.6 percent, or 4.1 million, are beer drinkers, who consume on an average of 23.7 gallons of beer (per capita) annually in California. Therefore, baby boomers in the state of California drink approximately 97.2 million gallons of beer annually, or 14 percent of the total 688.5 million gallons consumed.

Much of this consumption is of microbrewed and import beer. It is estimated that baby boomers make up 60.2 percent of the market for total microbrewed and import beer consumption in the state of California. All totaled, this would account for 673,485 31-gallon barrels, or 20.9 million gallons.

In addition to the baby boomer market, the post-baby boomers who can legally consume alcohol in the state of California, those individuals between the ages of 21 and 30, comprise the next largest market segment Backbay Brewing will tap. In the state of California, there are 4.3 million individuals in this age group, according to the U.S. Bureau of the Census. Of those, 1.4 million are beer drinkers who consume 33.2 million gallons of beer annually. Of that, microbrewed and import beer consumption in this age group is 7.2 million gallons, or 231,580 31-gallon barrels.

The third significant consumer market is the 50-to-64 age group. According to the U.S. Bureau of the Census, there are 3.9 million individuals in this age group residing in the state of California. Approximately 1.3 million of these individuals drink beer. Together, they account for 30.8 million gallons of beer consumed annually. Of that, microbrewed and import beer consumption in this age group is 6.6 million gallons, or 213,680 31-gallon barrels.

Altogether, the total market for Backbay Brewing's Diamond Tap Premium Lager would be the total of the three segments highlighted, which is 1.1 million 31-gallon barrels, or 34.7 million gallons. Figure A–2 shows a complete breakdown of the target market for Backbay Brewing.

With the introduction of Diamond Tap Premium Lager, Backbay Brewing Company will compete directly against other microbrewed beers for a share of the market just defined. Aside from being a premium microbrewed beer, the main attraction for Diamond Tap Premium Lager beer for this target group will be its lager heritage. Lager beers are the most popular type of beer brewed in North America. In fact, according to *Beverage Industry* magazine, all styles of lagers account for 89.6 percent of the total market, with premium lager beer at 37.3 percent. Using 37.3 percent as a barometer, the total feasible market for Diamond Tap Premium Lager would be 417,292 31-gallon barrels of beer. Of the total feasible market, it is estimated that Diamond Tap Premium Lager can

Figure A–2   Breakdown of Distribution Channels for
Backbay Brewing Company

capture 2.4 percent, for a total production of 10,000 31-gallon barrels during its first year for total sales of $2.1 million.

Distribution Strategies

Diamond Tap Premium Lager will be packaged in three different containers: a six-pack of 12-ounce bottles; 22-ounce bottles; and 15-gallon kegs. While all three products will be available through retail channels, the 15-gallon kegs will be marketed mainly toward bars and other drinking establishments with a reputation for serving quality beer.

To effectively reach our customers, Backbay Brewing Company will use a four-tiered channel of distribution through which Diamond Tap Premium Lager will be sold to a wholesale distributor, which will in turn sell the product to retail distributors for sale to consumers. See Figure A–2 for an illustration of our distribution channel.

Through this distribution channel, Backbay Brewing will target mainly liquor stores, as well as drinking establishments. In addition, Backbay Brewing will also target upscale convenience stores, supermarkets, and membership warehouses. Figure A–2 has a complete breakdown of distribution channels Backbay Brewing Company will be using.

Pricing Strategies

Since Backbay Brewing Company is positioning Diamond Tap as a premium lager, pricing will be based not only on a markup strategy to

Figure A–3   Promotional Schedule for 1995

	Cost	Jan	Feb	Mar	Apr	May	June	July	Aug	Sept	Oct	Nov	Dec
Sales promotion													
Counter-tabletop cards	$ 20,000												
Beer-tasting events/shows	33,500												
Marketing materials	16,500												
Cardboard displays & flyers	22,000												
Merchandising allowance program—Bars	22,000												
Merchandising allowance program—Stores	21,000												
Sales promotion total:	$136,500												
Advertising													
Coupon program	$ 30,000												
Radio advertising	20,000												
Other advertising expenses	13,000												
Advertising total:	$ 63,000												
Contingency fund total:	$ 10,500												
Total promotional budget:	$210,000												

186

cover our costs but it will also be geared competitively in order to produce an aggressive pricing strategy. The costs in order to produce a 31-gallon barrel of Diamond Tap Premium Lager are as follows:

Full-grain malt, yeast, hops, water, bottles, kegs, caps, labels, beer boards, printed boxes, direct labor, and brewing overhead	$75.50
Operating expenses	$68.00
State excise tax	$ 6.50
Federal tax	$ 7.00

Given the four-tiered distribution channel Backbay Brewing Company will be using, Diamond Tap Premium Lager will be sold to a wholesale distributor at the following prices:

- Six-pack of 12-ounce bottles, $3.85
- 22-ounce bottles, $1.20
- 15-gallon keg, $105

This pricing structure will allow Diamond Tap Premium Lager to be sold on a retail basis at a very competitive suggested price of:

- Six-pack of 12-ounce bottles, $6.99
- 22-ounce bottles, $2.20
- 15-gallon keg, $195

This pricing structure is very competitive with other premium brand lagers, which sell on an average between $5.99 at the low end and $8.99 at the high end for a six-pack of 12-ounce bottles, $1.99 to $3.99 for a 22-ounce bottle, and $150 to $225 for a 15-gallon keg.

Promotional Strategies

The main goals of the promotional strategy for Diamond Tap Premium Lager are to develop relationships with a core group of regional distributors with strong access to liquor stores, bars, convenience food stores, supermarkets, and membership warehouses; support the wholesale distributors in their sales efforts to the retailer; and, finally, to educate the consumer market as depicted in Figure A–3. The first step Backbay Brewing will adopt in its promotional efforts is to identify a group of wholesale distributors with sufficient clout in the distribution channels we've defined for Diamond Tap Premium Lager and enter into exclusive relationships with those distributors. Backbay Brewing will define exclusive areas for distribution of Diamond Tap Premium Lager by geographic area. Those areas will include:

- *Southern California.* Ventura down to San Diego and up through Palm Springs and Indio.
- *Central Valley.* Santa Barbara up to San Luis Obispo and over to the Mammoth Mountain area.
- *Central California.* Monterey up through the San Francisco Bay area over to Lake Tahoe.
- *Northern California.* From Ukiah up to the Oregon border and over to the Nevada border.

In order to enter into these relationships and service them afterward, Backbay Brewing will hire a sales manager prior to Diamond Tap Premium Lager's launch date. We will also develop, not only for our inside sales force, but also for our distributors, collateral marketing material, including a pricing sheet illustrating the various price breaks for volume purchases, and a brochure highlighting the brewery, the beer, the company's philosophy, and our commitment to brewing the best premium lager in North America.

Backbay Brewing's goal is to line up the southern California area during development and the Central Valley area no later than the first quarter after the launch of the product. Thereafter, we hope to add the central California area by the end of the second quarter, and finally, the northern California area by the end of the third quarter.

To support our distributors, Backbay Brewing will make available product samples as well as point-of-purchase displays and materials to draw attention to the product in the retail environment. These materials will include cardboard displays, flyers, bar mirrors, and so on. The final phase of our promotional strategy will consist of consumer education. The main objective in this phase is to stimulate initial purchases of the product and maintain those customers through repurchases. To accomplish this goal, Backbay Brewing will utilize a combination of advertising and sales promotion events. The promotional strategy aimed at the consumer market will consist of:

1. In-store display and price feature support obtained from retailers by implementing a merchandising allowance program where we will make contractual payments of $15 per day for a 20-six-pack in-store display at liquor stores, convenience food stores, and supermarkets. We will also institute a merchandising allowance program with bars to distribute counter- and table-top cards advertising Diamond Tap Premium Lager. We will also provide initial discounts of 15 percent for our distributors to pass along to bars on purchases of 15-gallon kegs, to initiate draft sales through this distribution.

2. A coupon program instituted through advertisements in local newspapers, direct mail, and local green sheets, as well as in conjunction with liquor stores and supermarkets for inclusion in their sales flyers, for which we will make coop money available. The coupons will offer a discount of $1 off the regular price. One million coupons will be distributed through newspapers, magazines, and the mail.

3. Along with the coupon program, we will participate in major beer-tasting events and shows that will serve to promote Diamond Tap Premium Lager, not only to compete but to have sampling booths as well.

During the first year of sales, 10 percent of projected sales will be set aside for promotional purposes, for a total of $210,000. Of this, 30 percent will be budgeted for advertising, 65 percent for sales promotion, and the remaining 5 percent will be held in a contingency fund. The table on p. 186 provides an example of the cost breakdown and schedule for the promotional strategy of Diamond Tap Premium Lager.

Sales Potential

The sales potential for Diamond Tap Premium Lager is based upon the following factors:

- Number of beer drinkers who *will* purchase a premium microbrewed beer.
- Number of units per customer.
- Average price per unit.
- Average price after discounts/commissions.

Figure A–4 illustrates the revenue projections for Backbay Brewing Company for its first three years of operation. For example, during its first year, the projections would be based upon the following:

- The target market is 1,118,746 31-gallon barrels.
- The feasible market is 37.3 percent of target, or 417,292 31-gallon barrels.
- A conversion rate of 2.4 percent is projected during the first year of operation for a market share of 10,000 31-gallon barrels.
- Revenue projected at $2.1 million.
- The total revenue potential after three years is $2.5 million.

Figure A–4 Revenue Model for Backbay Brewing

Revenue Summary	1995	1996	1997
Product One—Six-Packs			
No. of customers	13,778	14,742	16,510
Units/Customer	24	24	24
Total units	330,672	353,808	396,240
New customers	13,778	964	1,768
Price/Unit	$ 3.85	$ 3.85	$ 3.85
Revenue	$1,273,087	$1,362,161	$1,525,524
Product Two—22-Ounce Bottles			
No. of customers	11,273	12,062	13,508
Units/Customer	48	48	48
Total units	541,104	578,976	648,384
New customers	11,273	789	1,446
Price/Unit	$ 1.20	$ 1.20	$ 1.20
Revenue	$ 649,325	$ 694,771	$ 778,061
Product Three—15-Gallon Kegs			
No. of customers	172	178	199
Units/Customer	12	12	12
Total units	2,064	2,136	2,388
New customers	172	6	21
Price/Unit	$ 105	$ 105	$ 105
Revenue	$ 216,720	$ 224,280	$ 250,740
Total revenue	$2,139,132	$2,281,212	$2,554,325

COMPETITIVE ANALYSIS

The business outlined in this plan is one that relies on reaching the consumer market on a mass basis in an effective manner. In order to do this, the business will have to develop key assets and a distinct presence that will allow it to compete effectively within the retail market.

The Competition

The market for microbrewed premium lager beer can be divided into several strategic groups starting with the primary competitors that will compete directly against Backbay Brewing Company for a share of the market. These primary competitors include beers such as Alpine Village Hofbrau Lager from Alpine Village Hofbrau, Cable Car Lager from Thousand Oaks Brewing Company, Calistoga Lager from the Napa Valley Brewing Company, Cherokee Choice Lager from the Okie Girl Brewery, Eureka Lager from the Los Angeles Brewing Company, Loggers

Lager from Boulder Creek Brewing Company, Nevada City Brew (Dark & Gold) from Nevada City Brewing Company and Truckee Lager from the Truckee Brewing Company. In California, these companies control 14 percent of the target market.

The second strategic group is made up of secondary competitors that include domestic and import brewers of mass-produced premium lager beer such as Michelob and Budweiser from Anheiser-Busch, Lowenbrau, and Miller from Miller Brewing Company; Coors from Coors Brewing Company; Moosehead from Moosehead Breweries; and Henry Weinhard's from Blitz-Weinhard Brewing Company. This group of strategic competitors accounts for the majority of the target market at roughly 83.6 percent.

The last group of competitors we'll discuss include brewpubs. While these competitors are not a major competitive force since they do not distribute their product through the same channels as Backbay Brewing, they do, nonetheless, account for 2.4 percent of the market and are a significant factor in areas of California where they exert some influence. Refer to Figure A–1 for a complete breakdown of the microbrew and premium beer industry in California.

Key Assets and Skills

The success of Backbay Brewing Company will be contingent upon establishing key assets and skills in two major areas: marketing and production. The major factors that need to be present within the realm of marketing include:

- The formation of key alliances with several established wholesale distributors in California that will lead to the development of a statewide distribution network.
- The implementation of a statewide marketing campaign designed to support distributors as well as to educate consumers about Diamond Tap Premium Lager by promoting quality, taste, and freshness of the beer compared to its competitors. This marketing campaign will feature print advertising, couponing, and direct mail, as well as collateral material such as flyers, counter-cards and other point-of-purchase displays.

For production, the assets and skills required include:

- Brewing experience, especially at the microbrew level.
- Establishment of a strategic partnership with key suppliers of high-quality ingredients to produce Diamond Tap Premium Lager.

- Experience in package design for mass-marketed products, premium lager brewery production, and physical distribution as well as inventory.

Distinct Competitive Advantages

There are a number of competitors that Diamond Tap will compete against for a share of the consumer's dollar. Almost all the microbreweries defined as primary competitors produce and distribute a premium lager beer that boasts superior taste and quality as well as freshness. Many of these competitors do, in fact, produce a very good beer. The main differences that will set Diamond Tap Premium Lager apart from its competitors is better and more targeted marketing, as well as a more effective distribution. system. Pricing is another area where Diamond Tap will hold a competitive advantage. The suggested retail price for Diamond Tap will be $6.99 per six-pack, $2.20 for a 22-ounce bottle, and $195 for a 15-gallon keg. That is almost 10 percent less than 80 percent of our primary competitors. Clearly, quality coupled with an aggressive pricing will provide us with a distinct competitive advantage over our primary competitors.

As for our larger base of secondary competitors, Diamond Tap's main competitive advantage is the quality of the product. Without a doubt, mass-marketed beers will hold an advantage in price and distribution, as well as promotional efforts. One area they will not be able to compete against Backbay Brewing is in the quality department. Diamond Tap Premium Lager will have not only a more robust but smooth taste, it will also be more fresh. The premium quality of the Diamond Tap, as opposed to the mass-produced beers, has proven to be more of a selling point (rather than price) to the audience Backbay Brewing is targeting.

Competitive Strategies

Backbay Brewing Company will seek to establish a solid distribution network throughout the state of California in order to create a forceful presence in liquor stores, bars, convenience food stores, and supermarkets. We will undertake this goal by capitalizing on several key assets such as the quality of the product and a growing interest in premium microbrewed beer, as well as a very competitive price point. We will promote these key strengths in our marketing efforts designed to support wholesale distribution efforts, as well as our target audience of mostly upper-income beer drinkers who enjoy a quality brew.

DESIGN AND DEVELOPMENT PLANS

There are several areas of development that Backbay Brewing needs to consider in order to begin marketing Diamond Tap Premium Lager. Those areas include: develop Diamond Tap Premium Lager to perfect the brewing process so that the product meets our marketing goals; to establish and begin implementation of a premarket campaign to begin recruiting wholesale distributors and start building a solid base of customers; and, finally, to obtain the necessary expertise at all levels of the company in order to successfully develop and launch Diamond Tap Premium Lager.

It is important to recognize that, in terms of product development, Backbay Brewing has already formulated and registered its recipe for Diamond Tap as a *trade secret* with our patent attorney, Robert Pack, of Newport Beach, California. We intend to use this recipe to perfect the final brewed version of Diamond Tap Premium Lager.

Those steps include:

1. Gather ingredients.
    1.1. Choose the type barley malt.
        1.1.1. Select suppliers of barley malt.
        1.1.2. Test barley malt to determine which supplier's provide the best flavor, body, head, and color.
    1.2. Choose type of hops.
        1.2.1. Select suppliers of hops.
        1.2.2. Test hops to determine which suppliers provide the best flavor.
    1.3. Choose suppliers of dried lager yeast.
        1.3.1. Test lager yeasts to determine which suppliers is the best fermentation agent.
    1.4. Test Diamond Tap recipe with final selections for malt, hops, and yeast.
2. Set up brewing process.
    2.1. Determine optimum malting process.
    2.2. Gauge mashing temperature.
    2.3. Boil wort and add hops.
    2.4. Determine yeast amounts and fermentation period.
    2.5. Determine aging period.
    2.6. Carbonate the beer.
    2.7. Conduct taste tests.

3. Determine container development.

   3.1. Select bottle and keg style.

   3.2. Select bottle color.

   3.3. Test appeal of bottle with beer integrated.

   3.4. Delivery.

4. Design label and package.

   4.1. Create label and package design, which will require the recruitment of a freelance graphic.

   4.2. Integrate label with container.

   4.3. Develop prototype for six-pack product and 22-ounce bottle.

5. Test market prototypes.

   5.1. Enter into relationship with regional distributor of southern California market.

   5.2. Deliver prototype units.

   5.3. Gauge reactions.

   5.4. Make modifications as a result of test marketing.

6. Start production.

   6.1. Launch preproduction run.

   6.2. Conduct cost reduction check to achieve goal of $155 in costs per barrel.

   6.3. Begin brewing.

7. Make final delivery.

   7.1. Initiate distribution development, which will include the recruitment of a sales manager and account representatives to obtain purchase orders from targeted state distributors that service liquor stores, bars, convenience food stores, and supermarkets in the market areas defined in distribution strategies.

   7.2. Deliver initial orders for distributors and retailers.

   7.3. Implement the sales promotion campaign, which is budgeted at $210,000 during the first year of operation and is geared toward supporting wholesale distributors and raising consumer awareness at the retail level.

Figure A–5 illustrates the development program throughout the first year. The major benchmarks include:

- Select ingredients and suppliers for Diamond Tap Premium Lager.
- Perfect the brewing process.
- Design label and package.
- Test market to southern California market.
- Establish retail and distributor price points of $3.85 and $6.99 for a six-pack, $1.20 and $2.20 for a 22-ounce bottle, and $105 and $195 for a 15-gallon keg.
- Establish relationships with southern California and Central Valley distributors, and obtain purchase orders.
- Initiate a merchandising allowance program among liquor stores, bars, convenience food stores, and supermarkets.

Organizational Development

In order to properly develop Diamond Tap Premium Lager, it will be necessary to recruit a sales manager. This position will provide Backbay Brewing with the expertise needed to establish the type of distribution channels and promotional campaign that Diamond Tap needs to succeed. With the addition of this key position, company management will consist of the following:

- *Chief executive officer*—Will Gillette. Responsible for company operations as well as market development. An accomplished businessman with 15 years of experience in the malt brewing industry, Mr. Gillette has extensive contacts at all phases of product development as well as marketing.
- *President*—John Melrose. Reporting directly to the CEO, Mr. Melrose's responsibilities include brewery operations, including quality control and package design. Mr. Melrose has 10 years of experience managing brewing operations and developing product.
- *Vice president of operations*—William Barney. Reporting directly to the president, Mr. Barney's responsibilities include the management of all purchasing and inventory control operations. Mr. Barney has a tremendous amount of contacts among raw material suppliers, as well as knowledge of modern inventory control systems.
- *Sales manager.* A position that will be responsible for establishment of wholesale distribution accounts, product presentation, and customer service. The sales manager will work in

Figure A–5 Development Schedule

	JAN	FEB	MAR	APR	MAY	JUN	JUL	AUG	SEP	OCT	NOV	DEC
Choose barley malt	■											
Choose hops		■										
Choose suppliers of dried lager yeast												
Test Diamond Tap recipe			■									
Determine optimum malting process				■								
Gauge mashing temperature				■								
Boil wort and add hops												
Determine yeast amounts/fermentation period					■							
Determine aging period					■							
Carbonate beer												
Conduct taste tests						■						
Select bottle and key style							■					

Select bottle color	■												
Test appeal of bottle		■	■										
Delivery			■										
Creation of label/package design				■									
Integration of label with container					■								
Development of prototype						■							
Enter into relationship with regional distributor							■						
Deliver prototype units								■					
Gauge reactions									■				
Modifications as a result of test marketing										■			
Preproduction run											■		
Cost-reduction check												■	
Begin brewing													■

conjunction with the CEO in order to develop a statewide distribution network. This executive will need a successful track record in alcoholic beverage sales.

Risks

There are several risks associated with the development of Diamond Tap Premium Lager. They include:

- *Creating an efficient network of statewide distributors.* Backbay Brewing Company must quickly build relationships with key distributors throughout the state in order to sufficiently penetrate the markets it has defined. We will begin with the recruitment of a southern California distributor, then provide for a phased introduction of distributors over the first year of the product's introduction, making this risk minimal and controllable.
- *Obtaining sufficient shelf space and promotion at the retail end.* This is crucial to deliver the type of sales we have projected. It is the main reason why we will implement an aggressive merchandising allowance program with retailers as well as bars, greatly reducing this risk.
- *Product acceptance by consumers.* Product quality will be a major factor in overcoming this risk. That is why Backbay Brewing will launch a coupon program to introduce consumers to the product. We want them to try the product. If they do, we feel we will have high repeat sales. Backbay Brewing will also participate in major taste-testing contests and promote the success we experience at these events. In addition, through advertising and POP displays, we will create visibility at the retail level to provide consumers with an incentive to try the product. Through these programs, we feel the risk of product acceptance will be very small.
- *Product delays.* Backbay Brewing has already developed what we feel is an award-winning recipe for Diamond Tap Premium Lager. We also have the expertise in place to perfect the brewing process, making this risk acceptable.
- *Increased competition from major competitors.* There is very little doubt that large breweries are beginning to create premium beers to compete against microbrewed products; however, their attempts, while good for mass-produced products, do not have the same richness of flavor nor freshness. They cannot compete against a good microbrewed product in quality.

Figure A–6 Development Expenses

Item	Budgeted Amount
Materials	$ 129,000
Direct labor	21,840
Overhead	376,790
G&A	14,560
Equipment	485,000
Miscellaneous	2,000
Total	$1,029,190

Financials

Figure A–6 depicts the major development expenses.

OPERATIONS AND MANAGEMENT

Backbay Brewing Company will be organized as a microbrewery of high-quality beers, starting with Diamond Tap Premium Lager beer. The headquarters for Backbay Brewing will be located in Newport Beach, California, a coastal community located in Orange County, just 50 miles south of Los Angeles and 80 miles north of San Diego. Backbay Brewing has already concluded a lease agreement for a 15,000-square-foot facility in Newport Beach.

In the following section, the business operations and management requirements of Backbay Brewing Company are detailed, along with projections for operational expenses, capital requirements, and cost of goods.

Operations

The following details the organizational structure for Backbay Brewing Company.

Marketing

Managed by the CEO, Will Gillette, the scope of responsibilities that this department will cover revolve around sales promotional support at the wholesale and retail levels. The marketing department will define the markets, outline the prospective customers within those markets, plan the various sales and promotional campaigns, measure response, and analyze the market to produce competitive strategies that will generate sales leads and coordinate with brewery operations in order to meet the needs of the customer base.

Sales

As a microbrewer, sales for Backbay Brewing Company will occur at three different stages: brewer to distributor, distributor to retailer, and retailer to consumer. At the brewer to distributor level, a sales manager will be hired during the development phase to set up initial distributors for the southern California and Central Valley areas. During the course of the year, we will add one other account representative. This sales force will be responsible for all statewide sales to wholesale distributors in the following four key areas: southern California, Central Valley, central California and northern California.

In addition to initiating sales, the two salespeople will also be responsible for handling problems originating at the brewer-to-distributor level. This includes making sure distributors receive their shipments and that the billing and payment schedules are consistent with the agreements signed between both parties. They will also handle returns and other issues arising at the retail level. As sales grow, it is expected that an assistant will be needed to help with customer service.

Brewery Operations

Handled directly by the president, John Melrose, the function of brewery operations is to coordinate the actual brewing of Diamond Tap Premium Lager. The brewing process for Diamond Tap Premium Lager is as follows:

1. Purchase ingredients and conduct inventory control.
2. Malt the barley.
3. Mash the malted barley to produce the wort.
4. Boil the wort and add hops.
5. Add yeast to promote fermentation of the wort.
6. Remove carbon dioxide.
7. Sterilize the wort.
8. Add yeast to promote the second round of fermentation.
9. Carbonate the beer using previously removed carbon dioxide for natural carbonation (krausened).
10. Filter the wort.
11. Age the beer.
12. Chill the beer and filter to remove remaining yeast.
13. Package the beer for shipping.

14. At each step of the brewing process, the staff will be required to perform exact checks of measurements of ingredients; temperatures of the kilns, brew kettles, and bright beer tanks; and the levels in storage barrels, fermenter tanks, and so on. The goal behind these measurements and checks is to ensure the quality of the finished beer product. Each batch of beer, once it reaches the bright brewing tanks, and prior to packaging, will be taste-tested to ensure the highest quality of beer. See Figure A–5 for a depiction of the brewing process.

The costs associated with the brewery operations of Backbay Brewing are detailed in Figure A–10. The cost-of-goods breakout is based on two elements: ingredients and labor. During the brewing process, the product may be in any one of four stages:

1. Ingredients (I)
2. Partially brewed (PB)
3. Fully brewed (FB)
4. Sold (S)

Product that is sold is expensed as a cost of good, while product that isn't sold is placed in inventory.

In order to assure the finest-quality beer during the production process, Backbay Brewing will utilize state-of-the-art equipment from the initial malting process all the way through finishing and packaging. In addition, as we've mentioned, the president of the company will oversee production, and there will be three skilled brewers during the first year to control every aspect of beer production. The investment costs for the brewing equipment are depicted in Figure A–8.

Administration

Administration is in charge of those overhead functions that support operations such as accounting, legal, human resources, and other functions related directly to internal operations. The expenses for Backbay Brewing Company are illustrated in Figure A–9. They are divided according to the functional lines already detailed.

Management

As mentioned in the design and development phase of the business plan, there are four key management positions that will be strategic to the growth of the Backbay Brewing, as described here.

Figure A–7   Cost of Goods (Barrels)

	1995	1996	1997
Barrels sold	10,000	10,700	11,984
Begin FB	0	4,500	4,815
FB% Sales (Barrels)	45	45	45
End FB	4,500	4,815	5,393
Inventory/FB	4,500	315	578
Begin PB	0	3,500	3,745
PB% Sales (Barrels)	35	35	35
End PB	3,500	3,745	4,194
Inventory/PB	3,500	245	449
Begin I	0	2,000	2,140
1% Sales (Barrels)	20	20	20
End I	2,000	2,140	2,397
Inventory/I	2,000	140	257
Barrels sold	10,000	10,700	11,984
Barrels FBI	4,500	315	578
Barrels PBI	3,500	245	449
Barrels II	2,000	140	257
Total barrels inventory	20,000	11,400	13,268
Ingredients/Barrel ($)	32	32	32
Ingredient costs ($)	640,000	364,800	424,576
Barrels sold	10,000	10,700	11,984
Barrels FBI	4,500	315	578
Barrels PBI	3,500	245	449
Total L&OH barrels	18,000	11,260	13,011
Labor/PA % (Barrels)	50	50	50
Labor/Barrel ($)	39	39	39
OH/Barrel ($)	18	18	18
Labor costs ($)	633,750	434,363	498,674
OH Costs ($)	292,500	200,475	230,157
Total L&OH ($)	926,250	634,838	728,831
Inventory/I ($)	64,000	4,480	8,224
Production costs ($)	1,502,250	995,158	1,145,183
Inventory/PB ($)	211,750	14,823	27,165
COG Production ($)	1,290,500	980,334	1,118,018
Inventory/FB ($)	400,500	28,035	51,442
COG Sold ($)	890,000	952,299	1,066,576
COGS/Barrel ($)	89	89	89
Begin II ($)	0	64,000	68,480
Change II ($)	64,000	4,480	8,224
End II ($)	64,000	68,480	76,704
Begin PBI ($)	0	211,750	226,573
Change PBI ($)	211,750	14,823	27,165
End PBI ($)	211,750	226,573	253,738
Begin FBI ($)	0	400,500	428,535
Change FBI ($)	400,500	28,035	51,442
End FBI ($)	400,500	428,535	479,977
Begin inventory ($)	0	676,250	723,588
Change inventory ($)	676,250	47,338	86,831
End inventory ($)	676,250	723,588	810,419
Revenue/Barrel ($)	213.91	213.19	213.14
Revenue ($)	2,139,132	2,281,212	2,554,325
Inventory turn	3.16	3.15	3.15

Figure A-8 Capital Summary

	1995	1996	1997
Initial capital	$ 0	$ 0	$ 0
Net capital	0	370,476	358,395
Malting Equipment			
No. barrels	10,000	10,700	11,984
ME/Barrel	3,500	3,500	3,500
ME capital	11,500	11,500	11,500
ME capital requirement	32,857	35,157	39,376
New ME capital	32,857	2,300	4,219
Mashing/Brewing Equipment			
No. barrels	10,000	10,700	11,984
MBE/Barrel	1,700	1,700	1,700
MBE capital	15,500	15,500	15,500
MBE capital requirement	91,176	97,559	109,266
New MBE capital	91,176	6,383	11,707
Fermentation/Aging Equipment			
No. barrels	10,000	10,700	11,984
FAE/Barrel	840	840	840
FAE capital	10,500	10,500	10,500
FAE capital requirement	125,000	133,750	149,800
New FAE capital	125,000	8,750	16,050
Finishing Equipment			
No. barrels	10,000	10,700	11,984
FE/Barrel	3,500	3,500	3,500
FE capital	22,000	22,000	22,000
FE capital requirement	62,857	67,257	75,328
New FE capital	62,857	4,400	8,071
Packaging Equipment			
No. barrels	10,000	10,700	11,984
PE/Barrel	7,500	7,500	7,500
PE capital	75,000	75,000	75,000
PE capital requirement	99,750	107,000	119,840
New PE capital	99,750	7,250	12,840
Total new capital	411,640	29,083	52,887
Total capital	411,640	399,559	408,374
Depreciation	41,164	44,072	49,361

Figure A–9   Operating Expenses

	1995	1996	1997
Marketing expenses	85,000	90,950	101,864
Sales expenses	80,000	85,600	95,872
Brewery operations expenses	70,000	74,900	83,888
Administrative expenses	35,000	37,450	41,944
Overhead	410,224	438,940	491,613
Total expenses	$680,224	$727,840	$815,181

Chief Executive Officer

This position will be held by William Gillette. Mr. Gillette has been active in the brewing industry for the last 15 years, serving as a marketing director for a brewer of mass-produced beer. In the capacity of CEO for Backbay Brewing Company, Mr. Gillette will handle the marketing of Diamond Tap Premium Lager. His duties will include the compilation of market information as well as the formation of market strategies and materials. Mr. Gillette will also head Backbay Brewing's new product research and development. In addition, Mr. Gillette will provide direction in conjunction with Backbay Brewing's president and vice president of Operations concerning the management and overall operations of the business.

President

This position will be held by John Melrose. Mr. Melrose has over 10 years of experience managing brewery operations for a brewer of mass-produced beer. As the president of Backbay Brewing, Mr. Melrose will be responsible for all brewery operations. This not only includes the actual brewing process but purchasing and inventory control, as well as packaging and delivery to wholesale distributors. In addition, Mr. Melrose will provide direction in conjunction with Backbay Brewing's CEO and vice president of Operations concerning the management and overall operations of the business.

Vice President of Operations

This position will be held by William Barney. Mr. Barney has developed a number of contacts among suppliers of ingredients for the malt brewing industry as a purchasing director for a brewer of mass-produced beer. As the vice president of Operations, Mr. Barney will handle all of the purchasing and inventory control functions of Backbay

Brewing. He will report directly to the president in order to coordinate brewing operations with those of purchasing. In addition, Mr. Barney will provide direction in conjunction with Backbay Brewing's CEO and president concerning the management and overall operations of the business.

Sales Manager

The responsibilities of this position will include the management of all inside sales operations. This will include not only recruiting reputable wholesale distributors but maintaining those relations by acting as the liaison between Backbay Brewing and its network of wholesale distributors. This includes taking orders, making sure they are fulfilled according to the terms set forth in the distributor agreements, providing support for the distributors so they have appropriate marketing materials, and handling any type of problems that may occur at the wholesale level or that are passed along through the distribution channel from the retail level.

FINANCIAL COMPONENTS

The following section outlines the financial specifications for this business venture.

Income Statement

As detailed in Figure A–10, the net profit of Backbay Brewing Company is a healthy 27 percent during the first year of operation, indicating a strong product concept in a highly competitive market. With continued growth in the acquisition of market share, the net profit will continue to increase, thereby supporting the expansion plans of the company during the second and third years.

Cash Flow Statement

Figure A–11 shows the cash flow for the first three years of operation for Backbay Brewing Company. As detailed, the cumulative cash flow after the first year shows a positive that will be used in the second year for reinvestment into capital equipment and expansion of brewery operations. It also indicates a very attractive break-even point and ROI that will allow us to attract additional investment for expansion.

Figure A-10 Income Statement

	Jan	Feb	Mar	Apr	May	Jun	Jul	Aug	Sep	Oct	Nov	Dec	1995	Qtr 1	Qtr 2	Qtr 3	Qtr 4	1996	1997
Income	42,783	64,174	85,565	128,348	149,739	171,131	181,826	203,218	213,913	246,000	310,174	342,261	2,139,132	410,618	501,867	738,739	729,988	2,281,212	2,554,325
Cost of goods	17,800	26,700	35,600	53,400	62,300	71,200	75,650	84,550	89,000	102,350	129,050	142,400	890,000	171,414	209,506	266,644	304,736	952,299	1,066,576
Gross profit	24,983	37,474	49,965	74,948	87,439	99,931	106,176	118,668	124,913	143,660	181,124	199,861	1,249,132	239,204	292,361	372,096	425,252	1,328,913	1,487,749
Margin %	58	58	58	58	58	58	58	58	58	58	58	58	58	58	58	58	58	58	58
Expenses	34,011	40,813	47,616	47,616	49,656	52,377	55,778	63,261	71,424	71,424	72,104	74,144	680,224	160,125	167,403	196,517	203,795	727,840	815,181
Net profit	-9,029	-3,339	2,350	27,332	37,783	47,563	50,398	55,407	53,490	72,227	102,020	125,717	568,908	79,080	124,958	175,579	221,457	601,073	672,568
Margin %	-21	-5	3	21	25	28	28	27	25	29	35	37	27	19	25	27	30	28	28
Depreciation	3,430	3,430	3,430	3,430	3,430	3,430	3,430	3,430	3,430	3,430	3,430	3,430	41,164	11,018	11,018	11,018	11,018	44,072	49,361
Net profit before interest	-12,459	-6,770	-1,081	23,902	34,353	44,123	46,968	51,976	50,059	68,796	105,590	122,286	527,744	68,062	113,940	164,561	210,439	567,001	623,207
Margin %	-29	-11	-1	19	23	26	26	26	23	28	34	36	25	17	23	26	29	24	24
Interest	13,350	13,200	13,050	12,900	12,750	12,600	12,450	12,300	12,150	12,000	11,850	11,400	150,000	36,135	34,903	33,671	32,166	136,875	127,716
Net profit before taxes	-25,809	-19,970	-14,131	11,002	21,603	31,523	34,518	39,676	37,909	56,796	93,740	110,886	377,744	31,927	79,037	130,890	178,273	420,126	495,491

Figure A-11 Cash Flow Statement

	Jan	Feb	Mar	Apr	May	Jun	Jul	Aug	Sep	Oct	Nov	Dec	1995	Qtr 1	Qtr 2	Qtr 3	Qtr 4	1996	1997
Cash sales	17,113	25,670	34,226	51,339	59,896	68,452	72,730	81,287	85,565	98,400	124,070	136,904	855,652	164,247	200,747	256,496	291,995	912,485	1,021,730
Receivables	0	0	25,670	38,504	51,339	77,009	89,844	102,678	102,096	121,931	128,348	147,600	892,019	458,720	261,317	323,540	398,190	1,441,767	1,552,160
Other income	0	0	0	0	0	0	0	0	0	0	0	0	0	0	0	0	0	0	0
Total income	17,113	25,670	59,896	89,843	111,235	145,461	162,574	183,965	194,661	220,331	252,418	284,504	1,747,671	622,967	462,064	579,036	690,185	2,354,252	2,573,890
Material	0	0	0	0	0	0	0	0	0	0	0	0	0	0	0	0	0	0	0
Direct labor	7,800	11,700	15,600	23,400	27,300	31,200	33,150	37,050	39,000	44,850	56,550	62,400	390,000	91,806	95,979	112,671	116,844	417,300	467,376
Overhead	0	0	0	0	0	0	0	0	0	0	0	0	0	0	0	0	0	0	0
Marketing/Sales	8,250	9,900	11,550	11,550	12,045	12,706	13,530	15,345	17,325	17,325	17,490	17,985	165,000	38,841	40,607	47,669	49,434	176,550	197,736
Operations/R&D	3,500	4,200	4,900	4,900	5,110	5,390	5,740	6,510	7,350	7,350	7,420	7,630	70,000	16,478	17,227	20,223	20,972	74,900	83,888
G&A	1,750	2,100	2,450	2,450	2,555	2,695	2,870	3,255	3,675	3,675	3,710	3,815	35,000	8,239	8,614	10,112	10,486	37,450	41,944
Taxes	0	0	40,528	0	0	40,528	0	0	40,528	0	0	40,528	162,113	41,538	41,538	41,538	41,538	166,150	186,451
Capital	3,430	3,430	3,430	3,430	3,430	3,430	3,430	3,430	3,430	3,430	3,430	3,430	41,164	11,018	11,018	11,018	11,018	44,072	49,361

Balance Sheet

The balance sheet in Figure A–12 assumes that all cash generated by the business is reinvested back into the company. Since the accounts receivable and payable are kept short and are controlled, they will not lead to significant working capital requirements.

Figure A–12   Balance Sheet

	1995	1996	1997
Assets			
Current Assets			
Cash	$ 855,653	$ 912,485	$1,021,730
Accounts receivable	892,018	1,441,768	1,552,160
Inventory	676,250	723,588	810,419
Total Current Assets	$2,423,921	$3,077,841	$3,384,309
Fixed Assets			
Capital/Plant	$ 370,476	$ 399,559	$ 408,374
Investment	41,164	44,072	49,361
Miscellaneous assets	0	0	0
Total Fixed Assets	$ 411,640	$ 443,631	$ 457,735
Total Assets	$2,835,561	$3,521,472	$3,842,044
Liabilities			
Current Liabilities			
Accounts payable	$ 717,303	$1,034,785	$1,075,601
Accrued liabilities	660,000	706,200	790,944
Taxes	162,113	166,150	186,451
Total Current Liabilities	$1,539,416	$1,907,135	$2,052,996
Long-Term Liabilities			
Bond payable	$ 0	$ 0	$ 0
Notes payable	300,000	300,000	300,000
Total Long-Term Liabilities	$ 300,000	$ 300,000	$ 300,000
Total Liabilities	$1,839,416	$2,207,135	$2,352,996
Owner's Equity			
Owner's equity	$ 996,145	$1,314,337	$1,489,048
Total Liability/Equity	$2,835,561	$3,521,472	$3,842,044

Appendix B

BUSINESS RESOURCES

GENERAL SMALL BUSINESS RESOURCES

Associations

American Management Association, 135 West 50th Street, New York, NY 10020; (212) 586-8100

Center for Entrepreneurial Management, Inc., 180 Varick Street, 17th Floor, New York, NY 10014; (212) 633-0060

National Association for the Self-Employed, P.O. Box 612067, Dallas, TX 75261-2067; (800) 232-6273

National Management Association, 2210 Arbor Boulevard, Dayton, OH 45439; (513) 294-0421

Small Business Network, 10451 Mill Run Circle, Suite 400, Owings Mills, MD 21117; (410) 581-1373

Small Business Service Bureau, 554 Main Street, P.O. Box 15014, Worcester, MA 01615-0014; (508) 756-3513

Publications

Barron's National Business & Financial Weekly, 200 Liberty Street, New York, NY 10281; (212) 416-2700

The Business Owner, 383 S. Broadway, Hicksville, NY 11801; (516) 681-2111

Business Review, P.O. Box 777, Cypress, TX 77429; (713) 373-3535

BusinessWeek, 1221 Avenue of the Americas, 39th Floor, New York, NY 10020; (212) 512-3896

Entrepreneur Magazine, 2392 Morse Avenue, P.O. Box 19787, Irvine, CA 92714-6234; (800) 421-2300

Entrepreneurial Manager's Newsletter, 180 Varick Street, 17th Floor, New York, NY 10014; (212) 633-0060

Journal of Small Business Management, West Virginia University, College of Business Economics, Bureau of Business Research, P.O. Box 6025, Morgantown, WV 26506-6025; (304) 293-5837

Nation's Business, 1615 H Street NW, Washington, DC 20062-2000; (202) 463-5650

The Pricing Advisor, 3277 Roswell Road, #620, Atlanta, GA 30305; (404) 252-5708

The Wall Street Journal, Customer Service: (800) 568-7625

Books

The Entrepreneur and Small Business Problem Solver: An Encyclopedic Reference and Guide, William Cohen; John Wiley & Sons, 605 Third Avenue, New York, NY 10158

Minding Your Own Small Business, Nancy Holt, Joe Shuchat, and Mary Lewis Regal; CDC Education and Human Development, Inc., U.S. Printing Office, Department 33, Washington, DC 20402

HOME-BASED BUSINESS RESOURCES

Home Business Institute, Inc., P.O. Box 301, White Plains, NY 10605-0301; (914) 946-6600

National Association for the Cottage Industry, P.O. Box 14850, Chicago, IL 60614; (312) 472-8116

National Association of Home-Based Businesses, 10451 Mill Run Circle, Owings Mills, MD 21117; (410) 363-3698

Publication

Self-Employment Survival Letter, P.O. Box 2137, Naperville, IL 60567; (708) 717-4188

START-UP ASSISTANCE

Associations

American Bankers Association, 1120 Connecticut Avenue, Washington, DC 20037; (202) 663-5000

American League of Financial Institutions, 900 19th Street NW, Suite 400, Washington, DC 20006; (202) 628-5624

America's Community Bankers, 900 19th Street NW, Suite 400, Washington, DC 20006; (202) 857-3100

Association of Small Business Development Centers, 1050 17th Street NW, Suite 810, Washington, DC 20036; (202) 887-5599

Bancard Services Trust Company, 22311 Ventura Boulevard, Suite 125, Woodland Hills, CA 91364-1522; (818) 999-3333

Independent Bankers Association of America, One Thomas Circle NW, Suite 950, Washington, DC 20005; (202) 659-8111

National Association of Small Business Investment Companies (NASBIC), 1199 N. Fairfax Street, Suite 200, Alexandria, VA 22314; (703) 683-1601

National Commercial Finance Association, 225 West 34th Street, Suite 1815, New York, NY 10122; (212) 594-3490

National Venture Capital Association (NVCA), 1655 N. Fort Myer Drive, Suite 700, Arlington, VA 22209; (703) 351-5269

SBA Online—Telephone Assistance and General Information: (202) 205-6400; Direct-Dial Access: (202) 401-9600; 800-Number Access: (800) 697-4636; 900-Service Access: (900) 463-4636

SBA Small Business Answer Desk; (800) 827-5722

SCORE National Office, 409 3rd Street SW, 4th Floor, Washington, DC 20024; (202) 205-6762

Books

A Banker's Guide to Small Business Loans, American Bankers Association, 1120 Connecticut Avenue NW, Washington, DC 20036

Banking and Small Business, Derek Hansen, Council of State Planning Agencies, Hall of the States, 400 N. Capitol Street, Washington, DC 20001

Business Loans: A Guide to Money Sources and How to Approach Them Successfully, Rick Hayes, CBI Publishing Co., Inc., 135 W. 50th Street, New York, NY 10020

Encyclopedia of Banking and Finance, F. L. Garcia, Bankers Publishing Co., 210 South Street, Boston, MA 02111

Financing the Smaller Business, Thomas Martin, Center for Video Education, Inc., 103 S. Bedford Road, Mount Kisco, NY 10549

Financing Your Business, Price Waterhouse, 1251 Avenue of the Americas, New York, NY 10020

Handbook of Business Finance and Capital Sources, Dileep Rao, Inter Finance Corp., 511 11th Avenue, South, Minneapolis, MN 55415

How and Where to Raise Venture Capital to Finance a Business, Ted Nicholas, Enterprise Publishing Co., 725 Market Street, Wilmington, DE 19801

How to Ask for a Business Loan, Benton Gup, R. F. Dame, Inc., 1905 Huguenot Road, Richmond, VA 23235

How to Obtain Financing and Make "Your Best Deal" with Any Bank, Finance, or Lending Company!, I. M. Fytenbak, Cambrian Financial Corp., 2775 Park Avenue, Santa Clara, CA 95050

How to Raise Venture Capital, Stanley Pratt, Charles Scribner's Sons, 597 5th Avenue, New York, NY 10017

Maximizing Profits in Small- and Medium-Sized Businesses, Jerome Braverman, Van Nostrand Reinhold Co., Inc., 135 W. 50th Street, New York, NY 10020

Raising Cash: A Guide to Financing and Controlling Your Business, Sol Postyn and Jo Postyn, Lifetime Learning Publications, 10 Davis Drive, Belmont, CA 94002

Small Business and Venture Capital, Rudolph Weissman, Arno Press, 382 Main Street, P.O. Box 958, Salem, NH 03079

Small Business Financing, American Bankers Association, 1120 Connecticut Avenue NW, Washington, DC 20036

Small Business Financing: Federal Assistance & Contracts, Anthony Chase, McGraw-Hill Book Co., 1221 Avenue of the Americas, New York, NY 10020

Sourceguide for Borrowing Capital, Leonard Smollen, Mark Rollinson, and Stanley Rubel, Capital Publishing Co., 10 S. LaSalle Street, Chicago, IL 60603

The Small Business Guide to Borrowing Money, Richard Rubin and Philip Goldbert, McGraw-Hill Book Co., 1221 Avenue of the Americas, New York, NY 10020

Trade Financing, Charles Gmur, Business Press International, Ltd., 205 E. 42nd Street, New York, NY 10017

Understanding Money Sources, SBA, 1441 L Street NW, Washington, DC 10416

Up-Front Financing: The Entrepreneur's Guide, David Silver, John Wiley & Sons, 605 Third Avenue, New York, NY 10158

Venture Capital: The Complete Guide for Investors, David Silver, John Wiley & Sons, 605 Third Avenue, New York, NY 10158

Who's Who in Venture Capital, David Silver, John Wiley & Sons, 605 Third Avenue, New York, NY 10158

Magazines

American Banker, One State Street Plaza, 26th Floor, New York, NY 10004; (212) 803-8200

Bankers Digest, 7515 Greenville Avenue, Suite 901, Dallas, TX 75231; (214) 373-4544

Business Credit, 8815 Centre Park Drive, Suite 200, Columbia, MD 21045-2158; (410) 740-5560

Corporate Cashflow, 6151 Powers Ferry Road NW, Atlanta, GA 30339; (404) 955-2500

Corporate Finance, 1328 Broadway, New York, NY 10001; (212) 594-5030

Corporate Financing Week, 488 Madison Avenue, New York, NY 10022; (212) 303-3300

Credit, 919 18th Street NW, Third Floor, Washington, DC 20006; (202) 296-5544

Going Public: The IPO Reporter, 2 World Trade Center, 18th Floor, New York, NY 10048; (212) 227-1200

The Independent Banker, 518 Lincoln Road, P.O. Box 267, Sauk Centre, MN 56378; (612) 352-6546

Journal of Cash Management, 7315 Wisconsin Avenue, Suite 1250 West, Bethesda, MD 20814; (301) 907-2862

The Secured Lender, 225 W. 34th Street, Suite 1815, New York, NY 10122; (212) 594-3490

MARKET RESEARCH SERVICES

Dun & Bradstreet Small Business Services, 3 Sylvan Way, Parsippany, NJ 07054; (800) 544-3867; fax: (800) 525-5980

FIND/SVP, 625 Sixth Avenue, New York, NY 10011; (212) 645-4500

Gale Research, Inc., 835 Penobscot Bldg., Detroit, MI 48226; (313) 961-2242

Giga Information Group, One Longwater Circle, Norwell, MA 02061; (617) 982-9500

ONLINE SERVICES

America Online Incorporated, 8619 Westwood Center Drive, Vienna, VA 22182; (703) 448-8700 or (800) 827-6364

CompuServe, 5000 Arlington Centre Boulevard, Columbus, OH 43220; (800) 848-8990

Delphi, General Videotex Corp., 1030 Massachusetts Avenue, Cambridge, MA 02138; (800) 544-4005

Dow Jones News/Retrieval Service, P.O. Box 300, Princeton, NJ 08543-0300; (609) 452-1511

GEnie, P.O. Box 6403, Rockville, MD 20849-6403; (800) 638-9636

Knight-Ridder Information Services, Inc., 2440 El Camino Real, Mountain View, CA 94040; (800) 334-2564

NewsNet, 945 Haverford Road, Bryn Mawr, PA 19010; (215) 527-8030 or (800) 345-1301

Ovid Technologies, 333 7th Avenue, New York, NY 10001; (800) 955-0906

Prodigy Services Company, 445 Hamilton Avenue, White Plains, NY 10601; (800) 776-0845 (1-800-PRODIGY)

VU/TEXT Information Services, Inc., 1 Commerce Square, 2005 Market Street, Suite 1010, Philadelphia, PA 19103; (215) 587-4400

Publication

The Whole Internet User's Guide and Catalog, O'Reilly & Associates, 103-A Morris Street, Sebastopol, CA 95472; (800) 998-9938

ADVERTISING AND MARKETING

Associations

American Advertising Federation, 1101 Vermont Avenue NW, Suite 500, Washington, DC 20005; (202) 898-0090

American Marketing Association, 250 S. Wacker Drive, Suite 200, Chicago, IL 60606; (312) 648-0536

Association of National Advertisers, 155 East 44th Street, New York, NY 10017-4270

Cable Television Advertising Bureau, 757 Third Avenue, 5th Floor, New York, NY 10017; (212) 751-7770

Invention Marketing Institute, 345 W. Cypress Street, Glendale, CA 91204; (818) 246-6540

Marketing Research Association, 2189 Silas Deane Highway, Suite 5, Rocky Hill, CT 06067; (203) 257-4008

Outdoor Advertising Association of America, 12 East 49th Street, 22nd Floor, New York, NY 10017; (212) 688-3667

Point-of-Purchase Advertising Institute, 66 North Van Brunt Street, Englewood, NJ 07631; (201) 894-8899

Radio Advertising Bureau, 304 Park Avenue South, 7th Floor, New York, NY 10010; (212) 254-4800

Books

Advertising—How to Write the Kind That Works, David Nalickson, Charles Scribner's Sons, 597 5th Avenue, New York, NY 10017

Advertising and Communication Management, Michael Ray, Prentice-Hall, Inc., Route 9 West, Englewood Cliffs, NJ 07632

Advertising and Public Relations for a Small Business, Diane Bellavance, DBA Books, 77 Gordon Street, Boston, MA 02135

Advertising and Sales Promotion; Cost-Effective Techniques for Your Small Business, William Brannen, Prentice-Hall, Route 9 West, Englewood Cliffs, NJ 07632

Advertising Doesn't Cost . . . and Other Lies, L. S. Enterprises, 120 Enterprise Avenue, Secaucus, NJ 07094

Advertising Media Models: A Practical Guide, Roland Rust, Lexington Books, 125 Spring Street, Lexington, MA 02173

Advertising Small Business, Andrea Dailey, Bank of America, Department 3120, P.O. Box 37000, San Francisco, CA 94137

Big Paybacks from Small-Budget Advertising, Webster Kuswa, Dartnell Corporation, 4660 Ravenswood Avenue, Chicago, IL 60640

Essentials of Advertising Strategy, Don Schultz, Crain Books, 740 Rush Street, Chicago, IL 60611

Handbook of Small Business Advertising, Michael Anthony, Addison-Wesley Publishing Co., Reading, MA 01867

How to Advertise: A Handbook for Small Business, Sandra Linville Dean, Enterprise Publishing, Inc., 725 Market Street, Wilmington, DE 19801

How to Advertise and Promote Your Small Business, Connie Siegel, John Wiley & Sons, Inc., 605 Third Avenue, New York, NY 10158

How to Maximize Your Advertising Investment, Philip Johnson, CBI Publishing, 135 West 50th Street, New York, NY 10020

How to Promote Your Own Business, Gary Blake, New American Library, 1633 Broadway, New York, NY 10019

Marketing Management, Kenneth Kavis, John Wiley & Sons, Inc., 605 Third Avenue, New York, NY 10158

Profitable Advertising Techniques for Small Business, Harvey Cook, Entrepreneur Press, 3422 Astoria Circle, Fairfield, CA 94533

Profitable Methods for Small Business Advertising, Ernest Gray, John Wiley & Sons, Inc., 605 Third Avenue, New York, NY 10158

Step-by-Step Advertising, Cynthia Smith, Sterling Publishing Co., Inc., Two Park Avenue, New York, NY 10016

Strategic Advertising Campaigns, Don Schultz, Dennis Martin, and William Brown, Crain Books, 740 Rush Street, Chicago, IL 60611

Strategy in Advertising: Matching Media and Messages to Markets and Motivation, Leo Bogart, Crain Books, 740 Rush Street, Chicago, IL 60611

Streetfighting: Low-Cost Advertising/Promotion Strategies for Your Small Business, Jeff Slutsky and Woody Woodruff, Prentice-Hall, Route 9 West, Englewood Cliffs, NJ 07632

The 27 Most Common Mistakes in Advertising, Alec Benn, AMACOM, 135 West 50th Street, New York, NY 10020

The Secrets of Practical Marketing for Small Business, Herman Holtz, Prentice-Hall, Inc., Route 9 West, Englewood Cliffs, NJ 07632

Magazines

Adcrafter, 1249 Washington Boulevard, Detroit, MI 48226-1852; (313) 962-7225

Advertising Age, 220 East 42nd Street, New York, NY 10017; (212) 210-0100

Advertising Communications Times, 121 Chestnut Street, Philadelphia, PA 19106; (215) 629-1666

Adweek, 1515 Broadway, New York, NY 10036-8986; (212) 536-5336

American Advertising, 1101 Vermont Avenue NW, Suite 500, Washington, DC 20005; (202) 898-0089

American Demographics, P.O. Box 68, Ithaca, NY 14851; (607) 273-6343

Business Marketing, 740 N. Rush Street, Chicago, IL 60611; (312) 649-5200

Inside Media, Cowles Business Media, 911 Hope Street, Building 6, P.O. Box 4949, Stamford, CT 06907-0949; (203) 358-9900

Journal of Marketing Research, 250 S. Wacker Drive, #200, Chicago, IL 60606

Quirk's Marketing Research Review, 8030 Cedar Avenue South, Suite 229, Bloomington, MN 55425; (612) 854-5101

Tradeshow Week, 12233 W. Olympic Boulevard, Suite 236, Los Angeles, CA 90064; (310) 826-5696

RECORDKEEPING AND TAXES

Associations

American Accounting Association, 5717 Bessie Drive, Sarasota, FL 34233; (813) 921-7747

Independent Accountants International, 9200 S. Dadeland Boulevard, Suite 510, Miami, FL 33156; (305) 661-0580

International Credit Association, 243 N. Lindbergh Boulevard, P.O. Box 419057, St. Louis, MO 63141-1757; (314) 991-3030

Publications

Taxes: The Tax Magazine, 4025 W. Peterson Avenue, Chicago, IL 60646; (312) 583-8500

The Tax Adviser, Harborside Financial Center, #201 Plaza 3, Jersey City, NJ 07311-3881; (201) 938-3447

Appendix C

SMALL BUSINESS RESOURCES

Although the editors at Entrepreneur Group have made every effort to verify the following information to ensure its accuracy at the time of publication, businesses and other organizations do move or cease to conduct business. Due to these circumstances, Entrepreneur Group cannot be held responsible for the reliability of the sources listed herein. If you are unable to contact any of the following organizations, first try calling directory assistance in the area code listed, by dialing 1-Area Code-555-1212 and asking for the organization listed. If you are still unable to make contact, please write the Research Department at: Entrepreneur Group, 2392 Morse Avenue, Irvine, CA 92714. We will be more than happy to help you locate the organization if it still exists.

Associations

American Management Association, 135 West 50th Street, New York, NY 10020; (212) 586-8100

American Marketing Association, 250 S. Wacker Drive, Suite 200, Chicago, IL 60606; (312) 648-0536

Marketing Research Association, 2189 Silas Deane Hwy., Rocky Hill, CT 06067; (203) 257-4008

National Association of Investment Companies, 1111 14th Street, NW, Suite 700, Washington, DC 20005; (202) 289-4336

National Association of Small Business Investment Companies, 1199 N. Fairfax Street, Alexandria, VA 22314; (703) 683-1601

National Federation of Independent Business, 150 W. 20th Avenue, San Mateo, CA 94403; (415) 341-7441

National Venture Capital Association, 1655 N. Fort Myer Drive, Suite 700, Arlington, VA 22209; (703) 351-5269

Small Business Network, 10451 Millrun Circle, Suite 400, Owingsmills, MD 21117; (410) 581-1373

Conferences

Small Business Innovation Research Conferences, c/o Foresight Science and Technology, Inc., 6064 Okeechobee Boulevard, P.O. Box 170569, West Palm Beach, FL 33417; (407) 791-0720

Venture Capital Resource Centers

The Capital Institute (advises businesses on raising money), 477 Ninth Avenue, Suite 103, San Mateo, CA 94402; (415) 340-8753; fax: (415) 340-8610

Center for Venture Research, University of New Hampshire, Whittemore School of Business and Economics, Durham, NH 03824; (603) 862-3341

International Venture Capital Institute, Inc., P.O. Box 1333, Stamford, CT 06904; (203) 323-3143

Missouri Venture Forum, 222 S. Meramec Avenue, Suite 303, St. Louis, MO 63105; (314) 432-7440

New York State Science and Technology Foundation (Venture Line, Small Business Fund, Technology and Disabilities Fund), 99 Washington Avenue, #1730, Albany, NY 12210; (518) 473-9741

Oklahoma Investment Forum, 616 S. Boston, Tulsa, OK 74119; (918) 585-1201; fax: (918) 585-8386

Vankirk Business Information, 2800 Shirlington Road, #904, Arlington, VA 22206; (703) 379-9200

Venture Economics, Inc. (division of Securities Data Publishing Co.), 40 W. 57th Street, #1100, New York, NY 10019; (212) 765-5311

Venture Economics Investor Services Group, 11 Farnsworth Street, Boston, MA 02210; (617) 345-2504

Matching Services

The Capital Network, Inc., 8920 Business Park Drive, Austin, TX 78759-7405; (512) 794-9398

Capital Search Consulting, Inc., 701 Palomar Airport Road, Carlsbad, CA 92009; (619) 576-9693

The Investment Exchange, Suite 300, 700 Fourth Avenue, SW, Calgary, Alberta, Canada T2P 3J4; (403) 299-1770

Non-Traditional Financial Services, 4567 Prospect Street, Littleton, CO 80123; (303) 797-3734; fax: (303) 730-6698

Seed Capital Network, 8905 Kingston Pike, Suite 12, Knoxville, TN 37923; (615) 573-4655; fax: (615) 577-9989

Venture Capital Funds

The Capital Rose Perpetual Fund, Inc., 690 Sugartown Road, Malvern, PA 19355; (610) 644-4212

Inroads Capital Partners, 1603 Orrington Avenue, Suite 2050, Evanston, IL 60201; (708) 864-2000

New Era Capital Partners, 5410 Wilshire Boulevard, 9th Floor, Los Angeles, CA 90036; (213) 931-8238

Women's Equity Fund, Boulder, CO; (303) 443-2620 (for Colorado companies only)

Women's Business Ownership Assistance

Office of Women's Business Ownership, SBA, 409 Third Street SW, Washington, DC 20416; (202) 205-6673

Government Agencies

Advanced Technology Program, NIST, USDC, Building 101, Gaithersburg, MD 20899; (301) 975-2636; (800) 287-3863

American Indian Program, Assistant Director, Minority Business Development Agency, USDC, Office of Operations, 14th & Constitution Avenue, NW, Room 5063, Washington, DC 20230; (202) 482-1015

Business and Industrial Loans, FmHA-USDA (Farmers Home Administration-United States Department of Agriculture), Room 6304, South Building, 14th & Independence Avenue, SW, Washington, DC 20250; (202) 720-6903

Community Development Block Grants, Headquarters, Community Planning & Development, HUD, 451 7th Street, SW, Washington, D.C. 20410; (202) 708-2090

Copyright Clearance Center, 222 Rosewood Drive, Danvers, MA 01923; (508) 750-8400

Copyright Office, Library of Congress, Washington, DC 2055; (202) 287-9100

Division of Research Programs (Promotion of the Humanities—Texts/Translations), Texts/Translations, NEH, 1100 Pennsylvania Avenue, NW, Room 318, Washington, DC 20506; (202) 606-8207

Economic Injury Disaster Loans (EIDL), Headquarters Office, Office of Disaster Assistance, Small Business Administration, 409 Third Street SW, Washington, DC 20416; (202) 205-6734

Export-Import Bank of the United States, 811 Vermont Avenue, NW, Washington, DC 20571; (202) 565-3946

Indian Business Development Program, Deputy to the Assistant Secretary/Indian Affairs (Trust and Economic Development), BIA-DOI, 1849 C Street NW, Room 4513, Washington, DC 20240; (202) 208-3662

Indian Credit Program, Deputy to the Assistant Secretary, Office of Trust and Economic Development, BIA-DOI, 1849 & C Street NW, Room 2528, Washington, DC 20240; (202) 219-5274

Industrial Development Grants, FmHA—USDA, Room 6304, South Building, 14th & Independence Avenue, SW, Washington, DC 20250; (202) 720-6903

Loans for Small Businesses ("Business Loans 7(a)(11)"), Director, Loan Policy and Procedures Branch, SBA, 409 Third Street SW, Washington, DC 20416; (202) 205-6570

MTC Program, NIST Manufacturing Technology Center, USDC, Bldg. 222, Room B212, Gaithersburg, MD 20899-0001; (301) 975-5020

Nonprofit National Corporations Loan and Grant Program, FmHA-USDA, Room 6304, South Building, 14th & Independence Avenue, SW, Washington, DC 20250; (202) 720-6903

Office of Program Development, Minority Business Development Agency, USDC, 14th & Constitution Avenue NW, Room 5096, Washington, DC 20230; (202) 482-5770

Project Grants, Director, NEA, Literature Program, 1100 Pennsylvania Avenue NW, Washington, DC 20506; (202) 682-5451

Section 7j Development Assistance Program, Office of Associate Administrator/Minority Small Business and Capital Ownership Development (AA/MSB&COD), SBA, 409 Third Street SW, Washington, DC 20416; (202) 205-6420

Section 8a Program, Minority Business Development Agency, SBA, Room 5096, 14th & Constitution Avenue, NW, Washington, DC 20230; (202) 482-5770

Small Business Administration, 1441 L Street NW, Washington, DC 20416-0001; (202) 653-6823

Small Business Investment Companies, Associate Administrator for Investment, Investment Division, SBA, 409 Third Street, SW, Washington, DC 20416; (202) 205-6510

U.S. Department of Agriculture, 14th & Independence Avenue, SW, Washington, DC 20250; (202) 720-2791

U.S. Department of Commerce, Herbert C. Hoover Bldg., 14th Street & Constitution Avenue NW, Washington, DC 20230; (202) 482-2000

U.S. Department of Energy, 1000 Independence Avenue, SW, Washington, DC 20585; (202) 586-5000

U.S. Department of Interior, 1849 C Street, NW, Washington, DC 20240; (202) 208-3100

U.S. Department of Labor, 200 Constitution Avenue NW, Washington, DC 20210-0001; (202) 219-6666

U.S. Department of Labor, Office of Small Business and Minority Affairs, 200 Constitution Avenue, NW, Room C2318, Washington, DC 20210; (202) 219-9148

U.S. Department of Treasury, Internal Revenue Services, 1111 Constitution Avenue, Washington, DC 20224; (202) 622-5000

U.S. Patent and Trademark Office, Office of Public Affairs, Washington, DC 20231; (703) 557-4636

U.S. Printing Office, Dept. 33, Washington, DC 20402; (202) 512-1800

U.S. Securities and Exchange Commission, 450 Fifth Street, NW, Washington, DC 20549; (202) 942-8088

Women's Business Ownership Assistance, Headquarters Office, Office of Women's Business Ownership, SBA, 409 Third Street, SW, Washington, DC 20416; (202) 205-6673

General Start-Up Assistance

American Bankers Association, 1120 Connecticut Avenue, NW, Washington, DC 20036; (202) 663-5000

American League of Financial Institutions, 900 19th Street, NW, Suite 400, Washington, DC 20006; (202) 628-5624

Commercial Finance Association, 225 West 34th Street, Suite 1815, New York, NY 10122; (212) 594-3490

File Transfer Protocol: ftp://ftp.sba.gov

Independent Bankers Association of America, One Thomas Circle, NW, Suite 950, Washington, DC 20005; (202) 659-8111

Internet (Using Uniform Resource Locators—URLs)

National Council and Savings and Community Bankers of America, 900 19th Street, Suite 400, Washington, DC 20006; (202) 857-3100

National Venture Capital Association, 1655 N. Fort Myer Drive, Suite 700, Arlington, VA 22209; (703) 351-5246

SBA Gopher: gopher://gopher.sba.gov

SBA Home Page: http:www.sba.gov

SBA On-Line

SBA's electronic bulletin board service: 2400-baud modems, call (800) 859-INFO; 9600-baud modems, call (800) 697-INFO (limited access), or (900) 463-INFO (full access—14¢ per minute). DC metro area, call (202) 401-9600.

SBA Small Business Answer Desk; (800) 827-5722

SCORE National Office, 409 3rd Street SW, 4th Fl., Washington, DC 20024-3212; (202) 205-6762

Small Business Investment Companies (SBIC), Director of the Office of Investment, SBA, 409 Third Street SW, Washington, DC 20416; (202) 205-6510

Telnet: telnet://sbaonline.sba.gov

US Business Advisor (Being developed. Will provide interactive access to all federal business information and services): http://www.business.gov

Venture Economics Investor Services Group, 11 Farnsworth Street, Boston, MA 02210; (617) 345-2504

Market Research

BIS Strategic Decisions, One Longwater Circle, Norwell, MA 02061; (617) 982-9500

Dun & Bradstreet Small Business Services, 3 Sylvan Way., Parsippany, NJ 07054; (800) 544-3867; fax: (800) 525-5980

FIND/SVP, 625 Sixth Avenue, New York, NY 10011; (212) 645-4500

Gale Research, Inc., 835 Penobscot Bldg., Detroit, MI 48226-4094; (313) 961-2242

LINK Resources, 79 Fifth Avenue, Suite 1200, New York, NY 10003; (212) 620-3099

Business Information Centers (BICs)

US Small Business Administration Business Information Center, Attn. Adria Graham, 3600 Wilshire Boulevard Suite L100, Los Angeles, CA 90010; (213) 251-7253; fax: (213) 251-7255

US Small Business Administration San Diego District Office, Attn: Lisa DeMars, 550 West C Street, Suite 550, San Diego, CA 92101; (619) 557-7252; fax: (619) 557-5894

SBA/Bell Atlantic Business Information Center, Washington District Office, Attn: Claudette Ford, 1110 Vermont Avenue NW, Suite 900, Washington, DC, 20043-4500; (202) 606-4000 ext 266; fax: (202) 606-4225

US Small Business Administration Atlanta District Office, Attn: Katrina Winberg, 1720 Peachtree Road, NW, 6th Floor, Atlanta, GA 30309; (404)347-4749; fax: (404)347-2355

US Small Business Administration Boise District Office, Attn: Tom Bergdoll, 1020 Main Street, Boise, ID 83702-5745; (208) 334-9077; fax: (208) 334-9353

US Small Business Administration Chicago District Office, Attn: Phyllis Scott, 500 W. Madison Street, Suite 1250, Chicago, IL 60661-2511; (312) 353-1825; fax: (312) 886-5688

SBA/Nations Bank/MBDA/Bell Atlantic Small Business Resource Center, Attn: Rachel Walker, 3 West Baltimore Street, Corner of Charles & Baltimore, Baltimore, MD 21201; (401) 605-0990

US Small Business Administration Boston District Office, Attn: Andrea Ross, 10 Causeway Street, Room 265, Boston, MA 02222-1093; (617) 565-5615; fax: (617) 565-5598

US Small Business Administration Kansas City District Office, Attn: Kim Malcolm, 323 West 8th Street, Suite 104, Kansas City, MO 64105; (816) 374-6675; fax: (816) 374-6759

Online Services

America Online Incorporated, 8619 Westwood Center Drive, Vienna, VA 22182; (703) 448-8700; (800) 827-6364

CD Plus Technologies, 333 7th Avenue, 4th Floor, New York, NY 10001; (800) 955-0906

CompuServe Incorporated, 5000 Arlington Center Boulevard, Columbus, OH 43220; (614) 457-8600; (800) 848-8990

Delphi Internet Services Corp, 1030 Massachusetts Avenue, Cambridge, MA 02138; (800) 544-4005

DIALOG Information Services, Inc., Marketing Dept., 3460 Hillview Avenue, Palo Alto, CA 94304; (415) 858-3785; (800) 334-2564

Dow Jones News/Retrieval Service, P.O. Box 300, Princeton, NJ 08543-0300; (609) 452-1511

GEnie, G.E. Information Services, 401 N. Washington Street, Rockville, MD 20850; (800) 638-9636

NewsNet, 945 Haverford Road, Bryn Mawr, PA 19010; (215) 527-8030; (800) 345-1301

NEXIS, Mead Data Central, P.O. Box 933, Dayton, OH 45401; (513) 859-5398; (800) 543-6862

Prodigy Services Company, 445 Hamilton Avenue, White Plains, NY 10601; (800) 776-0845 (1-800-PRODIGY)

VU/TEXT Information Services, Inc., 325 Chestnut Street, Suite 1300, Philadelphia, PA 19106; (800) 258-8080

Publications

Arkebauer, James B., and Ron Schultz, *The Entrepreneur's Guide to Going Public*, 1994, Upstart Publishing Company, Inc., 155 N. Wacker Drive, Chicago, IL 60606-1719; (800) 235-8866

Berle, Gustav, *SBA Hotline Answer Book*, 1992, John Wiley & Sons, Inc., 605 Third Avenue, New York, NY 10158; (212) 850-6000

Blum, Laurie, *Free Money from the Federal Government: For Small Businesses and Entrepreneurs*, John Wiley & Sons, Inc., 1993, 605 Third Avenue, New York, NY 10158; (212) 850-6000

The Colorado Guide to Financing Sources, Financial Education Publishers, Inc., 4567 Prospect Street, Littleton, CO 80123; (303) 797-3734

Dawson, George M., *Borrowing for Your Business*, 1991, Upstart Publishing Company, Inc., 155 N. Wacker Drive, Chicago, IL 60606-1719; (800) 235-8866

Dumouchel, J. Robert, *Government Assistance Almanac 1995-96*, Omnigraphics, Inc., Penobscot Building, Detroit, MI 48226; (313) 961-1340

Fallek, Max, *Finding Money for Your Small Business*, 1994, Dearborn Publishing Group, Inc., 155 N. Wacker Drive, Chicago IL 60606-1719; (800) 235-8866

Gaston, Robert J., *Finding Private Venture Capital for Your Firm: A Complete Guide*, 1989, John Wiley & Sons, Inc., 605 Third Avenue, New York, NY 10158; (212) 850-6000

How to Raise Money for Your Business, Financial Education Publishers, Inc., 4567 Prospect Street, Littleton, CO 80123; (303) 797-3734

McKeever, Mike P., *Start-Up Money: How to Finance Your New Small Business*, 1984, Nolo Press, 950 Parker Street, Berkeley, CA 94710; (510) 549-1976

Nicholas, Ted, *Forty-Three Proven Ways to Raise Capital for Your Small Business*, 1991, Upstart Publishing Company, Inc., 155 N. Wacker Drive, Chicago, IL 60606-1719; (800) 235-8866

Owen, Robert R., Garner, Daniel R., and Bunder, Dennis S., *The Arthur Young Guide to Financing for Growth*, 1986, John Wiley & Sons, Inc., 605 Third Avenue, New York, NY 10158; (212) 850-6000

Pratt's Guide to Venture Capital Sources, Securities Data Publishing, Inc., 40 W. 57th Street #1100, New York, NY 10019; (212) 765-5311

Silver, A. David, *Up-Front Financing: The Entrepreneur's Guide*, 1982, John Wiley & Sons, Inc., 605 Third Avenue, New York, NY 10158; (212) 850-6000

Silver, A. David, *Venture Capital: The Complete Guide for Investors*, 1985, John Wiley & Sons, Inc., 605 Third Avenue, New York, NY 10158; (212) 850-6000

Vankirk's Venture Capital Directory, Vankirk Business Information, 2800 Shirlington Road, #904, Arlington, VA 22206; (703) 379-9200

Venture Capital Journal, Securities Data Publishing, Inc., 40 W. 57th Street #1100, New York, NY 10019; (212) 765-5311

Wright, Susan, *Raising Money in Less Than 30 Days: A Guide for Individuals and Organizations*, 1993, Citadel Press, 120 Enterprise, Secaucus, NJ 07094; (800) 447-BOOK

Related Books by Entrepreneur Group

To order any of the following business guides 24 hours a day, 7 days a week, call 1-800-421-2300, or fax your order to 1-714-851-9088

The Home-based Business Resource, #1804

Small Business Encyclopedia, #3500 (three-volume set)

Writing Effective Business Plans, #1800

Appendix D

GOVERNMENT LISTINGS

GOVERNMENT AGENCIES

Copyright Clearance Center, 222 Rosewood Drive, Danvers, MA 01923; (508) 750-8400

The Copyright Office, Library of Congress, Washington, DC 20540; (202) 707-3000

Export-Import Bank of the United States, 811 Vermont Avenue NW, Washington, DC 20571; (202) 565-3946

Internal Revenue Service, 1111 Constitution Avenue NW, Washington, DC 20224; (202) 622-5000

U.S. Department of Agriculture, 14th & Independence Avenue SW, Washington, DC 20013; (202) 720-7420

U.S. Department of Commerce, Herbert C. Hoover Building, 14th Street & Constitution Avenue NW, Washington, DC 20230; (202) 482-2000

U.S. Department of Energy, 1000 Independence Avenue SW, Washington, DC 20585; (202) 586-5000

U.S. Department of Interior, 1849 C Street NW, Washington, DC 20240; (202) 208-3100

U.S. Department of Labor, 200 Constitution Avenue NW, Room S-1004, Washington, DC 20210; (202) 219-6666

U.S. Department of Treasury, Main Treasury Building, 1500 Pennsylvania Avenue NW, Washington, DC 20220; (202) 622-2000

U.S. Patent and Trademark Office, Washington, DC 20231; (800) 786-9199

U.S. Printing Office, Washington, DC 20402; (202) 512-1800

U.S. Securities and Exchange Commission, 450 Fifth Street NW, Washington, DC 20549; (202) 942-8088

U.S. Small Business Administration, P.O. Box 34500, Washington, DC 20043-4500; (800) 827-5722

STATE COMMERCE AND ECONOMIC DEVELOPMENT DEPARTMENTS

Alabama Development Office, 401 Adams Avenue, Montgomery, AL 36130; (334) 242-0400

Alaska State Dept. of Commerce and Economic Development, State Office Building, P.O. Box 110800 Juneau, AK 99811-0800; (907) 465-2500

Arizona State Dept. of Commerce, Small Business Advocate, 3800 N. Central Avenue, Phoenix, AZ 85012; (602) 280-1480

Arkansas Industrial Development Commission, Minority & Small Business, One State Capitol Mall, Little Rock, AR 72201; (501) 682-1060

California State Department of Commerce, 801 K Street, Suite 1600, Sacramento, CA 95814; (916) 322-1394

Colorado Office of Economic Development, 1625 Broadway, Suite 1710, Denver, CO 80202; (303) 892-3840

Connecticut Economic Resource Center, 805 Brook Street, Building 4, Rocky Hill, CT 06067; (860) 571-7136

Delaware State Chamber of Commerce, 1201 N. Orange Street, Suite 200, Wilmington, DE 19801; (302) 655-7221

District Of Columbia: Office of Economic Development, 717 14th Street NW, 12th Floor, Washington DC 20005; (202) 727-6600

Florida Department of Commerce, 536 Collins Building, 107 W. Gaines Street, Tallahassee, FL 32399-2000; (904) 488-3104

Georgia Dept. of Community Affairs, Suite 1200, 100 Peachtree Street, Atlanta, GA 30303; (404) 656-2900

Hawaii: Business Action Center, 1130 N. Nimitz Hwy., Suite A-254, Honolulu, HI 96817; (808) 585-2600

Idaho State Dept. of Commerce, P.O. Box 83720, Boise, ID 83720; (208) 334-2470

Illinois Dept. of Commerce and Community Affairs, 100 W. Randolph Street, Chicago, IL 60601; (312) 814-7179

Indiana State Dept. of Commerce, One N. Capitol, Suite 700, Indianapolis, IN 46204-2288; (317) 232-8782

Iowa Department of Economic Development, 200 E. Grand Avenue, Des Moines, IA 50309; (515) 281-3251

Kansas Department of Commerce and Housing, Business Development Department, 700 SW Harrison Street, Suite 1300, Topeka, KS 66603; (913) 296-3483

Kentucky Dept. of Economic Development, Business Information Clearinghouse, 22nd Floor, Capitol Plaza Tower, Frankfort, KY 40601; (800) 626-2250

Louisiana Dept. of Economic Development, P.O. Box 94185, Baton Rouge, LA 70804-9185; (504) 342-5388

Maine: Business Answers, Dept. of Economic and Community Development, 33 Stone Street, 59 Statehouse Station, Augusta, ME 04333; (207) 287-2656

Maryland Department of Business and Economic Development, Division of Regional Development, 217 East Redwood Street, Baltimore, MD 21202; (410) 767-0095

Massachusetts Office of Business Development, 1 Ashburton Place, Boston, MA 02108; (617) 727-3221

Michigan Jobs Commission, Ombudsman, 201 N. Washington Square, Victor Office Center, 4th Floor, Lansing, MI 48933; (517) 335-1847

Minnesota Small Business Assistance Office, 500 Metro Square, 121 Seventh Place East, St. Paul, MN 55101; (612) 282-2103

Mississippi Dept. of Economic and Community Development, Division of Existing Industry and Business, P.O. Box 849, Jackson, MS 39205; (601) 359-3593

Missouri: Community and Economic Development, Business Information Program, P.O. Box 118, Jefferson City, MO 65102; (573) 751-4982

Montana: Dept. of Commerce, 1424 Ninth Avenue, Helena, MT 59620; (406) 444-4780

Nebraska: Department of Economic Development, P.O. Box 94666, Lincoln, NE 69509; (402) 471-3782

Nevada State Dept. of Business and Industry, Office of the Director, Center for Business Advocacy Services, 2501 E. Sahara Avenue, Suite 202, Las Vegas, NV 89104; (702) 486-4335

New Hampshire State Department of Resources and Economic Development, P.O. Box 330, Concord, NH 03302-1856; (603) 271-2591

New Jersey: State of New Jersey Dept. of Commerce and Economic Development, Division of Small Businesses, Women and Minority Businesses, CN 835, Trenton, NJ 08625-0835; (609) 292-3860

New Mexico Economic Development Department, P.O. Box 20003, Santa Fe, NM 87504; (505) 827-0300

New York: Division for Small Business, Empire State Development, One Commerce Plaza, Albany, NY 12245; (518) 473-0499

North Carolina: Small Business and Technology Development Center, 333 Fayetteville Street Mall, Suite 1150, Raleigh, NC 27601-1742; (919) 715-7292

North Dakota: Center for Innovation and Business Development, P.O. Box 8372, Grand Forks, ND 58202; (701) 777-3132

Ohio One-Stop Business Permit Center, 77 S. High Street, 28th Floor, Columbus, OH 43216; (614) 644-8748

Oklahoma: Department of Commerce, P.O. Box 29680, Oklahoma City, OK 71326-0980; (405) 843-9770

Oregon Department of Economic Development, 775 Summer Street NE, Salem, OR 97310; (503) 986-0123

Pennsylvania Business Resource Center, Room 404, The Forum Building, Harrisburg, PA 17120; (717) 783-5700

Rhode Island Economic Development Corporation, Seven Jackson Walkway, Providence, RI 02903; (401) 277-2601

South Carolina: Enterprise Development Dept., South Carolina State Development Board, P.O. Box 927, Columbia, SC 29202; (803) 737-0400

South Dakota: Governor's Office of Economic Development, 711 E. Wells Avenue, Pierre, SD 57501; (605) 773-5032

Tennessee: Office of Small Business, Dept. of Economic and Community Development, 320 Sixth Avenue North, 7th Floor, Nashville, TN 37243-0405; (615) 741-2626

Texas Department of Commerce, Small Business Division, P.O. Box 12728, Austin, TX 78711; (512) 936-0100

Utah Department of Community and Economic Development, 3600 Constitution Boulevard, West Valley City, UT 84119; (801) 963-3286

Vermont: Development and Community Affairs, 109 State Street, Montpelier, VT 05609-0501; (802) 828-3221

Virginia: Department of Economic Development, Office of Small Business and Financial Services, 901 E. Byrd Street, Suite 1800, Richmond, VA 23319. Call (804) 371-8253 for information on the Virginia Small Business Development Center in your area.

Washington: Business Assistance Division, Community Trade and Economic Development, 906 Columbia Street SW, P.O. Box 48300, Olympia, WA 98504-8300; (360) 753-4900

West Virginia Small Business Development Center, 950 Kanawha Boulevard, Charleston, WV 25301; (304) 558-2960

Wisconsin: Dept. of Development, 123 W. Washington Avenue, Madison, WI 53703; (608) 266-9467

Wyoming Dept. of Economic and Community Development, 6101 Yellowstone Road, Cheyenne, WY 82002; (307) 777-7284

STATE SMALL BUSINESS DEVELOPMENT OFFICES

Note: The following offices are the lead Small Business Development Centers for each state. Most states have other regional centers, as well.

Alabama Small Business Development Consortium, 1717 11th Avenue, South, Suite 419, Birmingham, AL 35294; (205) 934-7260

Alaska: UAA SBDC, 430 W. Seventh Avenue, Suite 110, Anchorage, AK 99501; (907) 274-7232

Arizona Small Business Development Center, 1414 W. Broadway, Suite 165, Tempe, AZ 85282; (602) 966-7786

Arkansas Small Business Development Center, University of Arkansas at Little Rock, 100 South Main, Suite 401, Little Rock, AR 72201; (501) 324-9043

California Small Business Development Center, Office of Small Business, 801 K Street, Suite 1700, Sacramento, CA 95814; (916) 324-5068

Colorado Small Business Development Center, 1625 Broadway, Suite 1710, Denver, CO 80202; (303) 892-3809

Connecticut: University of Connecticut, Connecticut Small Business Development Center, 2 Bourne Place, U-94, Storrs, CT 06269-5094; (203) 486-4135

Delaware Small Business Development Center, 005 Purnell Hall, Newark, DE 19716; (302) 831-2747

District of Columbia: Howard University, School of Business, Small Business Development Center, Room 125, Washington, DC 20059; (202) 806-1550

Florida Small Business Development Center, University of West Florida, 11000 University Parkway, Pensacola, FL 32514; (904) 474-2908

Georgia Small Business Development Center, University of Georgia, 1180 E. Broad. Street, Athens, GA 30602-5412; (706) 542-7436

Hawaii: University of Hawaii at Hilo, Small Business Development Center, 200 West Kawili Street, Hilo, HI 96720-4091; (808) 933-3515

Idaho Small Business Development Center, Boise State University, 1910 University Drive, Boise, ID 83725; (208) 385-1640

Illinois Small Business Development Center, 620 E. Adams Street, Springfield, IL 62701; (217) 524-5858

Indiana Small Business Development Center, One North Capitol, Suite 425, Indianapolis, IN 46204; (317) 264-6871

Iowa Small Business Development Center, 137 Lynn Street, Ames, IA 50014; (515) 292-6351

Kansas: Please call the Small Business Administration at (316) 269-6273.

Kentucky Center for Business Development, Room 225, Carol Martin Gatton Business and Economics Building, University of Kentucky, Lexington, KY 40506-0034; (606) 257-7668

Louisiana Small Business Development Center, College of Business Administration, Admin. 2-57, Northeast Louisiana University, Monroe, LA 71209-6435; (318) 342-5506

Maine: University of Southern Maine, Maine Small Business Development Center, 96 Falmouth Street, P.O. Box 9300, Portland, ME 04104-9300; (207) 780-4420

Maryland Small Business Development Center, 217 East Redwood Street, Baltimore, MD 21202; (410) 767-6552

Massachusetts: University of Massachusetts, Massachusetts Small Business Development Center, P.O. Box 34935, Amherst, MA 01003-4935; (413) 545-6301

Michigan Small Business Development Center, 2727 Second Avenue, Detroit, MI 48201; (313) 964-1798

Minnesota Small Business Development Center, Department of Trade and Economic Development, 500 Metro Square, 121 Seventh Place East, St. Paul, MN 55101-2146; (612) 297-5770

Mississippi Small Business Development Center, University of Mississippi, Old Chemistry Building, Suite 216, University, MS 38677; (601) 232-5650

Missouri Small Business Development Center, 300 University Place, Columbia, MO 65211; (314) 882-0344

Montana: Small Business Development Center, Dept. of Commerce, 1424 Ninth Avenue, Helena, MT 59620; (406) 444-4780

Nebraska Business Development Center, University of Nebraska—Omaha, 60th and Dodge Street, College of Business Administration, Room 407, Omaha, NE 68182; (402) 554-2521

Nevada Small Business Development Center, University of Nevada—Reno, College of Business/032, Reno, NV 89577-0100; (702) 784-1717

New Hampshire Small Business Development Center, 108 McConnell Hall, 15 College Road, Durham, NH 03824; (603) 862-2200

New Jersey Small Business Development Center, Ackerson Hall, 180 University Avenue, Newark, NJ 07102; (201) 648-1110

New Mexico Small Business Development Center, P.O. Box 4187, Santa Fe, NM 87502-4187; (505) 438-1237

New York Small Business Development Center, State University of New York, State University Plaza, S-523, Albany, NY 12246; (518) 443-5398

North Carolina Small Business and Technology Development Center, 3333 Fayetteville Street Mall, Suite 1150, Raleigh, NC 27601; (919) 715-7272

North Dakota Small Business Development Center, P.O. Box 7308, University of North Dakota, Grand Forks, ND 58202; (701) 777-3700

Ohio Department of Development, P.O. Box 1001, Columbus, OH 43216-1001; (614) 466-2480

Oklahoma Small Business Development Center, Station A, P.O. Box 2584, Durant, OK 74701; (405) 924-0277

Oregon Small Business Development Center Network, 44 W. Broadway, Suite 501, Eugene, OR 97401; (503) 726-2250

Pennsylvania Small Business Development Center, 3733 Spruce Street, Room 423, Vance Hall, Philadelphia, PA 19104; (215) 898-1219

Rhode Island Small Business Development Center, Bryant College, 1150 Douglas Pike, Smithfield, RI 02917; (401) 232-6111

South Carolina Small Business Development Center, College of Business Administration, Room 652, University of South Carolina, Columbia, SC 29208; (803) 777-5118

South Dakota Small Business Development Center, University of South Dakota, School of Business, 414 E. Clark Street, Vermillion, SD 57069; (605) 677-5498

Tennessee Small Business Development Center, University of Memphis, South Campus, Building No. 1, Memphis, TN 38152; (901) 678-2500

Texas Small Business Development Center, 1402 Corinth Street, Corinth, TX 75215; (214) 565-5837

Utah Small Business Development Center, 8811 South 700 East, Salt Lake City, UT 84070; (801) 255-5878

Vermont Small Business Development Center, 60 Main Street, Suite 103, Burlington, VT 05401; (802) 658-9228

Virginia Small Business Development Center, P.O. Box 798, Richmond, VA 23206-0798; (804) 371-8258

Washington: Community Trade and Economic Development, 906 Columbia Street SW, P.O. Box 48300, Olympia, WA 98504-8300; (360) 753-2200

West Virginia Small Business Development Center, 950 Kanawha Boulevard, Charleston, WV 25301; (304) 558-2960

Wisconsin Small Business Development Center, 432 Lake Street, Madison, WI 53706; (608) 262-3878

Wyoming Small Business Development Center, 111 W. Second Street, Suite 502, Casper, WY 82601; (307) 234-6683

SBA DISTRICT OFFICES

The Small Business Administration has several types of field offices. Of these, the district offices offer the fullest range of services to small businesses.

Alabama: 2121 8th Avenue North, Suite 200, Birmingham, AL 35203-2398; (205) 731-1344

Alaska: 222 W. 8th. Avenue, Room A36, Anchorage, AK 99513-7559; (907) 271-4022

Arizona: 2828 N. Central Avenue, Suite 800, Phoenix, AZ 85004-1093; (602) 640-2316

Arkansas: 2120 Riverfront Drive, Suite 100, Little Rock, AR 72202; (501) 324-5871

California: 2719 N. Air Fresno Drive, Suite 107, Fresno, CA 93727-1547; (209) 487-5189

330 N. Brand Boulevard, Suite 1200, Glendale, CA 91203-2304; (818) 552-3210

550 West C Street, Suite 550, San Diego, CA 92188-3540; (619) 557-7250

211 Main Street, 4th Floor, San Francisco, CA 94105-1988; (615) 744-6820

660 J Street, Suite 215, Sacramento, CA 95814-2413; (916) 498-6410

200 W. Santa Ana Boulevard, Suite 700, Santa Ana, CA 92701; (714) 550-7420

Colorado: 721 19th Street, Suite 426, Denver, CO 80202-2599; (303) 844-3984

Connecticut: 330 Main Street, 2nd Floor, Hartford, CT 06106; (203) 240-4700

Delaware: (branch office) 824 N. Market Street, Suite 610, Wilmington, DE 19801-3011; (302) 573-6294

District of Columbia: 1110 Vermont Avenue NW, Suite 900, Washington, DC 20005; (202) 606-4000

Florida: 1320 S. Dixie Hwy., Suite 501, Coral Gables, FL 33146-2911; (305) 536-5521

7825 Baymeadows Way, Suite 100-B, Jacksonville, FL 32256-7504; (904) 443-1900

Georgia: 1720 Peachtree Road NW, 6th Floor, Atlanta, GA 30309; (404) 347-4749

Hawaii: 300 Ala Moana Boulevard, Room 2314, Honolulu, HI 96850-4981; (808) 541-2990

Idaho: 1020 Main Street, Suite 290, Boise, ID 83702-5745; (208) 334-1696

Illinois: 500 W. Madison Street, Suite 1250, Chicago, IL 60661-2511; (312) 353-4528

   511 W. Capitol Avenue, Suite 302, Springfield, IL 62704; (217) 492-4416

Indiana: 429 N. Pennsylvania Street, Suite 100, Indianapolis, IN 46204-1873; (317) 226-7272

Iowa: 216 6th Avenue SE, Suite 200, Cedar Rapids, IA 52401-1806; (319) 362-6405

   210 Walnut Street, Room 749, Des Moines, IA 50309-2186; (515) 284-4422

Kansas: 100 E. English Street, Suite 510, Wichita, KS 67202; (316) 269-6616

Kentucky: 600 Dr. Martin Luther King Jr. Place, Room 188, Louisville, KY 40202; (502) 582-5971

Louisiana: 365 Canal Street, Suite 2250, New Orleans, LA 70130; (504) 589-6685

Maine: 40 Western Avenue, Room 512, Augusta, ME 04330; (207) 622-8378

Maryland: 10 S. Howard Street, Suite 6220, Baltimore, MD 21201-2525; (410) 962-4392

Massachusetts: 10 Causeway Street, Room 265, Boston, MA 02222-1093; (617) 565-5590

Michigan: 477 Michigan Avenue, Room 515, Detroit, MI 48226; (313) 226-6075

Minnesota: 100 North 6th Street, Suite 610, Minneapolis, MN 55403-1563; (612) 370-2324

Mississippi: 101 W. Capital Street, Suite 400, Jackson, MS 39201; (601) 965-4378

Missouri: 323 West 8th Street, Suite 501, Kansas City, MO 64105; (816) 374-6708

   815 Olive Street, Room 242, St. Louis, MO 63101; (314) 539-6600

Montana: 301 South Park Avenue, Room 334, Helena, MT 59626; (406) 441-1081

Nebraska: 11145 Mill Valley Road, Omaha, NE 68154; (402) 221-4691

Nevada: 301 East Stewart Avenue, Room 301, Las Vegas, NV 89101; (702) 388-6611

New Hampshire: 143 N. Main Street, Suite 202, Concord, NH 03301; (603) 225-1400

New Jersey: Two Gateway Center, 4th Floor, Newark, NJ 07102; (201) 645-2434

New Mexico: 625 Silver SW, Suite 320, Albuquerque, NM 87102; (505) 766-1870

New York: 111 West Huron Street, Room 1311, Buffalo, NY 14202; (716) 551-4301

    26 Federal Plaza, Suite 31-00, New York, NY 10278; (212) 264-2454

    100 South Clinton Street, Suite 1071, Syracuse, NY 13260; (315) 448-0423

North Carolina: 200 North College Street, Suite A-2015, Charlotte, NC 28202-2137; (704) 344-6563

North Dakota: 657 Second Avenue North, Room 219, Fargo, ND 58108-3086; (701) 239-5131

Ohio: 1111 Superior Avenue, Suite 630, Cleveland, OH 44114-2507; (216) 522-4180

    2 Nationwide Plaza, Suite 1400, Columbus, OH 43215-2592; (614) 469-6860

Oklahoma: 210 Park Avenue, Suite 1300, Oklahoma City, OK 73102; (405) 231-5521

Oregon: 222 SW Columbia Street, Suite 500, Portland, OR 97201-6695; (503) 326-2682

Pennsylvania: 475 Allendale Road, Suite 201, King of Prussia, PA 19406; (610) 962-3800

    960 Penn Avenue, 5th Floor, Pittsburgh, PA 15222; (412) 644-2780

Puerto Rico: 252 Ponce De Leon Avenue, Suite 201, Hato Rey, PR 00918; (809) 766-5572

Rhode Island: 380 Westminster Mall, 5th Floor, Providence, RI 02903; (401) 528-4561

South Carolina: 1835 Assembly Street, Room 358, Columbia, SC 29201; (803) 765-5377

South Dakota: 110 South Phillips Avenue, Suite 200, Sioux Falls, SD 57102-1109; (605) 330-4231

Tennessee: 50 Vantage Way, Suite 201, Nashville, TN 37228-1500; (615) 736-5881

Texas: 4300 Amon Carter Boulevard, Suite 114, Ft. Worth, TX 76155; (817) 885-6500

   10737 Gateway West, Suite 320, El Paso, TX 79935; (915) 540-5676

   9301 Southwest Fwy., Suite 550, Houston, TX 77074-1591; (713) 773-6500

   222 E. Van Buren Street, Room 500, Harlingen, TX 78550-6855; (210) 427-8625

   1611 Tenth Street, Suite 200, Lubbock, TX 79401-2693; (806) 743-7462

   727 E. Durango Boulevard, Room A-527, San Antonio, TX 78206-1204; (210) 229-5900

Utah: 125 South State Street, Room 2237, Salt Lake City, UT 84138-1195; (801) 524-5804

Vermont: 87 State Street, Room 205, Montpelier, VT 05602; (802) 828-4422

Virginia: 1504 Santa Rosa Road, Suite 200, Richmond, VA 23229; (804) 771-2400

Washington: 1200 Sixth Avenue, Suite 1700, Seattle, WA 98101-1128; (206) 553-7310

West Virginia: 168 W. Main Street, 5th Floor, Clarksburg, WV 26301; (304) 623-5631

Wisconsin: 212 E. Washington Avenue, Room 213, Madison, WI 53703; (608) 264-5261

Wyoming: 100 East B Street, Room 4001, Casper, WY 82602-2839; (307) 261-6500

Appendix E

BUSINESS BANKS

Knowledge is power, and in 1996, for the second consecutive year, the Small Business Administration's (SBA) Office of Advocacy is giving entrepreneurs a powerful tool to help them obtain loans from commercial banks.

In its just-released *Micro Business Lending in the United States*, 1995 edition, the Office of Advocacy found that since the 1994 study was released, commercial bank credit to microfirms (defined as companies seeking loans of $100,000 or less) has increased by $2.7 billion.

Jere W. Glover, Chief Counsel for Advocacy at the SBA, attributes the increase to the study and the SBA's LowDoc loan program. "Low-Doc got banks in the habit of making smaller loans and convinced them to change the procedure to make it faster," says Glover. "Also, the fact that there is published information about the amount of loans they are making and where they rank in their state is a competitive incentive for banks to be in this market."

Banks have also become much more serious about courting small businesses, contends Glover, and adds that he has been visited by a number of banking executives touting their new small-business programs. "Each looked me straight in the eye and said, 'Jere, this year it's real.'" For banks, the need to truly become small-business friendly is powerful, Glover says, because an entrepreneur whose institution doesn't make small-business loans might just move to a more welcoming bank.

The SBA's report, which for the first time provides the number and amount of small-business loans, relies on the call report data filed quarterly by financial institutions, although Glover acknowledges the study has its limitations. One problem is that call reports don't provide separate information on SBA-guaranteed lending. This means financial institutions that are active SBA lenders but sell the guaranteed portion of their loans in the secondary market are likely to be underrepresented in the rankings because the call reports contain only information on the unguaranteed portion of their SBA loans.

Some banks may also be making microloans through credit cards, second mortgages, or other forms of consumer credit, which again would preclude their small-business activities from appearing in the reports. Nor do call reports reflect demand conditions. Consequently, a bank with one or fewer branches in a geographic area, or one in a location where few people seek microloans, will appear not to be small-business friendly.

Even with these limitations, however, Glover believes the study can be a valuable tool for an entrepreneur seeking capital. In addition to helping pinpoint friendly banks, he says, the report might help turn around unfriendly ones. "You could go in and talk to a bank and say, 'Look, you only made 100 small-business loans. You ought to be making more, and I'm here to help you. Here's my application.'" And that's a powerful tool for an entrepreneur, concludes Glover.

Cynthia E. Griffin

The SBA defines microbusiness-friendly banks as those whose microloans (loans of under $100,000) comprise at least 25 percent of their total assets. Following is a list of the top banks in each state. Please note that not all states have lenders that meet this criterion.

Alabama

CB&T Bank of Russell City, P.O. Box 2400, Phenix City, AL 36838-2400; (334) 297-7000

First Bank of Dothan, 1479 W. Main Street, Dothan, AL 36301; (334) 794-8090

First National Bank of Union Springs, P.O. Box 570, Union Springs, AL 36089; (334) 738-2060

Independent Bank of Oxford, 402 Main Street, Oxford, AL 36203; (205) 835-1776

Peoples Exchange Bank of Monroe County, 1112 Main Street, Beatrice, AL 36425; (334) 789-2490

Southland Bank, 3299 Ross Clark Circle, Dothan, AL 36303; (334) 671-4000

Arizona

Bank of Casa Grande Valley, 1300 E. Florence Boulevard, Casa Grande, AZ 85222; (520) 836-4666

Arkansas

Bank of Eureka Springs, P.O. Box 309, Eureka Springs, AR 72632; (501) 253-8241

Bank of Little Rock, 305 E. Broadway, North Little Rock, AR 72116; (501) 228-9818

Calhoun County Bank, P.O. Box 8, Hampton, AR 71744; (501) 798-2207

First Bank of Arkansas, 500 N. Falls, Wynne, AR 72396; (501) 238-2265

First Bank of Arkansas, 825 Hwy. 463, Trumann, AR 72472; (501) 483-6433

Stephens Security Bank, 108 Ruby Street, Stephens, AR 71764; (501) 786-5416

California

Centennial Thrift & Loan Association, 18837 Brookhurst, #100, Fountain Valley, CA 92708; (714) 964-9111

Inland Community Bank, N.A., 851 W. Foothill Boulevard, Rialto, CA 92376; (909) 874-4444

Monument National Bank, 1450 N. Norma Avenue, Ridgecrest, CA 93555; (619) 446-3576

North State National Bank, P.O. Box 3235, Chico, CA 95927; (916) 893-0415

Redding Bank of Commerce, 1177 Placer Street, Redding, CA 96001; (916) 241-2265

Six Rivers National Bank, 402F Frank Street, Eureka, CA 95501; (707) 443-8400

Taft National Bank, 523 Cascade Place, Taft, CA 93268; (805) 763-5151

Colorado

Bank at Broadmoor, 4 Elm Avenue, Colorado Springs, CO 80906; (719) 633-2695

Bank of Durango, 15 Bodo Drive, P.O. Drawer G, Durango, CO 81302; (970) 259-5500

Bank of Grand Junction, 2415 F Road, Grand Junction, CO 81505; (970) 241-9000

Bank of the Southwest, N.A., 523 San Juan Street, Pagosa Springs, CO 81147; (970) 264-4111

Cheyenne Mountain Bank, 1580 E. Cheyenne Mtn. Boulevard, Colorado Springs, CO 80906; (719) 579-9150

Citizens Bank of Pagosa Springs, P.O. Box 1508, Pagosa Springs, CO 81147; (970) 264-2235

Clear Creek National Bank, P.O. Box 337, Georgetown, CO 80444-0337; (303) 569-2393

Eagle Bank of Broomfield, 1990 W. Tenth Avenue, Broomfield, CO 80020; (303) 460-9991

Farmers Bank, 100 Elm Avenue, Eaton, CO 80615; (970) 454-3434

First State Bank, P.O. Box 3309, Idaho Springs, CO 80452; (303) 567-2696

First State Bank of Colorado Springs, 1776 S. Nevada Avenue, Colorado Springs, CO 80906; (719) 475-1776

First State Bank of Hotchkiss, P.O. Box 38, Hotchkiss, CO 81419; (970) 872-3111

Fort Morgan State Bank, 520 Sherman Street, Fort Morgan, CO 80701; (970) 867-3319

Gunnison Bank & Trust Co., 232 W. Tomichi Avenue, Gunnison, CO 81230; (970) 641-0320

Lafayette State Bank, 811 S. Public Road, Lafayette, CO 80026; (303) 666-0777

Mountain National Bank, 361 W. Hwy. 24, Woodland Park, CO 80863; (719) 687-3012

Olathe State Bank, 302 Main Street, Olathe, CO 81425; (970) 323-5565

Florida

American Bank & Trust Co., 101 W. Garden Street, Pensacola, FL 32501; (904) 432-2481

Apalachicola State Bank, P.O. Box 370, Apalachicola, FL 32329; (904) 653-8805

C & L Bank of Blountstown, P.O. Box 534, Blountstown, FL 32424; (904) 674-5900

Dadeland Bank, 7545 N. Kendal, Miami, FL 33156; (305) 667-8401

First American Bank of Indian River County, 4000 20th Street, Vero Beach, FL 32960; (407) 567-0552

First National Bank of Southwest Florida, 2724 Del Prado Boulevard, Cape Coral, FL 33904; (941) 772-2220

First National Bank of Wauchula, 406 N. Sixth Avenue, Wauchula, FL 33873; (941) 773-4136

Putnam State Bank, 350 State Road, 19 North, Palatka, FL 32177; (904) 328-5600

Seminole National Bank, P.O. Box 2057, Sanford, FL 32772; (407) 330-5190

South Hillsborough Community Bank, P.O. Box 3430, Apollo Beach, FL 33572; (813) 645-0886

Wewahitchka State Bank, 125 N. Main Street, Wewahitchka, FL 32465; (904) 639-2222

Georgia

Adel Banking Co., P.O. Box 191, Adel, GA 31620; (912) 896-7402

Bank Atlanta, 1221 Clairmont Road, Decatur, GA 30030; (404) 320-3300

Bank of Dudley, P.O. Box 7, Dudley, GA 31022; (912) 676-3196

Bank of Milan, P.O. Box 38, Milan, GA 31060; (912) 362-4483

Bank of Thomas County, 2484 E. Pinetree Boulevard, Thomasville, GA 31799; (912) 226-5755

Bank of Toccoa, P.O. Box 430, Toccoa, GA 30577; (706) 886-9421

Bryan Bank & Trust, P.O. Box 1299, Richmond Hill, GA 31324; (912) 756-4444

Coastal Bank, P.O. Box 529, Hinesville, GA 31310; (912) 368-2265

Cordele Banking Co., 1620 16th Avenue E., Cordele, GA 31015; (912) 273-2416

Farmers & Merchants Bank, 301 W. Fourth Street, Adel, GA 31620; (912) 896-4585

First Bank & Trust, P.O. Box 545, Carnesville, GA 30521; (706) 384-4545

First National Bank of Alma, P.O. Box 2028, Alma, GA 31510; (912) 632-7262

First National Bank of Barnesville, 315 Thomaston Street, Barnesville, GA 30204; (770) 358-1100

First National Bank of Effingham, 501 S. Laurel, Springfield, GA 31329; (912) 754-6111

McIntosh State Bank, 210 S. Oak Street, Jackson, GA 30233; (770) 775-8300

Patterson Bank, 6365 Hwy. 84, Patterson, GA 31557; (912) 647-5332

White County Bank, 153 E. Kytle Street, Cleveland, GA 30528; (706) 865-3151

Idaho

Panhandle State Bank, P. O. Box 967, Sandpoint, ID 83864; (208) 263-0505

Twin River National Bank, 1507 G Street, Lewiston, ID 83501; (208) 743-2565

Illinois

Ashland State Bank, 9443 S. Ashland Avenue, Chicago, IL 60620; (312) 445-9300

Bank of Bourbonnais, 1 Heritage Plaza, Bourbonnais, IL 60914; (815) 933-0570

Bank of Edwardsville, 330 W. Vandalia, Edwardsville, IL 62025; (618) 656-0057

Banterra Bank of Gallatin County, P.O. Box 680, El Dorado, IL 62979; (618) 272-3151

Du Quoin State Bank, 15 E. Main, P.O. Box 468, Du Quoin, IL 62832; (618) 542-2111

First National Bank of Antioch, 485 Lake Street, Antioch, IL 60002; (708) 395-3111

First National Bank of Danville, 1 Town Center, Danville, IL 61832; (217) 442-0362

First National Bank of Wheaton, 1151 E. Butterfield Road, Wheaton, IL 60187; (708) 260-2200

Mercantile Trust & Savings Bank, 440 Maine Street, Quincy, IL 62301; (217) 223-7300

Northwest Bank of Rockford, 125 Phelps Avenue, Rockford, IL 61108; (815) 987-4550

Peoples National Bank, 108 S. Washington Street, McLeansboro, IL 62859; (618) 643-4303

State Bank of Geneva, P.O. Box 108, Geneva, IL 60134; (708) 232-3200

West Pointe Bank & Trust Co., 5701 W. Main Street, Belleville, IL 62223; (618) 234-5700

Indiana

Farmers State Bank, P.O. Box 455, Mentone, IN 46539; (219) 353-7521

Jackson County Bank, 125 S. Chestnut, Seymour, IN 47274; (812) 522-3607

Kansas

Admire Bank & Trust Co., 1104 E. 12th Avenue, P.O. Box 1047, Emporia, KS 66801; (316) 343-1940

Coffeyville State Bank, 313 W. 9th Street, P.O. Box 219, Coffeyville, KS 67337; (316) 251-1313

First National Bank of Wamego, P.O. Box 226, Wamego, KS 66547; (913) 456-2221

First National Bank, 2160 W. Hwy. 50, Emporia, KS 66801; (316) 343-1010

Peoples Bank & Trust Co., P.O. Box 1226, McPherson, KS 67460; (316) 241-2100

Kentucky

Bank of Ohio County, 11658 State Rte. 69 N., P.O. Box 127, Dundee, KY 42338; (502) 276-3631

Citizens Deposit Bank & Trust, 400 Second Street, Vanceburg, KY 41179; (606) 796-3001

Community First Bank, P.O. Box 198, Mount Olivet, KY 41064; (606) 724-5403

Farmers State Bank, P.O. Box 68, Main Street, Booneville, KY 41314; (606) 593-5151

First & Farmers Bank of Somerset Inc., 100 Public Sq., Somerset, KY 42501; (606) 679-7451

First Southern National Bank of Fayette County, 3060 Harrodsburg Road, Lexington, KY 40503; (606) 223-3743

First Southern National Bank of Jessamine County, 980 N. Main Street, P.O. Box 430, Nicholasville, KY 40356; (606) 885-1222

First Southern National Bank of Lincoln County, Main Street, P.O. Box 27, Hustonville, KY 40437; (606) 346-4921

First Southern National Bank of Wayne County, 216 N. Main Street, P.O. Box 489, Monticello, KY 42633; (606) 348-8421

Franklin Bank & Trust Co., 317 N. Main Street, Franklin, KY 42134; (502) 586-7121

Leitchfield Deposit Bank & Trust Co., 76 Public Sq., P.O. Box 188, Leitchfield, KY 42755-0188; (502) 259-5611

Peoples Bank & Trust Co., 524 Main Street, Hazard, KY 41701; (606) 436-2161

Louisiana

Acadian Bank, 1001 Canal Boulevard, Thibodaux, LA 70301; (504) 446-8161

Acadia State Bank, 2237 S. Acadian Thruway, #100, Baton Rouge, LA 70808; (504) 924-0984

Bank of Jackson, P.O. Box 248, Jackson, LA 70748; (504) 634-7741

First Bank of Natchitoches, 315 Royal, Natchitoches, LA 71457; (318) 352-9089

Gulf Coast Bank, 221 S. State Street, Abbeville, LA 70510; (318) 893-5010

Metro Bank, 3417 Williams Boulevard, Kenner, LA 70065; (504) 443-5626

Peoples State Bank, 880 San Antonio Avenue, Many, LA 71449; (318) 256-2071

Progressive National Bank of Desoto Parish, P.O. Box 233, Mansfield, LA 71052; (318) 872-3661

Sabine State Bank & Trust Co., P.O. Box 670, Many, LA 71449; (318) 256-7000

Southeast National Bank, P.O. Box 2488, Hammond, LA 70404; (504) 542-9700

Maine

United Bank, 145 Exchange Street, Bangor, ME 04401; (207) 942-5263

Katahdin Trust Co., Main Street, P.O. Box I, Patten, ME 04765; (207) 528-2211

Maryland

Commercial & Farmers Bank, 8593 Baltimore National Pike, Ellicott City, MD 21043; (410) 465-0900

Home Bank, 8305 Langmaid Road, P.O. Box 10, Newark, MD 21841; (410) 632-2151

Maryland Permanent Bank & Trust Co., 9612 Reisterstown Road, Owings Mills, MD 21117; (410) 356-4411

Massachusetts

Enterprise Bank & Trust Co., 222 Merrimack Street, Lowell, MA 01852; (508) 459-9000

Michigan

1st Bank, 502 W. Houghton, West Branch, MI 48661; (517) 345-7900

First Community Bank, 200 E. Main, Harbor Springs, MI 49740; (616) 526-2114

First National Bank in Ontonagon, 601 River Street, Ontonagon, MI 49953; (906) 884-4114

Grant State Bank, 10 W. Main, P.O. Box 38, Grant, MI 49327-0038; (616) 834-5685

MFC First National Bank, 1205 Ludington Street, Escanaba, MI 49829; (906) 786-5010

MFC First National Bank, 962 First Street, Menominee, MI 49858; (906) 863-5523

MFC First National Bank, P.O. Box 191, Iron River, MI 49935; (906) 265-5144

Peoples State Bank of Munising, 100 E. Superior, P.O. Box 158, Munising, MI 49862; (906) 387-2006

Minnesota

Chisago State Bank, 1135 Lake Boulevard, P.O. Box G, Chisago City, MN 55013; (612) 257-6561

CreditAmerica Saving Co., 2019 S. 6th Street, Brainerd, MN 56401; (218) 829-1484

First National Bank and Trust, 101 NW Second Street, P.O. Box 190, Pipestone, MN 56164; (507) 825-3344

Grand Marais State Bank, P.O. Box 100, Grand Marais, MN 55604; (218) 387-2441

Highland Bank, 701 Central Avenue E., Saint Michael, MN 55376; (612) 497-2131

Itasca State Bank, P.O. Box 160, Grand Rapids, MN 55744; (218) 327-1121

Lakes State Bank, P.O. Box 366, Pequot Lakes, MN 56472; (218) 568-4473

Mountain Iron First State Bank, P.O. Box 415, Mountain Iron, MN 55768; (218) 735-8201

Princeton Bank, 202 S. LaGrande Avenue, Princeton, MN 55371; (612) 389-2020

Roseville Community Bank, N.A., 1501 W. County Road, Suite C, Roseville, MN 55113; (612) 631-1040

Saint Stephen State Bank, 2 Central Avenue S, Saint Stephen, MN 56375; (612) 251-0902

State Bank of Delano, P.O. Box 530, Delano, MN 55328; (612) 972-2935

Town & Country Bank of Almelund, P.O. Box 88, Almelund, MN 55002; (612) 583-2035

United Community Bank, 155 2nd Street SW, P.O. Box 249, Perham, MN 56573; (218) 346-5700

Mississippi

Community Bank, P.O. Box 28, Indianola, MS 38751; (601) 887-4513

First Bank, P.O. Box 808, McComb, MS 39648; (601) 684-2231

Pike County National Bank, 350 Rawls Drive, McComb, MS 39648; (601) 684-7575

Union Planters Bank of Mississippi, P.O. Box 947, Grenada, MS 38902; (601) 227-3361

Missouri

Allegiant Bank, 2550 Schuetz Road, Maryland Heights, MO 63043; (314) 534-3000

Bank of Warrensburg, P.O. Box 477, Warrensburg, MO 64093; (816) 429-2101

Carter County State Bank, P.O. Box 129, Van Buren, MO 63965; (314) 323-4246

Centennial Bank, 9850 Street Charles Rock Road, St. Ann, MO 63074; (314) 423-6800

Central Bank of Kansas City, 2301 Independence Boulevard, Kansas City, MO 64124; (816) 483-1210

Citizens National Bank of Springfield, 1465 E. Sunshine, Springfield, MO 65804; (417) 887-4200

Commerce-Warren County Bank, 104 N. Hwy. 47, Warrenton, MO 63383; (314) 456-3441

Community Bank of Raymore, P.O. Box 200, Raymore, MO 64083; (816) 322-2100

Community Bank of the Ozarks, P.O. Box 43, Sunrise Beach, MO 65079; (314) 374-5245

First Bank of Kansas City, 3901 Main Street, Kansas City, MO 64111; (816) 561-8866

First Commercial Bank, P.O. Box 195, Gideon, MO 63848; (314) 448-3514

First Midwest Bank, P.O. Box 160, Poplar Bluff, MO 63902; (573) 785-8461

First Missouri State Bank, P.O. Box 430, Poplar Bluff, MO 63902; (573) 785-6800

First State Bank of Joplin, P.O. Box 1373, Joplin, MO 64802; (417) 623-8860

Lawson Bank, 401 N. Pennsylvania, Lawson, MO 64062; (816) 296-3242

Mercantile Bank of Poplar Bluff, P.O. Box 700, Poplar Bluff, MO 63902; (314) 785-4671

Northland National Bank, 99 N.E. 72nd Street, Gladstone, MO 64118; (816) 436-3500

Peoples Bank, P.O. Box H, Cuba, MO 65453; (573) 885-2511

Peoples Bank & Trust Co. of Lincoln County, P.O. Box G, Troy, MO 63379; (314) 528-7001

Rockwood Bank, P.O. Box 710, Eureka, MO 63025; (314) 938-9222

United Bank of Union, P.O. Box 500, Union, MO 63084; (314) 583-2555

Montana

BankWest, N.A., P.O. Box 7070, Kalispell, MT 59904; (406) 758-2256

Bitterroot Valley Bank, LoLo Shopping Center, P.O. Box 9, LoLo, MT 59847; (406) 273-2400

Citizens State Bank, P.O. Box 393, Hamilton, MT 59840; (406) 363-3551

First Bank of Lincoln, P.O. Box 9, Lincoln, MT 59639; (406) 362-4248

First Bank of Montana, 2801 Brooks, P.O. Box 4787, Thompson Falls, MT 59806; (406) 523-2300

First Boulder Valley Bank, P.O. Box 207, Boulder, MT 59632; (406) 225-3351

First Citizens Bank, N.A., P.O. Box 1728, Columbia Falls, MT 59912; (406) 892-2122

First Security Bank of West Yellowstone, P.O. Box 550, West Yellowstone, MT 59758; (406) 646-7646

Mountain Bank, Third & Spokane, Whitefish, MT 59937; (406) 862-2551

Mountain West Bank of Helena, 1225 Cedar Street, Helena, MT 59604; (406) 449-2265

Rocky Mountain Bank, 2615 King Avenue W., Billings, MT 59102; (406) 656-3140

State Bank and Trust Co., P.O. Box 1257, Dillon, MT 59725; (406) 683-2393

United States National Bank of Red Lodge, P.O. Box 910, Red Lodge, MT 59068; (406) 446-1422

Valley Bank of Glasgow, 110 Sixth Street S., Glasgow, MT 59230; (406) 228-4364

Valley Bank of Helena, 3030 N. Montana Avenue, Helena, MT 59601; 406) 443-7443

Valley Bank of Ronan, P.O. Box 129, Ronan, MT 59864; (406) 676-2000

Nebraska

American National Bank of Fremont, 99 W. Sixth Street, Fremont, NE 68025; (402) 727-8600

City State Bank, P.O. Box 370, Sutton, NE 68979; (402) 773-5521

Dakota County State Bank, 2024 Dakota Avenue, South Sioux City, NE 68776; (402) 494-4215

First National Bank, 100 W. Fletcher Avenue, Lincoln, NE 68521; (402) 435-7233

New Mexico

Bank Of The Southwest, 226 N. Main, Roswell, NM 88201; (505) 625-1122

Centinel Bank of Taos, P.O. Box 828, Taos, NM 87571; (505) 758-6700

First National Bank, P.O. Box 1107, Tucumcari, NM 88401; (505) 461-3602

Valley Bank Of Commerce, 217 W. Second, Roswell, NM 88201; (505) 623-2265

Valley National Bank, 333 Riverside Drive, Espanola, NM 87532; (505) 753-2136

New York

Continental Bank, 118 Seventh Street, Garden City, NY 11530; (516) 741-2400

Habib American Bank, 99 Madison Avenue, New York, NY 10016; (212) 532-4444

Solvay Bank, 1537 Milton Avenue, Solvay, NY 13209; (315) 468-1661

North Carolina

Bank of Currituck, P.O. Box 6, Moyock, NC 27958; (919) 435-6331

Old North State Bank, P.O. Box 995, King, NC 27021; (910) 983-0682

Triangle Bank, 4300 Glenwood Avenue, Raleigh, NC 27612; (919) 881-0455

United National Bank, 320 Green Street, Fayetteville, NC 28301; (910) 483-1131

Yadkin Valley Bank & Trust Co., 110 W. Market Street, Elkin, NC 28621; (910) 526-6300

North Dakota

First Southwest Bank of Bismarck, P.O. Box 777, Bismarck, ND 58502; (701) 223-6050

First Western Bank & Trust, 900 S. Broadway, Minot, ND 58701; (701) 852-3711

Kirkwood Bank & Trust Co., 919 S. Seventh Street, Bismarck, ND 58506; (701) 258-6550

Page State Bank, P.O. Box 5, Page, ND 58064; (701) 668-2261

Union State Bank of Fargo, P.O. Box 9399, Fargo, ND 58106-9399; (701) 282-4598

Ohio

Citizens National Bank of Norwalk, 12 E. Main Street, Norwalk, OH 44857; (419) 668-3736

First Bank of Marietta, 320 Front Street, Marietta, OH 45750; (614) 373-4904

New Richmond National Bank, 110 Front Street, New Richmond, OH 45157; (513) 553-3101

Peoples Banking Co., 1330 N. Main Street, Findlay, OH 45840; (419) 423-4741

Oklahoma

American State Bank, P.O. Box 280, Broken Bow, OK 74728; (405) 584-9135

Bank of Cushing & Trust Company, 224 E. Broadway, Cushing, OK 74023; (918) 225-2010

Bank of Inola, 11 W. Commercial, Inola, OK 74036; (918) 543-2421

Bank of Western Oklahoma, 201 E. Broadway, Elk City, OK 73644; (405) 225-3434

Citizens Bank of Tulsa, 2500 W. Edison, Tulsa, OK 74127; (918) 582-2600

Community State Bank, 103 S. Main, P.O. Box 220, Cashion, OK 73016; (405) 433-2675

First Bank of Hennessey, 101 N. Main, P.O. Box 724, Hennessey, OK 73742; (405) 853-2530

First National Bank of Roland, P.O. Box 308, Roland, OK 74954; (918) 427-7474

Peoples National Bank, P.O. Box 599, Kingfisher, OK 73750; (405) 375-5911

Union National Bank of Chandler, 1001 Manville, Drawer 278, Chandler, OK 74834; (405) 258-1795

Oregon

Bank of Astoria, 1122 Duane Street, Astoria, OR 97103; (503) 325-2228

Bank of Wallowa County, P.O. Box X, Joseph, OR 97846; (503) 432-9050

Columbia River Banking Company, 316 E. Third Street, The Dalles, OR 97058; (541) 298-6647

Valley Commercial Bank, P.O. Box 766, Forest Grove, OR 91716; (503) 359-4495

Pennsylvania

First Columbia Bank & Trust Co., 11 W. Main Street, Bloomsburg, PA 17815; (717) 784-1660

South Carolina

Anderson Brothers Bank, P.O. Box 310, Mullins, SC 29574; (803) 464-6271

Bank of Walterboro, 1002 N. Jefferies Boulevard, Walterboro, SC 29488; (803) 549-2265

Bank of York, P.O. Box 339, York, SC 29745; (803) 684-2265

Enterprise Bank of South Carolina, 206 E. Broadway, Erhardt, SC 29081; (803) 267-3191

M.S. Bailey & Son, Bankers, 211 N. Broad Street, Clinton, SC 29325; (803) 833-1910

Saluda County Bank, 200 N. Main Street, P.O. Box 247, Saluda, SC 29138; (803) 445-8156

Sandhills Bank, P.O. Box 127, Bethune, SC 29009; (803) 334-6241

South Dakota

American State Bank of Rapid City, P.O. Box 2530, Rapid City, SD 57709; (605) 348-3322

Tennessee

American City Bank, 340 W. Lincoln Street, Tullahoma, TN 37388; (615) 455-0026

Community Bank & Trust Co., P.O. Box 866, Lawrenceburg, TN 38464; (615) 762-5518

First State Bank, 301 Main Street, Jacksboro, TN 37757; (423) 562-7443

Lincoln County Bank, P.O. Box 677, Fayetteville, TN 37334; (615) 433-7041

Traders National Bank, 120 N. Jackson Street, Tullahoma, TN 37388; (615) 455-3426

Texas

Bloomburg State Bank, P.O. Box 155, Bloomburg, TX 75556; (903) 728-5211

Charter Bank—Northwest, 10502 Leopard Street, Corpus Christi, TX 78410; (512) 241-7681

Citizen State Bank, P.O. Box 4007, Corpus Christi, TX 78469; (512) 887-3000

East Texas National Bank, P.O. Box 8109, Marshall, TX 75671; (903) 935-1331

First Bank of Conroe, N.A., 1426 Loop 336, Conroe, TX 77304; (409) 760-1888

First Commercial Capital, 1336 E. Court, Seguin, TX 78155; (210) 379-8390

First International Bank, P.O. Box 629, Bedford, TX 76095; (817) 354-8400

First National Bank, P.O. Box 37, Newton, TX 75966; (409) 379-8587

First State Bank, 201 S. Old Betsy Road, Keene, TX 76059; (817) 645-7060

First Waco National Bank, 1700 N. Valley Mills Drive, Waco, TX 76710; (817) 776-0160

Founders National Bank, Skillman, 9696 Skillman, #150, Dallas, TX 75243; (214) 340-7400

Guaranty Bank, P.O. Box 1158, Mount Pleasant, TX 75456-1158; (903) 572-9881

Heritage Bank, 557 Ovilla Road, Red Oak, TX 75154; (214) 617-0222

Home State Bank, P.O. Box 219, Rochester, TX 79544; (817) 743-3511

Inter National Bank, 1700 S. Tenth Street, McAllen, TX 78505; (210) 630-1700

Justin State Bank, 412 S. Hwy. 156, Justin, TX 76247; (817) 648-2753

Lone Star National Bank, P.O. Box 1127, Pharr, TX 78577; (210) 781-4321

Midland American Bank, 401 W. Texas, Midland, TX 79701; (915) 687-3013

National Bank of Andrews, 1501 N. Main, Andrews, TX 79714; (915) 523-2800

North Texas Bank & Trust Co., P.O. Box 1299, Gainesville, TX 76240; (817) 665-8282

Security State Bank & Trust, P.O. Box 471, Fredericksburg, TX 78624; (210) 997-7575

Sundown State Bank, Fifth & Slaughter, Sundown, TX 79372; (806) 229-2111

Surety Bank, 600 S. First, Lufkin, TX 75901; (409) 632-5541

Texas Bank, 102 N. Main, Weatherford, TX 76086; (817) 594-8721

Texas Bank, 4101 John Ben Sheppard Pkwy., Odessa, TX 79762; (915) 368-0931

Texas Bank, P.O. Box 1990, Henderson, TX 75653; (903) 657-1466

United Bank & Trust, P.O. Box 3157, Abilene, TX 79604; (915) 676-3800

Van Horn State Bank, 100 E. Broadway Street, Van Horn, TX 79855; (915) 283-2283

Western National Bank, 8200A Nashville, Lubbock, TX 79423; (806) 794-8300

Woodhaven National Bank, 6750 Bridge Street, Fort Worth, TX 76112; (817) 496-6700

Utah

Advanta Financial Corp., 11850 S. Election Drive, Salt Lake City, UT 84020; (801) 264-2920

Bonneville Bank, 1675 N. 200 W., Provo, UT 84604; (801) 374-9500

Cache Valley Bank, 101 N. Main, Logan, UT 84321; (801) 753-3020

First Commerce Bank, 5 E. 1400 North, Logan, UT 84341; (801) 752-7102

Vermont

Union Bank, 20 Main Street, P.O. Box 667, Morrisville, VT 05661; (802) 888-6600

Virginia

Benchmark Community Bank, 100 S. Broad Street, Kenbridge, VA 23944; (804) 676-8444

First Bank & Trust Co., 236 W. Main Street, Lebanon, VA 24266; (540) 889-4622

Highlands Union Bank, P.O. Box 1128, Abingdon, VA 24212; (540) 628-9181

Marathon Bank, P.O. Box 998, Stephens City, VA 22655; (540) 636-9241

Virginia Community Bank, 408 E. Main Street, Louisa, VA 23093; (540) 967-2111

Washington

Bank of Fife, 1507 54th Avenue E., Fife, WA 98424; (206) 922-7870

Bank of Pullman, 300 E. Main, Pullman, WA 99163; (509) 332-1561

Bank of the West, P.O. Box 1597, Walla Walla, WA 99362; (509) 527-3800

Farmers State Bank, P.O. Box 489, Winthrop, WA 98862; (509) 996-2243

First American State Bank, 1100 Harrison Avenue, Centralia, WA 98531; (360) 736-0722

First National Bank of Port Orchard, 1488 Olney Avenue S.E., Port Orchard, WA 98366; (360) 895-2265

National Bank of Tukwila, 505 Industry Drive, Tukwila, WA 98138; (206) 575-1445

Pend Oreille Bank of Washington, P.O. Box 1530, Newport, WA 99156; (509) 447-5641

Towne Bank, P.O. Box 645, Woodinville, WA 98072; (206) 486-2265

West Virginia

Traders Bank, 303 Main Street, Spencer, WV 25276; (304) 927-3340

Wisconsin

Bank of Fort Atkinson, 200 Sherman Avenue W., Fort Atkinson, WI 53538; (414) 563-2461

Bank of Mauston, 503 State Road 82, Mauston, WI 53948; (608) 847-6200

Bank of Milton, P.O. Box 217, Milton, WI 53563; (608) 868-7672

Bradley Bank, 227-W. Wisconsin Avenue, Tomahawk, WI 54487; (715) 453-2112

Cambridge State Bank, 221 W. Main Street, Cambridge, WI 53523; (608) 423-3226

Citizens Bank, N.A., 129 E. Division Street, Shawano, WI 54166; (715) 526-6131

Community Bank and Trust Co., 1214 Tower Avenue, Superior, WI 54880; (715) 392-8241

Community Bank of Grafton, 2090 Wisconsin Avenue, Grafton, WI 53024; (414) 375-9150

Community First State Bank, 118 Elm Street, Spooner, WI 54801; (715) 635-2161

DeForest-Morrisonville Bank, 321 N. Main Street, DeForest, WI 53532; (608) 846-3711

F & M Bank, P.O. Box 890, Pulaski, WI 54162; (414) 822-3225

F & M Bank—New London, 401 N. Water Street, New London, WI 54961; (414) 982-4410

F & M Bank Kaukauna, Fourth Street Plaza, P.O. Box 920, Kaukauna, WI 54130; (414) 766-8160

F & M Bank Portage City, 31 Park Ridge, P.O. Box 808, Stevens Point, WI 54481; (715) 341-6691

F & M Bank Winnebego County, P.O. Box 501, Omro, WI 54963-0501; (414) 685-2771

Fidelity National Bank, 215 S. Eighth Street, Medford, WI 54451; (715) 748-5333

First National Bank, P.O. Box 269, Waupaca, WI 54981; (715) 258-5511

First National Bank Fox Valley, 161 Main Street, Menasha, WI 54952; (414) 729-6900

First National Bank of Hartford, 116 W. Sumner Street, Hartford, WI 53027; (414) 673-5800

First National Bank of New Richmond, 109 E. 2nd Street, New Richmond, WI 54017; (715) 246-6901

First National Bank of Park Falls, 110 N. Second Avenue, Park Falls, WI 54552; (715) 762-2411

First National Bank of Park Falls, P.O. Box 250, Park Falls, WI 54552; (715) 762-2411

First National Bank of Platteville, 170 W. Main Street, Platteville, WI 53818; (608) 348-7777

Green Lake State Bank, 515 Hill Street, Green Lake, WI 54941; (414) 294-3369

Headwaters State Bank, P.O. Box 149, Land O'Lakes, WI 54540; (715) 547-3383

Heritage Bank of Hayward, Hwy. 63 N., Hayward, WI 54843; (715) 634-2611

Ixonia State Bank, W. 1195 Marietta Avenue, Ixonia, WI 53036; (414) 567-2881

Lincoln County Bank, 401 W. Main Street, Merrill, WI 54452; (715) 536-8301

M & I Bank, 100 Main Street E., Ashland, WI 54806; (715) 682-3422

M & I Merchants Bank, 7 N. Brown Street, Rhinelander, WI 54501; (715) 369-3000

The Necedah Bank, 212 Main Street, Necedah, WI 54646; (608) 565-2296

Park Bank, 1200 Main Street, Holmen, WI 54636; (608) 526-2265

The RiverBank, 204 3rd Avenue, Osceola, WI 54020; (715) 294-2183

Security State Bank, P.O. Box 157, Iron River, WI 54847; (715) 372-4242

State Bank of Chilton, 26 E. Main Street, Chilton, WI 53014; (414) 849-9371

State Bank of Stockbridge, 401 W. Lake Street, P.O. Box 38, Stockbridge, WI 53088; (414) 439-1414

Stephenson National Bank & Trust, 1820 Hall Avenue, Marinette, WI 54143; (715) 732-1650

Wyoming

Equality State Bank, P.O. Box 1710, Cheyenne, WY 82003; (307) 635-1101

First Interstate Bank of Commerce, 4 S. Main Street, Sheridan, WY 82801; (307) 674-7411

Frontier Bank of Laramie County, 1501 S. Greeley Hwy., Cheyenne, WY 82007; (307) 637-7244

Riverton State Bank, 616 N. Federal, Riverton, WY 82501; (307) 856-2265

Western Bank Cheyenne, P.O. Box 127, Cheyenne, WY 82001; (307) 637-7333

GLOSSARY

accounts receivable: A record used to account for the total number of sales made through the extension of credit.

accrual basis: An accounting method used for recordkeeping purposes in which all income and expenses are charged to the period to which they apply, whether money has actually changed hands or not.

acid-test ratio: An analysis method used to measure the liquidity of a business by dividing total liquid assets by current liabilities.

asset earning power: A common profitability measure used to determine the profitability of a business by taking its total earnings before taxes and dividing them by total assets.

Audit Bureau of Circulation (ABC): A third-party organization that verifies the circulation of print media through periodical audits.

balance sheet: A financial statement used to report a business's total assets, liabilities, and equity.

bonding: Generally used by service companies as a guarantee to their clients that they have the necessary ability and financial backing to meet their obligations.

book-out policy: A policy whereby hotels "hold" meeting rooms for groups that also book blocks of guest rooms. Generally speaking, only hotels in major metropolitan areas employ book-out policies.

break-even analysis: An analysis method used to determine the number of jobs or products that a business needs to sell to pay its expenses and start making a profit.

business identity: A kind of *executive suite* arrangement without the offices, a business identity service provides mail collection and personalized phone answering services, along with copy centers and meeting rooms that can be scheduled when "tenants" need to meet with clients. Such a service can be useful for home-based entrepreneurs desiring a more professional image.

business plan: A plan used to chart a new or ongoing business's strategies, sales projections, and key personnel in order to obtain financing and provide a strategic foundation for growth.

Business Publications Audit (BPA): Like the Audit Bureau of Circulation, the BPA is a third-party organization that verifies the circulation of print media through periodical audits.

capitalization: Every company has capital, in the form of money, common stock, long-term debt, or in some combination of all three. It is possible to have too much capital (in which case the firm is overcapitalized) or too little capital (in which case the firm is undercapitalized).

cash basis: An accounting method used for recordkeeping in which income is logged when received, and expenses are charged when they occur.

chattel mortgage contract: A credit contract used for the purchase of equipment in which the purchaser receives title of the equipment upon delivery, but the creditor holds a mortgage claim against it.

collateral: Assets used as security for a loan.

commercial loans: Loans made to a business by a commercial bank.

conditional sales contract: A credit contract used for the purchase of equipment under which the purchaser doesn't receive title of the equipment until the amount specified in the contract has been paid in full.

cooperative advertising: Joint advertising strategy used by a manufacturer and another firm that distributes its products.

copyright: A form of protection used to safeguard original literary works, performing arts, sound recordings, visual arts, and renewals.

corporation: A legal form of operation that declares the business to be a separate legal entity guided by a group of officers known as the board of directors.

cost-of-living lease: A lease under which yearly increases are tied to the cost-of-living index.

cost per thousand (CPM): A measurement used in buying media. CPM refers to the cost it takes to reach a thousand people using a given medium.

current ratio: The ratio of total current assets to total current liabilities.

demographic characteristics: The attributes such as income, age, and occupation that best describe your target market.

depreciation: The lessening in value of fixed assets that provides the foundation for a tax deduction, based on either the declining-balance or straight-line method.

disability insurance: A payroll tax required in some states that is deducted from employee paychecks to ensure income during periods in which the employee is unable to work due to an injury or illness.

disclosure document program: A form of protection that safeguards an idea while it is in its developmental stage.

dollar control system: A system used in inventory management that reveals the cost and gross profit margin of individual inventory items.

Dun & Bradstreet: An agency that furnishes clients with market statistics and financial standings and credit ratings of businesses.

equipment loan: A loan used for the purchase of capital equipment.

equity capital: A form of financing in which private investors buy equity in a business.

exploratory research: Research used to gather market information in which targeted consumers are asked very general questions intended to elicit lengthy answers.

Fair Labor Standards Act: A federal law that enforces minimum standards by which employers must abide when hiring.

Federal Insurance Contributions Act (FICA): This law requires employers to match the amount of social security tax deducted from an employee's paycheck.

fictitious name: A business name other than that of the owner(s) or partner(s).

first in, first out (FIFO): An accounting system used to value inventory for tax purposes. Under FIFO, inventory is valued at its most recent cost.

fixed expenses: Expenses that must be paid each month and do not fluctuate with the sales volume.

flat lease: A lease under which the cost is fixed for a specific period of time.

401(k) plan: A retirement plan for employees that allows them to deduct money from their paychecks and place it in a tax-sheltered account.

frequency: The number of times you hope to reach your target audience through your advertising campaign.

income statement: Also called a profit-and-loss statement, an income statement charts the sales and operating costs of a business over a specific period of time, usually a month.

inventory loan: A loan that is extended based on the value of a business's inventory.

inventory turnover: An analysis method used to determine the amount of capital invested in inventory and the total number of times per year that investment will revolve.

investment tax credit: A federal tax credit that allows businesses to reduce their tax liability if they purchase new equipment for business use.

investment turnover: A profitability measure used to evaluate the number of times per year that total investment or assets revolve.

Keogh: A pension plan that lets business owners contribute a specific portion of their profits toward a tax-sheltered account. There are several Keoghs to choose from, including profit-sharing and defined-contribution plans.

last in, first out (LIFO): An accounting system used to value inventory. Under LIFO, inventory is valued according to the remaining stock in inventory.

leasehold improvements: The repairs and improvements a lessee makes to rented property. These improvements become the property of the lessor at the end of the lease.

liability: The legal responsibility for an act, especially as pertaining to insurance risks. While there are numerous comprehensive and special coverages for almost every possible liability, there are three forms of liability coverage that insurers will usually underwrite. The first is *general liability,* which covers any kind of bodily injury to nonemployees except that caused by automobiles and professional malpractice. The second is *product liability,* which covers injury to customers arising directly from goods they purchased from your business. The third is *public liability,* which covers injury to members of the public when they are on your premises.

market survey: A research method used to define the market parameters of a business.

markup: The amount added to the cost of goods or cost of service to produce the desired profit.

measure of liquidity: An analysis method used to measure the amount of liquid assets available to meet accounts payable.

media plan: A plan that details the usage of media in an advertising campaign including costs, running dates, markets, reach, frequency, rationales, and strategies.

net leases: There are three kinds of net leases: the net lease, the double-net lease and the triple-net lease. Under a net lease, the lessee pays a base rent plus an additional charge for taxes. A double-net lease adds another charge for insurance. Under a triple-net lease, the lessee pays yet another charge for common area expenses.

net profit on sales: A profitability measure in which you divide the net income before taxes by gross sales.

Occupational Safety and Health Act (OSHA): A federal law that requires employers to provide employees with a workplace that is free of hazardous conditions.

open to buy: This is the dollar amount budgeted by a business for inventory purchases for a specific time period.

overhead: All nonlabor expenses you need to meet to operate your business.

partnership: A legal form of business operated by two or more individuals who act as co-owners. The federal government recognizes several types of partnerships. The two most common are general and limited partnerships.

patent: A form of protection that provides a person or legal entity with exclusive rights to exclude others from making, using, or selling a concept or invention for the duration of the patent. There are three types of patents available: design, plant, and utility.

percentage lease: Under this type of lease, the landlord charges a base rent plus an additional percentage of any profits the business tenant produces.

personal loans: A loan made to a person based on the credit rating of that person.

profit: There are generally two kinds of profit: gross profit and net profit. Gross profit is the difference between gross sales and cost of sales, while net profit is the difference between gross profit and all costs associated with operating a business.

reach: The total number of people in your target market that you contact through your advertising campaign.

return on investment (ROI): A profitability measure that evaluates the performance of a business by dividing net profit by total assets.

return on owner's equity: A profitability measure used to gauge the earning power of the owner's total equity in the business by dividing the average equity investment of the owner by the net profit.

signature loans: See *personal loans.*

sole proprietorship: A legal form of operation in which one person owns and operates the business.

specific research: Research used to perform a market survey in which targeted consumers are asked very specific and in-depth questions intended to solve problems found through exploratory research.

Standard Rate and Data Service (SRDS): A company that produces a group of directories for each different type of advertising medium, listing rates, circulation, contacts, markets serviced, and so on.

step lease: A type of lease outlining annual rent increases based on the landlord's estimates of increases in his or her expenses.

subchapter-S: A portion of the Internal Revenue Code that allows small corporations to be taxed as partnerships. The corporations distribute income directly to their shareholders, who then claim the income on their personal income taxes.

variable expenses: Business costs that fluctuate from one payment period to another according to sales volume.

venture capital: Start-up or expansion capital, which a business obtains from private investors in exchange for equity positions within the business.

worker's compensation: State and federal insurance funds that reimburse employees for injuries they suffer on the job.

working capital: Net current assets available for the company to carry on with its work.

NOTES

Chapter 1   Introduction

1. *Vankirk's Venture Capital Directory*, vol. 1, Online Publishing, Inc., Arlington, VA, 1994.

Chapter 2   Business Plan

1. *Monthly Failure Report*, Dun & Bradstreet Corporation, New York, NY (1994).
2. David A. Aaker, *Developing Business Strategies*, John Wiley & Sons, Inc. (Second Edition, 1988).
3. Terence P. McCarty, *Business Plans That Win Venture Capital*, John Wiley & Sons, Inc. (1988).
4. Terence P. McCarty, *Business Plans That Win Venture Capital*, John Wiley & Sons, Inc. (1988).

Chapter 3   Start-Up Financing

1. Dan Steinhoff and John F. Burgess, *Small Business Management Fundamentals*, McGraw-Hill (4th ed., 1986).
2. Jack Zwick, *A Handbook of Small Business Finance*, U.S. Small Business Administration, 1981.
3. Erika Kotite, "High-Tech Handouts," *Entrepreneur*, November 1993.
4. Jeffrey E. Sohl, Center for Venture Research, Whittemore School of Business and Economics, University of New Hampshire, Durham, NH, January 1995.
5. Jeffrey E. Sohl, Center for Venture Research, Whittemore School of Business and Economics, University of New Hampshire, Durham, NH, January 1995.

Chapter 4   SBA Loans

1. Erskine Bowles, "Bite-Sized Loans," *Entrepreneur*, December 1993.
2. Michael Selz, "SBA May Cut Portion of Loan It Backs," *Wall Street Journal*, January 26, 1995.
3. Elizabeth Wallace, "Bank On It," *Entrepreneur*, May 1993.
4. Shannon Hill, "Help Line," *Entrepreneur*, February 1994.
5. Erskine Bowles, "Bite-Sized Loans," *Entrepreneur*, December 1993.
6. William Cohen, *The Entrepreneur and Small Business Problem Solver*, John Wiley & Sons, Inc. (1990).

Chapter 5   Bootstrap Financing

1. U.S. Small Business Administration Office of Management Assistance, "Understanding Money Sources."
2. Udayan Gupta, "Factoring and Venture Firms' Roles in Financing Growth," *Wall Street Journal*, June 15, 1994.

Chapter 6   Credit

1. U.S. Census Bureau, *County Business Patterns*, Cendata (Online Service), June 1991.

Chapter 7   Expansion Financing

1. Coopers & Lybrand, *Growing Your Business*, July/August 1994.
2. John Freear, Jeffrey Sohl, and William E. Wetzel Jr., "The Private Investor Market for Venture Capital," *The Financier*, ACMT, Vol. 1, No. 2, May 1994.

INDEX

Accounts receivable, 60, 152
Accutrade, Inc., 176
Acid-test ratio, 58
Acquisition, 4
Adjustable-rate mortgage, 111
Advanced Research Projects Agency
    (ARPA), 175
Aerospace industry, 115
Agricultural industry, SBA loan
    requirements, 92
Alliances, 150
American Collectors' Association (ACA),
    130
American Commercial Collectors
    Association (ACCA), 130
American Council of Life Insurance, 140
America Online, 140, 147
Annual meeting, 139–140
Apple Computer, 27, 161
Assets:
    assessment of, 53–54
    in balance sheet, 45–46
    protection of, 114
    sale of, 140
Assets-to-liabilities ratio, 58
Assignment of Claims Act, 131
Associated Credit Bureaus, Inc., 133
AT&T, 175

Bad credit, cleaning up, 132–136
Balance sheet, 39, 44–47, 146
Bankcard Holders of America, 136
Bankers' acceptances, 148
Bank loans, as financial resource, 5,
    62–63, 148
Bankruptcy, 13, 67, 114, 156
BBN, 175
Ben Ezra, Weinstein & Co., 177
Berkovich, Doren, 75–76
Best efforts, 170
Billing methods, 115–116
Bintz, John, 77
Blind pool, 141
Boeing Co., 177

Bonds, 149
Bookkeeping methods, 125
Bootstrap financing:
    advantages to, 108
    cash flow management, 114–116
    customers, 111
    defined, 107
    equipment suppliers 112
    expansion capital, 150–151
    factoring, 110
    leasing, 112–114
    real estate, 111–112
    trade credit, 108–110
Bottom line, 12
Breaking even, 15
Bridge phase, 4, 158
Bucceli, Lou, 140
Budgets:
    cash, 157
    cash flow, 143, 145
    development of, 31
    expansion capital/plans, 142, 149
Bulletin boards, 2
Business angels, 5, 71–72, 157
Business banks:
    listing by state, 242–261
    microloans, 241–242
Business cycle, 153
Business development, phases of, 4–5
Business failure, 13–15, 135
Business Opportunities Online Inc., 140
Business partners, as financial resource,
    5
Business plan:
    financial projections, 25–26
    financial statements:
        balance sheet, 44–47
        cash flow statement, 42–44
        income statement, 39–42
    form, 8–9
    goods *vs.* services, 9–10
    importance of, 7–8, 133–134
    lack of, 13
    as management tool, 15

Business plan: *(Continued)*
  for new start-up, 9
  personnel, 31, 33–34
  professional preparation of, 48
  purpose of, 10–13
  sample, 179–209
  SBA loan application, 92–93
  structure of:
    business defined, 17
    business description 18–20, 142
    competitive analysis, 26–28, 142
    design and development plans,
      28–32, 142
    executive summary, 17–18
    financial components, 39–47, 143
    market strategies, 20–26, 142
    operations and management, 32–39,
      142
    table of contents, 16–17
    title page, 16–17
Business Plans That Win Venture Capital
  (McCarty), 30, 33
Business resources:
  advertising, 215–217
  home-based businesses, 210–211
  marketing, 215–217
  market research services, 214
  online services, 214–215
  recordkeeping and taxes, 217–218
  small businesses:
    associations, 209–210, 219–220
    business information centers (BICs),
      225–226
    books, 210
    conferences, 220
    general start-up assistance,
      224–225
    government agencies, 222–224
    market research, 225
    matching services, 221
    online services, 226
    publications, 210, 227–228
    related books, 228
    venture capital funds, 221
    venture capital resource centers,
      220–221
    women's business ownership
      assistance, 221
  start-up assistance, 211–214,
    224–225
Buyouts, 4, 158

Callot, Anne Gene, 147
Calvin, Bob, 75–77
Capital equipment, 145
Capital Network, Inc., 147

Capital requirements:
  SBA loans, 100–103
  table, 32, 35–37, 143
Capital Search Marketing, 147
CAPLines, 82–83
Case, Daniel H., III, 177
Cash budget, 157
Cash flow:
  budget, 143, 145
  cycle, 138, 144
  evaluation of, 39
  expansion and, 138
  leasing and, 114
  management of, 114–116
  projections, 93, 95, 98–100, 157
Cash flow statement, 42–44, 58–59,
  144–145
Cash-only accounts, 134
CERFnet, 175
Certified lenders, 89
Certified and Preferred Lenders
  Program, 87, 90
Chattel mortgage, 60, 112, 153
Chicago Corp., 176
Cloherty, Patricia, 161, 163, 165
Closing, going public process, 17
C.O.D. accounts, 108, 116, 134
Collateral:
  in business plan, 18
  expansion capital, 148, 152
  SBA loans, 93
  types of, 152–153
Collections:
  aging receivables, 125, 127–128
  bad debt, incidence of, 124–125
  invoicing, 125
  laws on, 131–132
  process:
    personalized letters, 128–129
    phone calls, 129–131
    Small Claims Court, 131
Comaker, 60, 152
Commercial lenders, 63, 154
Commercial paper, 148
Common stock, 149
Competition, credit policy and,
  120
Competitive pricing, 24
Competitive strength grid, 27
CompuServe, as information resource,
  140, 147
Conditional sales contract, 112
Consequential goals, 29
Construction industry:
  billing practices, 116
  SBA loan requirements, 92

Consumer Credit Counseling Services, 135–136
Consumer Credit Protection Act, 131
Contracts:
 conditional sales, 112
 credit, 112
 going public and, 168–169
Corporations, 18, 68–69, 156
Cost-of-goods table, 32, 37–39, 143–144
Cost of sales, 95, 138
Cost-plus pricing, 23
Cotsakos, Christos M., 177
Credit, generally:
 collections, *see* Collections
 establishing, 123–124
 five C's of, 120
 policies, 118–120
 trade, *see* Trade credit
 use of, generally, 117–118
Credit cards:
 as financial resource, 1, 15, 62
 secured, 135–136
Credit line, establishment of, 123–124
Credit policy, establishment of, 119–120
Credit rating, 119
Credit report, 55–56, 119, 130
Credit reporting agencies, 55, 133
Creditworthiness, 55–56, 124
Cristich, Cristi, 105
Crouse, Tim, 140
Current assets, 45–46, 146
Current liabilities, 46, 146
Current ratio, 146
Customers, generally:
 in collection process, 127–128
 as financial resource, 5, 111, 151

Data General, 161
Debt financing:
 expansion capital, 50–155
 types of, generally, 60–64
Debt management, 55, 135
Debt-to-equity ratio, 146, 148
Defense industry, 115
Delinquent accounts, 127–128
DELTA (Defense Loan and Technical Assistance Program), 83–84
Demand pricing, 23
Demographics, 20
Department of Defense (DoD), 83–84
Department of Energy (DOE) loans, 65, 155
Department of Housing and Urban Development (HUD) loans, 65, 155
Department of the Interior (DOI) loans, 65, 155

Depreciation, 37
Developing Business Strategies (Aaker), 26
Development expense table, 143
Direct Access Notes, 176
Directed goals, 29
Direct labor, 144
Direct loans, 64, 78, 106
Direct Stock Market, 177
Discounts, 123, 157
Discretionary income, 58
Display merchandise, as collateral, 61, 153
Disposable income, 58
Distribution channels, 24
Dolan, Tim, 134
Double taxation, 69
Down payments, 111, 113–114
Dun & Bradstreet, 119

Economic Development Administration (EDA) loans, 65, 155
Economic Opportunity Loan (EOL) program, 154
Edwards, Mace, 110
Edwards Directory of American Factors (Edwards), 110, 141
ElectriCiti, 175
Endorser, 60, 152
Entrepreneur and Small Business Problem Solver, The (Cohen), 91
Entrepreneurs, personal traits of, 2–3
EOM (end of the month) credit terms, 122
Equal Credit Opportunity Act, 132
Equifax, 55, 133
Equipment and machinery:
 as collateral, 60, 153
 government loans for, 64
 suppliers, as financial resource, 112, 151
Equity, real estate, 58, 122
Equity financing:
 expansion capital source, 147, 155–156
 function of, 67
 venture capital and, 160
Equity investors, 5, 68
Ervin, Jim, 76–77
E Trade Group, Inc., 177
Executive summary, in business plan, 17–18
Expansion capital, sources of, 148–149
Expansion financing:
 business financial position, evaluation of, 145–146, 148
 cash flow considerations, 143–145
 expansion capital, 148–156

Expansion financing: *(Continued)*
  expansion plans, 139, 142–143
  preparation for, 138–139
  timing of, 137–138
  venture capital, 156–161
Export-Import Bank (EXIMBANK), 66,
    141, 155
Export Revolving Line of Credit
    Program, 66, 155
Export Working Capital Program
    (EWCP), 83
External funding, 56–57

Factoring, 110, 141, 151
Fair Credit Bill Act, 131
Fair Credit Reporting At, 131–132
Fair Debt Collection Act, 132
Family, as financial resource, 1, 5, 15, 62,
    75–77, 136
Farmers Home Administration (FmHA)
    loans, 64–65, 155
FA$TRAK, 85, 87
Feasible goals, 29
Finance companies, as financial
    resource, 135, 148
Financial plan:
  SBA loan applications, 94–100
  trade credit and, 109
Financial projection, marketing
    strategies, 25–26
Financial situation, evaluation of,
    50–53
Financial sources:
  list of, generally, 5–6
  selection factors, 149
Financial statements:
  balance sheet, 44–47, 146
  cash flow statement, 42–44, 144–145
  expansion capital and, 149
  income statement, 39–42, 146
  SBA loan application, 93
  year-end, 139
Financiers, 6
Firm commitment, 170
First Analysis Corp., 162
First stage, business development, 4
504 Certified Development Company
    Program, 84, 87–88
Fixed assets, 46
Fixed expenses, 34
FOB (free on board) credit terms, 122
Food Fund, 164–165
Food-service industry, 163–164
Form 8-K, 173
Form S-1/S-18/SB-1/SB-2, 172
Form S-R, 173

Form 10-K, 173
Form 10-Q, 173
Form U-7, 174
Friends, as financial resource, 1, 5, 15,
    62, 76–77, 136

General Motors Acceptance Corp.
    (GMAC), 176
General partner, 68
General partnerships:
  in business plan, 18
  defined, 67
  as financial resource, 140
  liabilities in, 67–68
  private venture capital, 157
Gentry, Phil, 106
Glover, Jere W., 241
GNI Group, Inc., 162–163
Goal-setting, 28–29, 139
Going public:
  advantages/disadvantages of,
    166–169
  cost of, 168
  for expansion capital, 160–161
  public offerings, *see* Public offerings
Golden Rule, 1
Government agencies:
  debt financing, 64–67
  expansion financing, 155
  as financial resource, generally, 5, 15
  listing of, 229–230
Government listings:
  government agencies, 229–230
  SBA district offices, 237–240
  state commerce and economic
    development departments,
    230–233
  state small business development
    officers, 233–236
Gross profit, 95
Growing Your Business (Coopers &
    Lybrand), 150
Guarantor, 60, 152

HAL-1/HAL-2, handicapped assistance
    loans, 154
Hambrecht & Quist, 177
Handbook of Small Business Finance, A
    (Zwick), 64
Hard product, 9
Harrison, Arthur, 164
Hostile takeovers, 169
Howard, Graeme, 140
Huffman, Frances, 75
Hughes, Paul, 132
Huttner, Rich, 163

IBM, 27
Income:
  disposable, 58
  loan applicants', 55
Income statement, 39–42, 146
Industrial venture capitalists, 157–159
Infrequent participant lenders, 89
Initial Public Offering (IPO), 6, 15, 71,
  167–168, 170–171
Institutional investors, 6
Insurance policies, as collateral, 61, 153
Intel, 161
Interest rate, 4, 57, 63, 80–81, 148, 152.
  See also specific types of loans
Interim loans, 152
Intermediate-term financing, 61, 148, 153
Intermediate-term loan, *see*
  Intermediate-term financing
Internal funding, 56–57
Internal Revenue Service, 132
International Trade Loan Program, 83
Internet:
  electronic financial services, 177–178
  growth of, 176–177
  history of, 175–176
Inventory, as collateral, 61, 148
Investment banking firms, venture
  capital, 159
Investment Exchange, 147
Investors, *see* Venture capitalists
  initial public offering (IPO), 171
  public offerings, 169
Invoices, 118, 125–127

Job descriptions, 31
Jobs, Steve, 8
Job specifications, 31
Joint ventures, 5

Klein, Andrew, 177–178
Kotite, Erika, 105, 161–165
Kumnick, Jon, 76

Labor expense, 33–34
Lawsuits, 168
Lease:
  as collateral, 61, 153
  negotiation of, 111
Leasing:
  advantages to, 113–114
  cash flow and, 114
  equipment, 113
  as financial resource, 5, 112–114
  ownership *vs.*, 113
  term of lease, 114
Lenders, SBA loans, 89–90

Leveraged buyout, 4, 158
Leveraging, 73
Liabilities:
  in balance sheet, 46–47, 146
  in general partnerships, 67–70
  in limited partnerships, 156
Life insurance policy, as financial
  resource, 140
Limited liability companies (LLCs),
  69–70
Limited partners, 67
Limited partnerships, 67–70, 140–141, 156
Liquid assets, 146
Liquidity, 146, 160
Loan applicants, good characteristics in,
  55–56
Loan proposal, elements of, 153–154
Local Development Companies (LDCs),
  66, 155
Lock boxes, 116
Logos, 17
Logos Research Systems, Inc., 176
Lombard Brokerage, Inc., 176
Long-term assets, 46
Long-term financing, 62, 65, 146,
  148–149, 153
Long-term liabilities, 47
Long-term loan, *see* Long-term financing
LowDoc Loan program, 85–86

Magnuson, Norm, 133
Management buyout, 5, 158
Manufacturing:
  capital requirements, 35, 49
  SBA loan requirements, 92
Marketing plans, 139
Marketing strategy, 25–27
Market research, 22
Market share, 21
Markup pricing, 24
Materials, cost of, 144
Maxwell, Brett, 162, 165
MCI, 175
MESBIC (Minority Enterprise Small
  Business Investment Company), 73,
  159
Mezzanine, business life cycle, 4
Micro Business Lending in the United States
  (Office of Advocacy), 241
MicroLoan program, 79
Microsoft, 27, 161
Milestone billing, 115
Minorities and the Women's
  Prequalification Loan programs,
  84–85
Minority entrepreneurs, 147

Money management, 55
Mortgages, 111–112
Motion Technology, Inc., 164–165

National Association of Investment
    Companies (NAIC), 147
National Association of Securities
    Dealers (NASD), 168
National Foundation for Consumer
    Credit, 135
Net profit on sales, 146
Nicklin, Oliver, 162, 165
Nonbank lending, 5
Norrid, Jennifer, 106

OEM (Original Equipment
    Manufacturer), 24
Online services, financial resource
    research, 140, 147
Operating expenses:
  bootstrap financing and, 115
  in financial plan, 95–98
  table, 32, 35, 143, 144–145
Operations:
  in business plan, 32–39
  expansion plans, 142
Orders to pay, 121, 123
Organizational chart, 32
Other People's Money (OPM), 57
Overhead expenses, 34
Owner funding, 150
Ownership, going public and, 168–169

Partnerships, *see* General partnerships;
    Limited partnerships
Passive activity, 69
Patricof & Co. Ventures Inc., 161, 163
Payables financing, 118
Payment provisions, negotiation of,
    115–116
Personal financial statement, 53–54,
    93–94
Personal loan, 61, 153
Personnel, assessment of, 31, 33
Portfolio diversification, 161–162
Positioning strategy, 22–23
Postal regulations, 132
Preferred lenders, 89
Preferred stock, 149
Pricing strategies, 23–24
Private investors, venture capital, 159
Private placement, 5, 15
Private venture capitalists, 157–158
Procedures, 29–30
Prodigy, 140
Product life cycle, 6, 28
Product review, 30

Profitability, 138, 146
Pro forma balance sheet, 95
Progress billings, 115–116
Projections:
  cash flow, 157
  expansion plans and, 139
  in SBA loan application, 93, 95–100
Promises to pay, 118, 121, 123
Promotion strategy, 24–25
Prospectuses, going public, 167, 171–173
Psychographics, 20
Public offerings:
  advantages/disadvantages of, 166–169
  do-it-yourself, 173–174, 176
  going public process, 170–173
  operating as public company, 167, 173
  preparation of, 169
  venture capital source, 160–161
Public shell, 141

Quantifiable goals, 29
Quick ratio, 58, 146

Rate of return, 4
Real estate:
  as collateral, 60, 153
  expansion capital source, 151
  as financial resource, 111–112
Recapitalization, 4
Receivable financing, 148
Red herring, 172
Registration:
  initial public offering, 171–172
  limited partnerships and, 68
Research and development, 4
Restrictive covenants, 148–149
Retailing industry, SBA loan
    requirements, 92
Return on investment, 157–158
Reverse merger, 6, 141
Risk:
  amount of, 4, 58
  in venture capital, 165
Robinson Patman Act, 131
ROG (receipt of goods) credit terms, 122
Rush, Carl, 162

Sales/revenue table, 143–144
Savings account:
  as collateral, 60, 153
  as financial resource, 5, 136
SBA-guaranteed loan, 64
SBA loans:
  application form, 103–104
  application requirements:
    collateral, 103–104
    financial plan, 94–100

generally, 79
personal financial statement, 93–94
capital requirements, 100–103
collateral, 103
generally, 108–109
lenders, types of, 89–90
rejection, 105
repayment ability, 105
restrictions, 90–92
structure of, 92–94
types of:
  CAPLines, 82–83
  Certified and Preferred Lenders
    Program, 87, 90
  DELTA (Defense Loan and Technical
    Assistance Program), 83–84
  direct, 78
  Economic Opportunity Loan (EOL)
    program, 154
  Export Working Capital Program
    (EWCP), 83
  FA$TRAK, 85, 87
  504 Certified Development
    Company (CDC) Program, 84,
    87–88
  generally, 64, 78–79
  International Trade Loan Program, 83
  LowDoc Loan program, 85–86
  Minorities and the Women's
    Prequalification Loan programs,
    84–85
  7(a) Loan Guaranty, 80–82, 85–86, 106
  7(m) MicroLoan program, 79, 88
  Small Business Investment Company
    (SBIC) Program, *see* SBICs
    (Small Business Investment
    Corporations)
  specialized programs, 84–89
  Surety Bond program, 89
SBDCs (Small Business Development
  Companies), 73–74, 78, 159
SBICs (Small Business Investment
  Corporations):
function of, generally, 72–73, 88–89
loans from, 72–73, 107–108
venture capital, 159
SBIDCs (State Business and Industrial
  Development Corporations), 65–66
SBIR (Small Business Innovation
  Research Program), 66, 141, 155
Scheduling, 30–31
SCOR (Small Corporate Offering
  Registration) form, 141, 174
Second stage, business development, 4
Secured credit cards, 135–136
Secured loans, 152–153. *See also*
  Collateral

Securities, as collateral, 60. 153
Securities and Exchange Commission
  (SEC):
electronic financial services and, 178
filing fees, 168
registration with, 171–172
role of, generally, 68, 70–71, 167
Seed phase, 4, 158
Self-financing, 57–58, 60, 150
Selling stock, 170, 172–173
Service Corps of Retired Executives
  (SCORE), 78
Service industry:
capital requirements, 35
SBA loan requirements, 92
Service product, 9
7(a) Loan Guaranty:
Low-Doc Loan Program, 85–86
overview, 80–81
popularity of, 106
specialized loan and lender delivery,
  81–82
7(m) MicroLoan program, SBA, 79, 88
Short-term financing, 61, 148, 153
Short-term loan, *see* Short-term
  financing
Signature loan, 61, 153
Silicon Graphics, Inc., 177
Slow-paying customers, 127
Small Business Administration (SBA):
bulletin board, 2
development of, 78
district offices, listing of, 237–240
expansion capital source, 154
loans, *see* SBA loans
Local Development Companies (LDCs)
  and, 66
Maximum Size Standard, 91
Small Business Fundamentals
  (Steinhoff/Burgess), 61
Small business loans, 63
Snyder, Tom, 76
Sole proprietorships, 18, 67, 156
Specialty venture capitalists, 165
Spring Street Brewery, 176–177
Sprint, 175
Stability, in loan applicants, 55
*Standard Industrial Classification (SIC)
  Manual,* 91
Start-up financing:
financial situation, evaluation of, 50–53
investor requisitions, 55–57
raising money, methods of:
  business angels, 71–72
  corporation, 68–69
  debt financing, 60–64
  equity financing, 67

Start-up financing: *(Continued)*
  government debt financing, 64–67
  limited liability company (LLC),
    69–71
  limited partnerships, 67–68
  MESBICs (Minority Enterprise
    Small Business Investment
    Company), 73, 159
  partnership, 67
  SBDCs (Small Business Development
    Companies), 73–74, 159
  SBICs (Small Business Investment
    Corporations), 72–73, 159
  self-financing, 57–60
  sole proprietorship, 67
  subchapter S corporation, 69
  trade credit, 74
  venture capitalists, 71
Start-up phase, 4, 158
Statement of account, 125
State regulation:
  collection processes, 132
  going public, 172
Stockholders, 168
Stone, Kent, 134
Strategic planning, 138–139
Strengths, in business plan, 11
Subchapter S corporation, 69–70, 156
Subline item billings, 116
Surety bond program, 89
Synchographics, 20–21
Syndications, 67, 156

Target market, 20–21
Taxation:
  debt financing, 69
  information resources, 217–218
  leasing, 113
  property, 113
Term loans, 152
Total sales, 95
Trade credit:
  cost of, 109–110
  credit policy, 118–121
  defined, 108
  discounts, expensive, 123
  expansion financing through, 148, 151
  negotiation of, 109
  procedures, 108–109
  start-up businesses and, 74
  terms of, 122
  tips and traps, 118
  types of, 121–122
Trade secrets, 19
Trade shows, 164

Transferability restriction test, 70
Trans Union Corp., 55, 133
Trucano, John, 163–165
TRW, 55, 133

ULOR (Uniform Limited Offering
    Registration) form, 174
Underwriter:
  in do-it-yourself public offerings,
    173–174
  selection of, 170–171
Underwriting, SBA loan requirements, 94
Uniform Commercial Code, 131
Unsecured loans, 61–62, 153
USP (unique selling proposition), 19

Variable expenses, 34
Vendors, as financial resource, 5
Venture capital:
  case illustrations, 161–165
  defined, 156
  as financial resource, generally, 5–6
  food-service industry, 163–164
  funding sources, 158–159
  going public, 160–161
  meeting with investor, 160
  online research, 147
  popular investment areas, 157–158,
    162
  return on investment, 157–158
  timing of investment, business life
    cycle, 158
Venture Capitalist, 2
Venture capitalists:
  meeting with, 160
  role of, generally, 15, 71
  types of, 158–159
Venture Economics, 162
Vision, in business plan, 12

Waiting period, in going public process,
    172
Wallman, Stephen, M. H., 176
Warehouse inventory, as collateral, 153
Weaknesses, in business plan, 11
Wholesaling industry, SBA loan
    requirements, 92
Wit Capital, 177
Womack, Clay, 177
Work assignments, 29–31
Working capital:
  expansion planning and, 141
  loans, 65, 152

Zwick, Jack, 64